Patropadeśa

Instructive Letters

Books Authored by Bhakti Vikāsa Swami

A Beginner's Guide to Kṛṣṇa Consciousness
A Message to the Youth of India
Brahmacarya in Kṛṣṇa Consciousness
Glimpses of Traditional Indian Life
Jaya Śrīla Prabhupāda!
My Memories of Śrīla Prabhupāda
On Pilgrimage in Holy India
On Speaking Strongly in Śrīla Prabhupāda's Service
Patropadeśa
Śrī Bhaktisiddhānta Vaibhava (three volumes)
Śrī Caitanya Mahāprabhu
Śrī Vaṁśīdāsa Bābājī
Vaiṣṇava Śikhā o Sādhana (Bengali)

Books Edited or Compiled by Bhakti Vikāsa Swami

Rāmāyaṇa
The Story of Rasikānanda
Gauḍīya Vaiṣṇava Padyāvalī (Bengali)

Patropadeśa

Instructive Letters

Volume One

1990–2010

Bhakti Vikāsa Swami

ISBN 978-93-82109-03-7

www.bvks.com
books@bvks.com

First printing (2015): 2,000 copies

Published by Bhakti Vikas Trust, Surat, India
Printed in India

Contents

Preface

Patropadeśa (*patra*—letter; *upadeśa*—instruction, advice) consists of selected correspondence with disciples and other devotees. Circa 1997, I considered that some of the content of my letters to individuals might be useful for others also, and thus I started to collect relevant texts with the intention of later publishing them as an anthology. Now, some fifteen years later, this volume is the result.

This compilation is intended primarily for my direct disciples and others who are familiar and comfortable with my stringent approach to Kṛṣṇa consciousness. Many of the letters featured herein deal with grave and sensitive topics and therefore offer insights into the practical application of the teachings of Kṛṣṇa consciousness in today's highly disturbed world. However, I have chosen not to include most of the polemic missives that I have written over the years regarding various contentious issues within ISKCON, as I feel that such matters require comprehensive analyses rather than decontextualized and incomplete perspectives. Nonetheless, this book is evidence that gurus in ISKCON must contend with many weighty topics and do not, as some persons seem to believe, merely bask in adulation.

The several hundred letters presented herein represent only a fraction from the tens of thousands (including short notes) that I have written over the last two decades. Before about late 1994, almost all of the many letters that I composed were written by hand, and are now lost. Since then, and now practically exclusively, my correspondence has mostly been by email.

As can be seen from some of the earlier entries in *Patropadeśa*, previously I often composed extensive replies to philosophical, polemic, and practical queries. But nowadays I prefer to respond verbally whenever lengthy answers are warranted. Modern technology makes for easy dissemination of such replies.

The perspectives and advice contained in this volume were offered to different individuals under varied circumstances and hence should not necessarily be considered universally applicable to all my disciples. Moreover, usually what I state in letters is unlikely to represent the whole gamut of my outlook on any given topic. Another important point is that my views and directions on some issues have changed since originally having been written. Most significantly, while still acknowledging the principle of respecting authority within ISKCON, nowadays I am more likely than previously to advise devotees to be cautious in dealing with ISKCON authorities in general, and particularly with certain devotees holding position within the institution.

The letters in this book are generally presented largely as they were written, although in many cases only excerpts are given. Formalities (such as "Dear So-and-so," and "Yours sincerely") have been elided, spelling errors corrected, abbreviations expanded, and footnotes provided to clarify certain points. Variant spelling styles have not been standardized, and diacritical marks are largely absent.

Sometimes, to make it easier to understand the context of my replies, the letter (or a portion thereof) to which I was replying is placed contiguously with my answer. And (as is common in email correspondence) often my replies include quoted text from the letter to which I am replying; such quoted text is featured in gray type.

In most cases, names of recipients of the letters have been withheld, and other names (of persons or places) have been substituted by a series of asterisks (***), a series of plus signs

(+++), or simply an initial (which does not necessarily correspond to the first letter of the name being withheld). And sometimes "Sri Sri Radha Krsna" has been used instead of the actual name of the Deities in a particular temple.

This edition is designated as "volume one," as I hope to publish at least one more volume after some years.

Bhakti Vikāsa Swami

1990

1 January 1990

*** Prabhu told me that since my visit to H and the unfortunate exchange with your uncle there, that your previous warm welcome to our devotees has cooled off and that you no longer want them to stay in your house. Which surprised me to some extent because of what I perceived to be our continued good relationship after the incident, and because you never wrote me a letter after I left expressing appreciation of my visit.

Anyway, I'm very sorry if you became discouraged in Krsna consciousness because of a disagreement between your uncle and myself. Of course, at that time I could have kept the atmosphere more congenial by simply agreeing with your uncle. I think that you were not there for much of the conversation. But, (at least as I perceived it) as your uncle was aggressively and unreasonably critical of our society, my response was thus.

Sometimes people think that a sadhu or a sannyasi should never become angry. That is generally true—for his own sake a sadhu or a sannyasi should not become angry. But when Krsna or His devotees are becoming the subject of criticism, the devotees should become angry (cf. Nectar of Instruction, Text 1, purport). Srila Prabhupada himself sometimes became angry at his disciples or at the nonsensical protestations of nondevotees. Such anger is pure and transcendental and is meant for rectification and uplift of others. This is an absolute fact which may not appeal to the sentiments of the less informed.

1

Now, I am not claiming to be on such an elevated platform: I can state frankly that I am not. And the fact that I was intolerant of your uncle's attitude was probably influenced by the fact that I was feeling the strain of fasting. But even then, it is unfortunate that because of one devotee's impropriety you should deprive yourself of the association of those saintly persons who had nothing to do with this incident.

I understand that some embarrassment may have been caused within your family and within your community—but even that is not a good reason to estrange yourself from the devotees, whose association is so vital to help us advance in Krsna consciousness. I would be interested to get your views on this.

I am now travelling in Andhra Pradesh and neighboring states with a built-up second hand DCM Toyota vehicle for preaching, and book distribution.

1 February 1990

I have received your letter (forwarded to me at ***) and have noted its confident, enthusiastic contents with some relief. I doubted that you had been disturbed in your Krsna consciousness so now my mind is at ease on this point.

And, if this whole incident develops circumstantially into the cause of establishing a FOLK centre at H, is it all not Krsna's way of turning the apparently adverse into the positive? In S there is an ISKCON centre which functions as a FOLK meeting house—a group of enthusiastic, educated young men come together weekly for bhajans and readings, arati and prasadam, give each other association, arrange house programs and spread Krsna consciousness to their best capacity. If you want my advice it is: do it! We cannot wait for fulltime devotees or sannyasis to come and start a centre in every village. Wherever there is enthusiasm, let the work begin.

The only thing you have to be very careful about is becoming caught up in too much committees, positions, and politics. That tendency is there wherever there is any organization. But as long as the simple basics are kept in the forefront—i.e. hearing and chanting about, and serving, Lord Sri Krsna; then all auspiciousness is guaranteed.

So, let us forget again the less fortunate incident in H and go forward positively in our march back to Godhead, accepting all such disturbances as educational and meant for our purification.

28 September 1990

I'm writing to find out about purchasing a Matador van. I don't have money now but I'd like to know how much I would have to raise. Of course, our party has a DCM Toyota vehicle, but I'm thinking that if we had another vehicle we could organize our preaching much more efficiently. An advance party could arrange programs and then when we reach the town, the DCM could go on with book distribution in the bazaar while the Matador takes me to the programs.

1 November 1990

Regarding the Ramajanmabhumi issue, ISKCON's position is that there should be a Rama temple there, and indeed in every town and village; to this end ISKCON's members are always busy spreading the names of Lord Krsna and Lord Rama all over the world. Although individual members of ISKCON will tend to sympathize with the kar-sevaks, ISKCON as an organization is not taking a stand on the issue.[1]

There are several reasons for this. One is that it has produced highly sectarian feelings between Hindus and Muslims. But

1. *Kar-sevak*—Voluntary worker. During the period in which the Babri Masjid in Ayodhya was demolished, this common term was particularly in vogue for volunteers committed to build a Rama temple at that site.

our preaching is for all classes of people. Our first instruction (the first instruction of Lord Krsna in Gita) is that we are not these bodies. We are not Hindus or Muslims. Religion without philosophy is sentimentalism or fanaticism. Human life is meant for cool headed consideration of the Absolute Truth. No one has ever thought of discussing philosophy in this whole issue. So we are not to put ourselves at the disposal of fanatics.

Another point is that the movement has been highly politicized for the gain of a few individuals. ISKCON also cannot be party to this.

Another point is that spiritual heads of these movements are all Mayavadis who do not actually believe in the supremacy of Rama and who do not accept the Deity in the temple as being the Supreme Lord Himself. What kind of temple will they build?

Another point is that ISKCON's mission is to spread pure love of God as taught by Lord Caitanya. We cannot divert all our energies into this issue—we have the most important work to do.

This issue does, however, show that devotional feelings are still strong in many Indian people, despite the atheistic and materialistic leaders who always want to stifle Indian culture and religion. It is a fact that the Hindus had to make some reaction to the government-abetted Islamization and Christianizaton of India; otherwise Vedic culture in India was doomed. This issue could be a turning point in the social and religious life of India. Unfortunately, it is in the hands of the Mayavadis; so we cannot hope for anything ultimately auspicious from it.

This letter is a private letter meant for your reading only.

By the way, your writing of "Sri Sri Sri Radha Krsna Balaram" is technically a rasabhasa, a mixing of devotional sentiments not approved by Lord Caitanya or His followers. This a complex subject explained in the concluding chapters of Nectar of Devotion. You may write:

"All glories to Sri Sri Krsna Balaram.

All glories to Sri Sri Radha Krsna."

See the last paragraph of Bhagavatam 4.20.15 purport for the cause of communal riots.

11 December 1990

Enclosed please find 3 new books published by BBT. "Endless Love" and "Krsna Consciousness and Christianity" are reprints of books printed in America which I thought could be valuable for our preaching here. "The Hare Krsna Challenge" is a book which I compiled and is printed in this format for the first time in the world.

Regarding Sri Ramajanmabhumi—we are all wondering what Srila Prabhupada's response would have been; though it is interesting to note that, despite being personally sent by Krsna to spread bhakti throughout the world, he always emphasized the spreading of the chanting of the Holy Names and decried all types of sectarian bodily identification (such as that between Hindus and Muslims) as animal-like ignorance and never talked about re-establishing Ramajanmabhumi. In fact, he said that our ISKCON temple at Mayapur was more important than that at the birth site of Lord Caitanya because it was much more involved in activities of Lord Caitanya; the karma of the Lord, in this case, preaching Krsna consciousness being more important than the janma (cf. Gita 4.9).

Notwithstanding, the agitation has got many people all over the world talking and thinking of Rama and Ayodhya and chanting the holy names. From a sociopolitical point of view (which actually we have nothing directly to do with) it was long overdue for Hindus to wake up lest they were lost to Islam, Christianity, atheism and gross materialism. Actually, the present wave of Hindu revivalism has probably been sparked off over the recent years by Indians seeing Westerners taking up their culture (which they had an enormous inferiority complex about) and especially because of the activities of ISKCON.

So we can say that for those who were forgetting Rama, or not very strongly remembering Him, the current agitation has been good for them. However, the communal violence which has erupted in the wake of the agitation cannot at all be pleasing to Rama and in fact, gives a very bad name to India and Hinduism. Why people mercilessly kill each other is described in Bhagavatam 4.26.5 purport. Because people are sinful meat eaters (both Hindus and Muslims) they think nothing of killing each other. But why don't the famous religious and political leaders get out into the streets and use their influence to stop these killings? Would that not also create a suitable atmosphere for the masjid/mandir issue to be settled? Or is the death of lakhs of people part of the temple construction program?

Because people are thinking "I am Hindu," I am Muslim," "I am black," "I am white," "I am a Brahmin," "I am American," "I am Chinese," and so on, they remain entrenched in the bodily concept of life and cannot make any proper spiritual progress, even though they identify themselves as staunch followers of particular religions. They have to come to the sense that, "I am not this body. I am atma, an eternal servant of Krsna."

Distributing this knowledge is the main function of ISKCON. That is especially established by distribution of transcendental books. Books are the basis of this movement. All over the world, during December, devotees hold the Prabhupada book distribution marathon, working morning to night to please Srila Prabhupada by distributing his books. Srila Prabhupada said, "If you really want to please me, then distribute my books." The Prabhupada marathon is a chance to get lots of Prabhupada's mercy.

Here in T our bus is distributing books from 6 am to 10 pm and the response is good. In a few days I will make a quick tour of some towns in A.P. to visit life members who I know and entreat them to donate each 5,000 or 10,000 rupees or whatever they can (most will give about 2,000 rupees) to purchase books which they can then distribute freely to their friends, employees, to schools or they can let us arrange the free distribution.

You also please help us in this way. Send us a donation for Vidya-dan and take books to distribute. Actually the idea of doing a book on Krsna consciousness and Christianity came after speaking to you on the subject in H so I think you should now take as many copies of this book as you can and induce your friends also to do so, distribute these books as you see fit, and thus get all the spiritual benefit of participating in the all-auspicious Prabhupada marathon.

23 December 1990

I was sorry to hear of the major loss due to fire; but, as you noted, there was no loss of life which would have been worse. Such is the nature of this world. "Grasisnu prabhavisnu ca" (Bhagavad-gita, chapter 13: Krsna devours and develops all). Sometimes He gives, sometimes He takes away; our only duty is to surrender to Him under all circumstances.

Sometime I will and must visit Udupi. But I want to go with devotees. It may not be so practical to take our whole bus party down there. Let us see what the future brings.

1991

11 January 1991

Srila Prabhupada wrote in one purport that "all the activities in our Krsna consciousness movement are centered on distributing books" so let us all continue to do so more and more. I'm sending under separate cover a nice cassette for more inspiration on book distribution right from the source: Srila Prabhupada himself!

30 January 1991

Thank you for the article in the Soviet Union magazine. I showed it to some Soviet devotees visiting here. Things have certainly changed dramatically in the USSR and in other parts of the world and are continuing to do so. Is this Krsna's plan to prepare a situation in the world favorable for spreading Krsna consciousness? If so, are we ready to meet the challenge?

Regarding the Gulf war I've just been giving several lectures in colleges in Gujarat on the subject. Some major themes have been 1) War is the inevitable outcome of mass sinful activity 2) therefore Bush, Saddam etc. are not the actual controllers of events; rather they are as instrumental puppets in the hands of maya 3) meaningless violence is a symptom of mercilessness so prominent in Kali-yuga 4) The real solution is not peace talks but chanting Hare Krsna and acting on the platform of spiritual knowledge taught in Bhagavad-gita As It Is. This may sound impossibly idealistic but really it is factual and unless and until the people of the world wake up to it they must suffer repeated war, earthquakes, famine etc.

18 February 1991

I very much want to make a book on "Gods, Demigods and incarnations" and many more books also. But I am seriously inhibited by continuing headaches. As and when Krsna allows me to be freed from the problem, I can start to work intensely on new publications. Until then whatever little I can do, I shall continue to do so.

I'll try to get you some foreign japa-mala bags at the Mayapur Festival, to which I'll be going soon. Please try and come one year to this festival. Srila Prabhupada liked as many devotees as possible from all over the world to come and glorify Lord Caitanya at His birthplace. It's a wonderful opportunity to associate with and hear from devotees all over the world.

On the subject of hearing, why not listen to the greatest acarya of the modern age, the savior of humanity in its darkest hour? I mean of course His Divine Grace A.C. Bhaktivedanta Swami Prabhupada, whose lecture tapes are available from BBT Bombay.

13 March 1991

Thank you for your kind sentiments regarding my health and service. Fortunately my health is not so bad that I can't keep busy in service. Definitely I have committed unlimited sinful activities in this and previous lives so present reactions are Krsna's mercy as a reminder not to fall into that nastiness again.

6 July 1991

Thankyou for your appreciation of the brahmacari book. All you brahmacaris who are out there distributing Srila Prabhupada's books are doing the most wonderful service, so it is a great mercy upon me if by reading this book you can all become more inspired.

If we can just stick to this program: stay brahmacari, live simply, dedicate our lives to preaching and distributing books; then our life is already perfect. It is definitely best to make the determination just to stick to this ashram. Then we can very easily make progress on the path back to Godhead and help others also along the path.

Distribute Srila Prabhupada's books, study them very deeply, and live by them; what more do we want?

All glories to the sankirtan devotees.

7 July 1991

The addition of Srila Prabhupada to your new letterhead is very nice, as is the news that you have given up onions and garlic. Actually, onions and garlic are foodstuffs in the mode of ignorance. According to the Puranas they were produced originally from the intestines of a dog.

Each kind of food that we eat affects our consciousness, so onions and garlic, being in the mode of ignorance, influence our consciousness towards ignorance. Therefore, they are not suitable for Vaisnavas or anyone wanting to elevate their consciousness. Of course, they are said to be valuable medically. However, a few years ago, the government of the USSR sent out a warning to their citizens to stop eating garlic—which they were accustomed to do in large quantities—having found by research that garlic is actually very bad for health. This I heard from devotees preaching there. Exactly what they found bad in it I don't know. Anyway, Krsna doesn't eat it, so we also don't.

It is very good that you are enthusiastic to distribute books. This is the best method of spreading Krsna consciousness—Srila Prabhupada said this many times.

You may have been distributing mostly amongst your acquaintances, but now why not spread your net to reach out to all the citizens of H? It may be a little more difficult to distribute to all different kinds of people, but it is very much possible.

Friends of yours who are now avoiding you because of their lack of interest in Krsna consciousness may be replaced with better friends who you will come into contact with by this book distribution. It is not at all unusual that materialistic friends avoid someone who becomes Krsna conscious. It happens in every case with someone who takes up Krsna consciousness seriously.

Of course, in India most people have some degree of Krsna consciousness, but the vast majority are not interested in taking it up seriously, and they would rather avoid those who are taking up Krsna consciousness seriously, feeling threatened in their material status quo. In this regard please consult Srimad-Bhagavatam: 7.5.30.

"The Hare Krsna Challenge" is a book which people can easily read and understand, and it's sure to start them thinking. Please try to distribute this book very widely. Then people will know our movement is not simply theoretical but that we have a very strong voice on all kinds of issues.

I agree that the BJP is a much better party than all others in as much as they propose to stop all cow slaughter. In this and many other ways they are a welcome alternative to the other parties, who have no interest in Vedic culture except to destroy it. Of course, the BJP members are not Krsna conscious as they are more or less all heavily influenced by Mayavada. Therefore, we also have to be somewhat cautious of them.

It is a fact that our movement should be giving dictation to politicians. We are the only ones with the truth "as it is." But quite frankly, I don't see any sign of this happening in the near future. The politicians generally promise people that which appeals to their sense gratification—our movement is not for sense gratification. So, although we should and do, to a limited extent, preach to politicians, we can't expect that they will take us very seriously unless and until Krsna consciousness begins to be accepted (at least in some way or other) by the masses of Indian people. Who knows what the future will bring? Lord Caitanya has great plans for this movement. He said that it will spread all over the world—therefore it will! Exactly how and when that happens is to be seen. I personally feel that our movement could and should be more strongly preached. There is great potential at the present time for spreading Krsna consciousness. Just see the rise of "Hindutva."

Regarding tea at Hare Krsna Land: Apparently Srila Prabhupada had authorized it, on the grounds that if it was not served so many people wouldn't come, and that tea drinking, although strictly not allowed for serious Vaisnavas, was not such a great vice as, for instance, smoking cigarettes, etc. Anyway, it's not very nice and is a controversial point.

Yes, Srila Prabhupada used snuff. Snuff has its medicinal use to clear the nose and head, and Srila Prabhupada used it for this. Even alcohol has its usage in many Ayurvedic medicines, and even tobacco is commonly used for brushing teeth. Everything has its usage. However, Srila Prabhupada's usage of snuff does not authorize foolish, less intelligent people to indulge in all kinds of nonsense. Srila Prabhupada was a goswami (that is, one in full control of his senses) and could therefore use such things without any danger of becoming involved in their misuse. However, snuff taking is not for everybody, nor is it necessary to widely let it be known that Srila Prabhupada used snuff, lest there be misunderstandings.

It is quite acceptable to offer puja to Tulasi in the evening. In fact, this is a regular practice in many of our ISKCON centres around the world.

Unfortunately I don't have any photo of myself to send to you. Maybe when you come to Vrindavan we can have a photo taken together. That would be very nice.

Anyway, one peculiarity of Vrindavan is that the Brijbasis' see Srimati Radharani as even more important than Lord Sri Krsna!

21 August 1991

If you have a tape copying machine you could bring about 30 cassettes (blanks) and copy some Prabhupada lectures.

Another item of good news is that you are now preparing seriously for taking formal initiation into Krsna consciousness. This is a serious commitment that, "Now let me prepare to fully enter into Krsna consciousness, to enter Krsna's eternal abode, never to return again to this condemned material world. Let me do whatever is necessary to that end." Initiation means becoming very serious so it is very good that you are coming to this point. Of course, initiation is not the end, but rather the beginning, of our real life of deep absorption in Krsna consciousness.

As you have asked if there is anything you can bring from B, please bring a little maha-prasadam from the Deities. If there is any special style of cloth being made there you might want to bring some as a gift for Srimati Radharani on Her birthday. You can consult the pujaris there as to what might be suitable.

14 October 1991

I have been travelling out of Vrindavan—to Chitrakut, Naimisaranya and Karoli (where the original Madan Mohan Deity worshiped by Srila Sanatana Goswami is) for the purpose of making articles for "Back to Godhead."

In one letter Srila Prabhupada wrote that, "If you really appreciate and love me, then try to preach vigorously like me." And once he said, that his disciples should not only distribute his books, but should read them also. So let us read his books, distribute them, follow their instructions, and make them our life and soul.

13 November 1991

Right now I'm sitting in a meeting—Indian continental committee meeting of ISKCON. I will shortly be making a presentation to the body about book distribution and production in India. It is sad to note that, even though all of Srila Prabhupada's books have been translated even in languages like Bulgarian, still in India we don't have all the books translated in even one language.

However one bright note is that in Kannada, the whole Bhagavatam has been translated up to the 12th Canto (complete). Now funds have to be raised for printing this monumental work. I hope that you may get involved in this most important project which is factually more important for preaching than temple construction.

I thank you for your appreciation of the book "Brahmacarya in Krsna Consciousness." It has been well received by devotees all over the world for which I am grateful to Srila Prabhupada for letting me do this service to him and to all the devotees.

So now you will be busy distributing Srila Prabhupada's books again. December is marathon month for book distribution so let us all put our energy into distributing as many books as possible, especially in this month.

17 December 1991

Now your books have come a little late but you can just start your one month marathon from the date you got your books. No special cassettes or T-shirts came out this year. What is coming out special is one lakh gitas. ISKCON B have their one lakh Gita Prachar Sankalpa. By approaching Life Members they are passing out one lakh Gitas. Some members take 1,000 Gitas, some 500, some 100, like that, to give to their friends, employees etc. Some give back to ISKCON (having paid for them) for free or cheap distribution. Now that's real big-time preaching. Surely Srila Prabhupada is satisfied with this. If you want Hare Krsna Challenge, order immediately for the next few months, because the reprint is almost out of stock. It is the most popular English small book by far.

1992

2 February 1992

It is very good news that you have received Srimad-Bhagavatam Maha-purana complete set. Srila Prabhupada said that we should make Srimad-Bhagavatam our life. That means we should read it, absorb it, speak about it, remember it, and preach it especially by distributing it to others. Within a few months BBT Bombay should have printed a cheaper English edition so you can look forward to distributing it. Certainly you will get all blessings to understand Bhagavatam because you not only appreciate this literature as being non-different from Krsna, but you are very eager to serve the message of Bhagavatam by distributing it.

So go on distributing books. What more can I say? It is a very simple formula to please Srila Prabhupada. You are personally feeling the ecstasy of serving His Divine Grace. Your efforts will not go in vain. As you pump more and more books out to the people of H, it will have its effect. Schools, colleges, outlying villages, factories, offices, homes—there are so many places to distribute books. Now you have caught the idea to inspire others. So in this way our movement can spread, person to person.

Thank you for putting your score for book purchases to me. But actually I am now giving my book score to whichever temple happens to be close by. But your sovereign efforts should not go unrecorded. I suggest you send your book sale scores every month to ISKCON B; otherwise BBT Bombay Mail order.

ISKCON B's great endeavor to put out one lakh Gitas fell short. They distributed 65,000 Gitas during December. That is still a tremendous figure. Their buses are out again now to get up towards the one lakh mark. They deserve all congratulations for this great work. And we should go on also doing whatever we can. You wish to distribute Srila Prabhupada's books forever is simply wonderful. Pray for Prabhupada's blessings and he will surely heap them on you.

About this book, "A Beginner's Guide to Krsna Consciousness." Subjects include: How to set up altar at home, how to use a japa-mala, how to put on tilak, the importance of Srila Prabhupada, the difference between Krsna consciousness and general Hinduism, etc., etc.

There is definitely a need for this book. Many people want to learn the practical techniques of Krsna consciousness, but lack guidance. I made such a book a few years ago in Bangladesh, and it became the top seller.

One thing is that I have to finance the printing of this book myself. BBT will distribute it, but I will have to put up the capital for paper and printing. I plan to print about 10,000 copies (depending on how much funds I raise) which would cost about Rs 60,000. So I have been writing to devotees I know who have helped me in the past.

If you could also make some financial contribution, to help me in this service to Srila Prabhupada, I would of course be most grateful.

17 February 1992

Yes, Krsna has been kind to you by giving you the association of devotees. Krsna is very merciful and is always heedful to the prayers of His devotees. According to our sincerity, Krsna will gradually reveal everything about Himself to us.

But patience is also required. Although we may desire earnestly, we cannot expect to achieve Krsna within a day. After all, great yogis meditate for thousands of years just to get a glimpse of the toe of His beautiful lotus feet. Still, that earnestness is our best qualification for achieving Krsna quickly. But also, patience is essential. In this regard, please consult Nectar of Instruction verse no. 3 (by Srila Prabhupada).

That you are considering the association of nondevotees to be a suffocation is a very good sign. Association of materialistic people is most unpalatable for pure devotees. Our solace is to associate with Krsna by reading His books, such as Bhagavad-gita and Srimad-Bhagavatam.

Also, by distributing these books, we get so much blessing from Srila Prabhupada, who so much wanted to uplift all the poor fallen conditioned souls by distributing these books. Srila Prabhupada said, "There is no comparison, there is no competition within the whole universe, with Srimad-Bhagavatam. Every word is for the benefit of human society. Somehow or other if the book goes in his hand he will be benefitted. If he reads even one sloka—or even one word—his life will be successful. Therefore we stress so much on the book distribution. Please distribute books, distribute books, distribute books."

Regarding an easy introductory book on Lord Caitanya— actually I had already decided to make such a book. There is a great need for it. I will start work as soon as possible (which may not be for 6–8 weeks). Let us introduce people to their best friend, Lord Caitanya.

You are welcome to write to me as and when you like. Or if you prefer, you may wish to correspond with any lady devotee. You could try writing to ISKCON B. For devotees like yourself living away from ISKCON temples correspondence is a valuable method to stay inspired.

15 March 1992

Anyway, I got the chance to participate in the Navadvipa Mandala Parikrama. 7 days of walking, chanting, dancing, and feasting in the glorious land of Lord Caitanya. About 500 devotees from all over the world participated. You also please come next year. You will certainly enjoy it and get tremendous spiritual benefit.

Yes, go on reading Srimad-Bhagavatam. Slowly doesn't matter. It is the most sublime literature and cannot be read like a modern novel.

Please contact ISKCON B or BBT Mail Order directly about sending your book scores, they know the new points system. The benefit is that we see how many books are being distributed in different places and offer our scores to Srila Prabhupada. Every little counts.

It is good news that you want to take initiation and I think you should do so. I don't think there should be any problem as your background is very pious. You might just consider that you only stopped onions and garlic quite recently. When sure that you are fully ready, go ahead with full enthusiasm.

Your gift of Sri Raghavendra Swami's maha-prasada, I was able to share with many devotees including some of our top leaders.

Distribute Books, Distribute Books, Distribute Books.

16 April 1992

I am working on the computer here making that book ready and pray for the blessings of the Vaisnavas that it may be published soon, for the pleasure of Prabhupada.

All glories to your book distribution! May it increase always. By now you may be initiated so that is further impetus to serve the parampara by this most important service. Srila Prabhupada is always with us in the preaching mission so go on getting his blessings by distributing books more and more, and inspiring others to do so.

Good news you got Caitanya-caritamrita. It's a really ecstatic book with very deep philosophy also. As well as distributing Srila Prabhupada's books we must read them thoroughly also so it is good that you are awakening your taste for that also. Read again and again Prabhupada's books.

Caitanya Mahaprabhu's appearance falls on Holi so we celebrate it by chanting Hare Krsna.

16 April 1992

Further discussion on Nectar of Instruction verse no. 3. An important point in this verse for those newly coming to devotional service is patience. We cannot expect immediately full success, but we have to go on patiently, expecting Krsna's mercy.

Regarding not associating with nondevotees. This is very difficult for persons such as yourself. What to do in such a situation? We can pray for the association of devotees. Although we may not be able to disassociate ourselves from nondevotees, we should at least not get caught up in their nonsense talk and activities. Remember Prahlad Maharaj and pray for his mercy. Prahlad had only demons as associates but he preached and was able to convert some of the young boys to Krsna consciousness.

So you also preach and make some devotees. Then you will have nice association. There must be many devotees in your area, you just have to uncover their inclination towards Krsna by preaching to them. Preaching means first and foremost distributing books and then also speaking about the books. For this we must read Srila Prabhupada's books carefully so as to be able to explain these teachings to others. In this regard please consult Sri Caitanya-caritamrita, Madhya-lila, chapter 7, texts

126–129. M has a set of Caitanya-caritamrta. So you can borrow from him.

12 May 1992

It is good to see also that you have printed up some mahamantra handbills. Your enthusiasm to preach will be appreciated by Krsna.

Regarding RK: no doubt he said some good things which he may have picked up here and there. But some of his teachings were very bad. For instance, he taught that meat-eating is not bad and personally ate meat even as a "sadhu." By mixing apparently good teachings with nonsense concocted ideas he has confused many good people including yourself. He also said "yata mat tata path"—"As many opinions, that many paths" which is directly opposite to Krsna's instruction, "mam ekam saranam vraja"— "surrender unto Me only."

There is much more which could be said about this but in brief I request you to understand that RK and V were both cheaters and that no bona fide Vaisnava (Gaudiya, Sri, Madhva or whatever) accepts them.

Now this is a test for you. Are you ready to accept Krsna's instruction: "sarva dharman parityajya" or will you remain attached to this so-called RK?

Please refer to Prabhupada's indirect references to the RK mission as follows (see the purports) : Gita 10.42, Bhagavatam 7.15.14, 7.15.37, 4.27.11, 3.15.19, 4.19.22, 6.18.19, 8.16.55, Isopanisad pp. 70–72.

12 May 1992

Attachment to RK mission is most unconducive for Krsna-bhakti so she has to be preached to on that point. She is a good soul, no doubt, and is doing valuable service; but may need careful preaching to so that this sentimental pseudo-devotional attachment be broken.

Good to hear that you are recruiting helpers for book distribution. Krsna is giving you transcendental intelligence how to spread His mission. Srila Prabhupada always told his disciples to "double it!" Whatever book distribution you are doing now, double it. And then again, double it. So one way to increase the distribution is to recruit helpers. Another way is to expand your field of activities to outlying towns and villages. Another way is to sell more and more books to those who already have them.

Blessings to be a good disciple? Chant 16 rounds, distribute books, and study them also. That is a good disciple.

26 May 1992

Regarding putting books into stores–do it. This is a very good program which Srila Prabhupada very much wanted. The book stores always require a rebate. ISKCON M regularly distributes books to stores at BBT price. They make no profit, but the books get distributed. In book distribution, at least in poor countries like India, profit is not our aim. We just want to see the books widely distributed.

Again you ask me to bless you to become a perfect disciple. Becoming a perfect disciple is not simply a matter of blessings. One has to hear and follow the instructions. When one is prepared to surrender fully, then blessings will act. Mercy is there for everyone to take but we also have to become eager enough to receive that mercy.

In our parampara, especially since the time of Srila Bhaktisiddhanta Sarasvati Thakura, emphasis has been firmly on the brhad-mrdanga: publishing and distributing transcendental books. Srila Prabhupada was personally told by Srila Bhaktisiddhanta: "If you ever get money, print books."

Srila Prabhupada stressed so much the importance of book distribution. Therefore, in parampara, his disciples and grand-disciples can easily get the mercy if they also stress on this secret of preaching success: distribute books, distribute books, distribute books.

You are personally experiencing the bliss of book distribution. Krsna is reciprocating and giving you the intelligence how to expand, by recruiting other book distributors, distributing books as prizes, to clubs, to shops etc.

Now, if you want to be a perfect disciple, try to do something to satisfy the parampara. You have made a group. Sit down together and seriously discuss how to increase your book distribution. You have intelligence, youthful energy, prestige and many material advantages. If you engage all these assets to distribute Srila Prabhupada's books, that will be the perfection of your life.

Think big. Whatever book distribution you are doing now, aim to increase many times over. Go back to people who have shown interest, give them a little prasad, speak to them nicely, and induce them gradually to take more and more books.

Set yourselves quotas. "This month we have to do one thousand books." Fulfill your quota come what may; increase every month. Don't just order a few books at a time. You should start distributing thousands of rupees worth of books every month. You are not limited to H and D but can expand your field of activities.

Book distribution is unlimited. When devotees first started distributing big books in America, they thought it would be impossible. But some devotees started doing 1 or 2 a day. After a few years some devotees were doing over 100 big books every day! Even now some German and Swiss devotees sell several hundred, sometimes a thousand books a day, on the streets, in the Christmas season.

So see what you can do. If we are sincere, Krsna will surely help us. It is time to move up gear and get into some serious book distribution.

Regarding S. I sent her a strong letter openly stating the fact that RK and V were meat-eaters, misleaders, and rascals and that she should not be attached to them. No doubt S is a very good devotee but, like so many others, misled due to wrongly-placed sentiment. Now you please preach to her also. When a devotee actually understands what is what and who is who, understanding philosophically how Krsna is the Supreme Personality of Godhead and we are all His eternal servants, and when he rejects everything bogus—at that time he (or she) can really make a strong commitment to Krsna consciousness and become a fixed-up devotee.

6 June 1992

The ISKCON Hare Krsna Gift Shop is a superb idea. Do it and be blessed. Make it at least break even financially and you could be opening a new frontier in preaching. Don't sacrifice purity for the sake of profit, though. Pictures of demigods and other religious items not conducive towards Krsna consciousness should not be sold.

Regarding the ekasloki Ramayana etc. I don't know anything about it. Srila Prabhupada has not mentioned it in his books. Prabhupada gave us the 18,000 verse Bhagavatam, full of variegated topics of Krsna. Why should we be anxious to get it over within one minute? What is the evidence that this is actually by Vedavyasa? And even if we were to get the same punya from the "ekasloki-Bhagavatam," we are not interested in punya, but in bhakti. In Hinduism, so many people say so many things, it can be bewildering. I just stick to what Prabhupada has given us and feel safe and protected by that.

Regarding book distribution, double it. Try to do it and you won't. Resolve—"I must do it"—and with this mood, praying to guru and Krsna, surely you will.

26 June 1992

This is real preaching: distributing books, convincing people to give up Mayavada, making a shop for preaching. Canakya Pandit says that one good flower can make a whole forest fragrant. Similarly, if there is one fired-up preacher, he can have tremendous impact on the whole area around him.

You have done a great service to S by cutting away the nasty weeds or sentimental attachment to Mayavada. Srila Prabhupada will be so happy as he personally detested this nonsense RK. Don't repeat this publicly, but Srila Prabhupada once said, "If I had been in power at the time, I would have killed RK."

His influence has been so perfidious; now it is our duty as preachers of Krsna consciousness to save people from the influence of these Mayavadis. Go on distributing these books that will have the best effect.

Always preach, always teach, and simultaneously keep yourself strong by regularly chanting 16 rounds of the Hare Krsna maha-mantra carefully on beads, and also studying Srila Prabhupada's books daily.

6 July 1992

On the path of Krsna consciousness there may be many upheavals. We cannot know what to expect. Krsna is anxious to see the obstacles in the path of devotion removed from His devotees' lives so that they can worship Him purely. Sometimes removal of those obstacles may seem painful. Just as in surgery, the pain is necessary but short-lived, and afterwards the patient continues to enjoy the benefit.

One other lesson from this incident is that Krsna's mercy manifests through His devotees. To be attached to Krsna means to be attached to His devotees. We can only approach Krsna through His devotees, not directly.

You have understood correctly. Read Srila Prabhupada's books. Follow his divine instructions and thus make sure steps towards Him. Krsna will help you.

You have also noted that many points may be better cleared by personal association. For that please approach *** Prabhu or any other ISKCON devotees. But do also study Srila Prabhupada's books carefully—all questions are answered therein.

Achieving perfection in chanting the Hare Krsna mantra can be achieved in course of time by any devotee who sincerely attempts to chant inoffensively and who follows the standard rules and regulations under the directions of a bona fide spiritual master.

20 July 1992

I am sending along with this one cassette which will form the basis of one chapter of an upcoming book on Vaisnava culture, etiquette, and behavior.

Regarding building big, expensive temples. Big temples are also meant for preaching. Many people will be attracted to come and take darshan, prasadam etc. A big temple does not necessarily mean that the devotees living there are not living simply. For themselves, they may have simple facilities; for Krsna everything opulent. Srila Prabhupada himself put much endeavor into establishing our temples at Mayapur, Vrindavan, and Bombay. He felt that big centers were required to establish our movement in the eyes of the public. It is a fact that most people take us more seriously because of these big centers.

On the other hand, much endeavor and money goes into building them (although the 10 crores you quoted sounds like an exaggeration). In B it may be understood, as we should have a model centre in each state. In P, I don't see the necessity. It is not that "ISKCON is encouraging." Our society is loosely-knit. There is much autonomy for local leaders. So if, in a few years, they can collect enough to build a big centre which will stand as a landmark for our society maybe for hundreds of years, it should be a good thing.

Of course, the main thing is to build the character of the devotees living in the temple. A big building without spiritual substance is meaningless. As far as I know the endeavor to build the devotees up spiritually is not lacking in B.

Regarding taking donations from rich people. Srila Prabhupada considered that we were helping such people by engaging their wealth in Krsna's service, thus saving them from going to hell. In the modern age to do anything substantial an organization is needed. Organization means buildings, books, vehicles, legal matters, computers, etc. All these require money. Srila Prabhupada himself demonstrated how to use all of these in Krsna's service without being affected. Whatever donations he got he used for printing books and building temples yet he always remained pure and simple. This is called yukta-vairagya (please consult "Nectar of Devotion" for a full explanation of yukta-vairagya).

29 August 1992

Worshipers of Shirdi Sai Baba are all foolish people who have no knowledge of, or interest in, sastra. This Baba maybe had some mystic power, and out of ignorance people accept him as God, although they have no idea of what is the meaning of the term "God." You can try telling such people what is the actual definition of the word "God" (see Bhagavad-gita As It Is 2.2 purport). But this type of person is usually hopeless to preach to because they want to remain cheated forever. If possible, induce them to purchase Prabhupada's books. That is the best preaching always.

Due to baldness over most of his head in later years, Srila Prabhupada did not have a sikha, for some time; later he grew a sikha at the bottom of his divine head where there was still some hair.

Krsna is eternal and is eternally worshiped, even by Prahlad Maharaj in Satya-yuga (before Lord Rama's advent) (see Srimad-Bhagavatam 7.5.30).

Please tell S, as she has asked, that certainly more than 16 rounds can be chanted daily. The more the better. But other services should not be neglected.

It is to your credit that you have found out one sincere soul by your preaching. The more you preach, the more Krsna will respond; that is a fact.

It is good also that you are relishing the nectar from Srila Prabhupada's books. Read, chant, preach, serve, associate with devotees—this is the simple and effective process given by Sri Caitanya Mahaprabhu.

7 October 1992

Not all the names of Visnu are equal in potency. In one sense, yes, in another, no. Names of Krsna like Nandasuta, Vrindavanchandra, Gopinath are more pleasing to Him than names like Vibhu, Prajapati, or Lokaswami as they are more intimate. In Caitanya-caritamrita it is described that chanting the name of Rama is equivalent to chanting a thousand names of Visnu, and chanting Krsna once is equivalent to chanting Rama three times. In one sense, all are absolute and therefore equal. In another, deeper understanding, there are also gradations in the Absolute.

You understand that Visnu is different from Krsna, but He is not different. He is non-different, yet also different. Caitanya Mahaprabhu's philosophy of acintyabhedabheda tattva explains all these points and resolves all other philosophies, such as visistadvaita, suddha-dvaita, and even kevaladvaita.

Krsna has unlimited names. Different Vaisnava acaryas have made up lists such as Balgopal Sahasranama. Some of them have been translated into English by one of our American godbrothers. They are available in America and are expensive. I suggest you not worry too much about this at present. Try to understand Krsna consciousness as presented in Srila Prabhupada's books, by reading them repeatedly.

Who said ISKCON devotees are not allowed to read about Tukaram, etc? This year Back to Godhead magazine ran a major article in one of its issues on Pandharapur in which praise was given to the Vaisnava saints of Maharashtra. Of course, we put more emphasis on studying the philosophy and saints of the Gaudiya Vaisnava sampradaya. There have been many pure devotees throughout India from different sampradayas. But the philosophical conclusion, and especially the levels of appreciation of Krsna, found in the Gaudiya Vaisnava sampradaya, is incomparable. But that does not mean that we have anything less than the highest respect for great Vaisnava saints in any sampradaya. Incidentally, Tukaram is understood to be initiated by Caitanya Mahaprabhu. One point is that those who are nowadays presenting the lives and teachings of the Maharastrian saints are almost all influenced by Mayavada. So whom shall we hear from?

The six Goswamis of Vrindavan were dear to both the gentle and the ruffians because they were not envious of anyone. We saw that even though Srila Prabhupada spoke so strongly, he held no personal grudge against anyone and was charming, expert in bringing people round. Still, he never compromised, and therefore he sometimes became angry with foolish rascals, and sometimes fools became angry with him.

7 October 1992

Wonderful news that you have now opened the Hare Krsna Gifts shop. I am sure that your combination of business acumen and devotional fervor will be blessed by Krsna to make it a great success.

Very good news that you have found another soul for Krsna. Better, though, if you personally encourage her now. If you like that she should get some inspiration by letter I suggest that you contact one of the matajis at ISKCON B to correspond with her. The main thing is to absorb what is in Prabhupada's books, which I am sure you are competent to direct her in, at least in the basic philosophy.

Srimati Radharani's name is not mentioned in Bhagavatam because Sukadeva Gosvami had limited time to speak to king Pariksit and he was afraid of becoming stunned with ecstasy if he spoke the name "Radha."

Ivory is considered pure but is not commonly used for Murtis, at least not in our sampradaya. Be careful in selling Murtis. The real system for Deity worship is that one should be trained by a competent acarya who is satisfied that the devotee is a bona fide candidate for doing puja. The forms of God are not like dolls. They should be worshiped properly or not at all. In the beginning we ask people to chant Hare Krsna. If selling Deities, best sell Gaura-Nitai. We want to spread Krsna consciousness widely, but not cheaply.

Thank you for your kind appreciation. You speak of my mercy but I am simply a peon repeating what Prabhupada emphasized most: distribute books.

I suggest that in your Gift shop you keep books at a minimum price and make profit from other items. People mostly prefer to purchase paraphernalia. We have to push them to take books. In India, Srila Prabhupada wanted to keep the price of his books low so that the common man could afford them. The real success of the Hare Krsna Gift shop will be in how many books you distribute.

1 November 1992

The story of the demise of the Gaudiya Math is certainly not pleasant. Still, it is a reality, and serves as a reminder of the danger of personal ambition, which can cause havoc in the spiritual life not only of the individual, but of the whole organization.

1 November 1992

About selling murtis. The proper process of keeping murtis at home is to worship Them with love. It should be done by initiated, trained devotees. To keep a murti on the wall like a piece of furniture or a statue is offensive.

Congratulations also on enlisting another devotee and book distributor. This is a sign of spiritual health, that your activities are expanding.

16 November 1992

I must thank you for your help. I know it is a painstaking task to transcribe cassettes. But it is helping to make these books. Making books is a long and laborious process, but the end result is worth it all if people feel inspired in Krsna consciousness.

The history of Gaudiya Math after 1935 is certainly not very palatable. Considering your response—one of dismay and some confusion—I am considering either publishing it as a separate booklet or not publishing it at all. There is much instruction to be had from it, but those who do not have firm faith in the sankirtan movement of Lord Caitanya may take it otherwise. It has been valuable for me to get your response and I shall now consider seriously about the publication of this information.

A godbrother, S Prabhu, has requested me to send him my research material on the history of the Gaudiya Math as he wishes to write a book on it. So maybe I will leave the task on him.

Please don't feel discouraged. Just understand that due to the mighty influence of Kali-yuga, even in a society of devotees, desires for power may enter and pollute. Our ISKCON has not been free from this phenomenon, although by Krsna's grace we are going on much better than the Gaudiya Math.

The best thing is to keep ourselves pure by chanting Hare Krsna with faith, and praying for strength to overcome the mighty force of Kali-yuga.

16 November 1992

Certainly Krsna is reciprocating with you. Krsna wants His message spread. Those who help this most important work are certainly favored by Him. You are distributing books, you have a Hare Krsna gift shop, and you are cultivating people to take up devotional service. And all this while overseeing a business! You always ask for my blessings, but it seems as if Srila Prabhupada is bestowing his blessings on you profusely. What is there for me to add? Rather I should take blessings from those who are favored by Krsna.

"Beginners' Guide to Krsna Consciousness" is printed but I don't want it distributed yet. I saw an advance copy and the printing is not good. At least one format will have to be reprinted and for this I have come to Bombay.

26 November 1992

Great news you sold a Bhagavatam set. That is real preaching. Soon, 2000 Bhagavatam sets will be available from BBT Bombay. See how many you can distribute. The way things are developing in your preaching, it just seems that Krsna is blessing your endeavors to increase more and more. December is coming—time for the special push.

28 November 1992

Some years ago I asked a devotee who had taken formal training in Ayurveda, about garlic. He said that because it is tamasic (strongly) it should never be taken, even for medicinal purposes, by devotees. Many ayurvedic medicines contain alcohol. Srila Prabhupada recommended that Western devotees in India use kalmegh "liquor." The idea is to take only a tiny quantity with plenty of water, not to indulge and get drunk. Once when I was very weak I asked an ayurvedic doctor about mrtyu-sanjivani, an ayurvedic "wine" mentioned in Bhagavatam which invigorates even those who are practically dead. He told me that it is not for Vaisnavas; its effect is not sattvic.

Once a devotee asked Prabhupada if he could take an ayurvedic medicine containing meat. The cryptic reply: "Only if it is guaranteed to cure you." The idea is that to facilitate Krsna's service, anything maybe done. But there is no such thing as a guaranteed cure. There are dozens of medicines in Ayurveda for combating cold and flu. It is not necessary to ingest garlic. Try Sudarshan Churna.

You must remember that you had presented me with a Kashmiri wool chaddar. Up until now, I did not use it—it had not been cold enough. Yesterday I thought to use it but saw that the Deities of Sri Sri Radha-Giridhari had no chaddar. So, happy news for you is that I have presented it to Them. We also bought new chaddars for the big Deities.

25 December 1992

Advice to Bh. U, same advice to everyone: try to increase love for Krsna by chanting His holy names with reading Prabhupada's books.

Unknown date

I am going to be basing at our small ISKCON Radha Giridhari temple here as there are 15,000 students living all around us and it is a golden opportunity for preaching.

Your remarks about the devotees at ISKCON P planning to build a huge expensive project are interesting. I had not heard of such plans before. I agree with your observations. Better to concentrate on publishing and distributing books, that is the most important part of preaching.

How to give Lord Caitanya's message to poor and illiterate people? Induce them to chant Hare Krsna and take Krsna Prasad.

Go on chanting Hare Krsna, read Srila Prabhupada's books and associate with devotees as much as possible. Make yourself strong in Krsna consciousness and make yourself fit to preach to others. All of us have important work to do in spreading Srila Prabhupada and Lord Caitanya's mission.

Unknown date

It is very encouraging and enthusing to hear of your increased plans for book distribution. Krsna is enlivening your transcendental intelligence to find out novel ways to distribute Srila Prabhupada's all-important books more and more and more.

Caitanya Mahaprabhu was approached by one brahmin in South India who wanted to follow Him on His divine tour but

Mahaprabhu told him, "No! Stay here and make all the people of your area Krsna conscious." So you can take up the same advice by making all of H Krsna conscious. And the best way to do that is to profusely distribute Srila Prabhupada's books. Srila Prabhupada said, "You should know it for certain that there is no better way to preach than to distribute my books." Increase it more and more and more. Krsna will give you more and more intelligence and transcendental realizations how to do it and how to depend on Him to cross over all obstacles in this big fight against maya.

Then we can discuss so much Krsna conscious philosophy, chant Hare Krsna together, take prasadam together, go for bath in the Yamuna, and most important of all, work out how to always distribute more and more books.

Jai! The mercy of Srila Prabhupada is raining on your lead.

Some things you could bring for the Deities is mangoes (a good local variety) and avacados, and some first class Bangalore incense.

Unknown date

Regarding Jesus Christ, the best thing is to read East West Dialogues (Krsna Consciousness and Christianity) available from BBT Bombay. Jesus did say, "No one comes to the Lord but through me," but this has been misinterpreted. For the time and place in which he was speaking it was true. No one but he was preaching amongst those people at that time. But so-called Christians quote this as if to say that all the acaryas (Madhva, Ramanuja, Rupa Gosvami etc.) are bogus which is of course untrue.

Basically, most, almost all, of what goes on in the name of religion in this Kali-yuga, be it Hinduism, Christianity or Islam or whatever, is all distorted, incomplete, and full of contradictions.

Prabhupada gave the real thing, bhagavat-dharma, by the simple process of chantng Hare Krsna, speaking from sastra, distributing Krsna-prasada.

1993

2 March 1993

It is very good news that you are tasting the sweet nectar of Sri Caitanya-caritamrita. I also think it to be the most ecstatic book.

How is it possible that Caitanya-caritamrita seems even sweeter than the Srimad-Bhagvatam? This is a very deep question which is not easy for everyone to understand. We get a clue from Caitanya-caritamrita, Adi-lila, Chapter 1, text 4 which is explained fully by whole of Adi-lila, chapter 3.

22 April 1993

It is very nice to know that you are continuing to relish the nectar of Srimad-Bhagavatam and Caitanya-caritamrita. Preaching is difficult work, but when we uncover one sincere soul like yourself, it all becomes worthwhile. So you also preach and make more devotees.

15 June 1993

Karnataka seems to be a prime state for Krsna consciousness.

15 June 1993

Still now I haven't got any reply from the devotee in Australia who was supposed to be doing that book on Lord Caitanya. So probably I shall have to do it myself, which of course will be a pleasure. But now I am involved in several books at once so we shall have to see when I can do such a book. At least encouragement from yourselves and others helps maintain my enthusiasm for going on with this writing work.

You ask about preaching. Please read the book, "Preaching is the Essence" just published by BBT Bombay. The essence is to depend on guru and Krsna and sincerely try to bring others to Krsna. Of course, for a committed preacher, knowledge of scripture is also essential. Otherwise, what will he/she preach?

Your desire to hear from devotees is very nice. Whenever you get the chance, please visit ISKCON temples to associate with devotees. In the meantime you can go on reading Prabhupada's books. By reading Prabhupada's books, you directly associate with the greatest pure devotee of our time and take instructions from him.

Have you read Srila Prabhupada Lilamrita also? Please do it, it is really inspiring.

25 June 1993

Thanks for your letter of 21st with the excellent news that now you have 14 devotees chanting 16 rounds daily. Just see how Prabhupada is blessing your book distribution! When you started you were afraid of losing friends. Now you have spiritual association more than you could have imagined, and certainly it will increase. Anandambudhi-vardhanam. The ocean of Lord Caitanya's sankirtan ecstasy is always increasing, never decreasing.

You are speaking also. This is correct. Study Prabhupada's books, practice, and preach. Simple formula but ever effective.

Bhaktivinoda Thakura may have taken babaji initiation from Gaura-kisora dasa Babaji, not sannyasa. Vaisnava sannyasa was introduced in our sampradaya by Bhaktisiddhanta Sarasvati

Thakura, after the disappearance of both Bhaktivinoda and Gaura Kisora. This is a little technical point, when we meet, I can explain.

19 July 1993

Everywhere I've been so far in Europe devotees are greeting me nicely. They are generally much more happy to receive a visiting sannyasi than at our temples in India. The general level of enthusiasm is considerably higher, also, although Western devotees, especially newer ones, have the problem of shaking off the contamination of Western sense gratification culture. I'm surprised to note, also, how some of them are strongly attached to their family, even if the family members are staunch nondevotees. Times have changed since I joined ISKCON.

3 October 1993

Nice to know that they are now becoming more and more enthusiastic. That is a sign of advancement in Krsna consciousness, when we want to serve more and more. Are the young ladies cooking also? They should learn.

About the book, "The Divine Name" by Raghava Caitanya Das. When Prabhupada was asked about it, he said it is more or less alright, although there may be a few minor discrepancies in it.

8 October 1993

It is a great help in my work. Just now I am very busy in publishing different books, but gradually I hope to be able to bring out all these planned books, one by one. Please pray to Krsna to give me the physical, mental, and spiritual strength to continue doing this service to Him.

You are very anxious for the book on Lord Caitanya Mahaprabhu. You are a devotee, so surely Krsna will fulfill your desire. As I explained in my last letter, I am still trying to get another devotee to take up this task as I am overloaded with other writing projects just now. Anyway, let us see. If I had some more strength, purity, and intelligence I could do more work, but being very limited, I am just trying to do what little I can.

15 October 1993

Sometimes Krsna leaves Radha to go to Chandravali. Chandravali always tries to entice Krsna away from Radha. This is just to increase the divine deliciousness of Krsna's love for Radha. Actually, Krsna's real object of affection is Radha and Radha only, but to increase Her feelings for Him and to enhance transcendental loving ecstasies of jealousy, pride, neglect etc., Krsna sometimes pretends to prefer Chandravali over Radhika.

Chandravali, although one of the two main gopis, is not one of the asta-sakhis because the asta-sakhis are assistants of Radhika. The staunch followers of Radhika do not even like to hear the name of Chandravali!

This is all going on the highest transcendental plane of ecstatic bliss of Krsna consciousness. It is not possible for those tinged with mundane desires to even begin to understand these dealings. Still, our ultimate aim is the service of Srimati Radhika, so there is no harm for us to know these things, even if our power of appreciation is very little.

The position of the followers of Caitanya Mahaprabhu in their previous appearance as followers of Lord Krsna is described in a book called "Gaura-ganoddesa-dipika" by Kavi Karnapura. It is a Sanskrit book. It has been translated in Bengali and also English. The English edition is available in USA and is very costly.

The names of Lord Caitanya's associates and their previous positions in Krsna-lila have been given in Srila Prabhupada's Caitanya-caritamrita edition in English. All the main devotees are listed there. See especially Adi-lila, volumes 2 and 3.

3 November 1993

In December devotees all over the world will be participating in the Prabhupada's book distribution marathon so I hope the H branch will be "fired up" also! One way to distribute many books is to ask businessmen to individually purchase 1,000 or more (or less, even 100 or even 50 or even 20) Gitas for free distribution to friends, schools etc: it can be done in the name of a departed relative, if desired. In that case a handbill or rubber stamp can be inserted saying, "In memory of ..." or whatever. Distribute books! Distribute books! Distribute books!

You often write that you like to hear me speak so I suggest that if possible you come to Vrindavan for the Govardhana-puja and Prabhupada's disappearance festival. I may not be speaking myself, but there will be many senior devotees whose discourses you can be enlightened by. I may try to come to H in January. If I come, some public function should be arranged.

17 November 1993

The Hare Krsna mahamantra is particularly recommended in the sastra (Kalisantarana Upanisad), by Lord Caitanya Mahaprabhu, and by our acaryas. Some of our acaryas have elaborately analyzed the meaning of the mahamantra. All names of Krsna are equal, but the Hare Krsna mahamantra is a prayer to Krsna along with the internal potency, (Srimati Radharani) that particularly pleases Him.

1994

21 January 1994

Regarding all these technical questions, I advise you to write directly to him, as his knowledge of scripture is far deeper than mine. When I have questions, I write to him he can guide you properly.

The best news you have given is of your continued enthusiasm in distributing Srila Prabhupada's books. This is always pleasing to Srila Prabhupada and you are no doubt experiencing his blessings. Please continue in this way and your advancement in Krsna consciousness will go on and on very nicely.

I am a very small and useless person, but if I have received any mercy from Srila Prabhupada, I extend my blessings to the devotees of H for their ever advancement in Krsna consciousness.

6 February 1994

Now I am concentrating mainly on writing and publishing, not so much travelling and preaching. Of course, next month I am scheduled to go to Pakistan, UAE, and Bahrain, then after that Mayapur, probably Orissa, and Andhra Pradesh also.

Please continue this transcription work. It is of a great help to me. I am much looking forward to the next one you will do,

H. H. Narmada Swami's memories of life in India before full modernization so badly damaged the old culture.

22 March 1994

You please go on with your preaching work! Be careful also to find time to chant daily 16 rounds and to read Srila Prabhupada's books.

29 May 1994

I do not at all deserve such nice treatment. It is all Prabhupada's mercy, and your kindness.

10 October 1994

Let this be our goal of our life: always to remember the lotus feet of Lord Sri Krsna, and never to forget Them.

30 November 1994

It's nice that you want to preach; I appreciate your efforts in this regard. Unfortunately, it seems that your idea of preaching is different from that of your husband. You should not think, however, that your husband is not preaching. The proofs are: Janmastami celebration held at your place, exhibitions organized by your husband and people in *** that started to practise Krsna consciousness. It seems your husband doesn't like to go out to preach, preferring to stay at home and bring up +++ in Krsna consciousness. I don't think it's bad. For family people in Krsna consciousness it's important to set a good example to others. Therefore, grihasthas may preach and spend enough time with their family, especially if they have small children.

Another point—for the preaching to be effective we have to show people how Krsna consciousness practically improves their lives. It doesn't look good if practising Krsna consciousness the husband and wife don't get on together. Conversely, if grihastha devotees can show how they can live together, it would attract others to follow their example. Srila Prabhupada has stated that a psychology of a man is that he always wants to feel superior to his wife, and, therefore, peace in the family can be maintained if the wife always remains submissive to the husband and tries to please him in all respects. It may be your opinion that what you're doing is more Krsna conscious, but if as a result of that there's tension in the home, then gains made in preaching on one side are lost in another way. It isn't that your husband is a bad person and he is asking you to do anything wrong. You're very lucky to have a husband who is a devotee and who is serious about Krsna consciousness. There are many women-devotees who either don't have husbands or whose husbands are against their being devotees. Simply your husband has a different opinion on how you should live in Krsna consciousness. As you're not being able to change his opinion, I think that for the long-term development of your Krsna consciousness, his Krsna consciousness and your son's Krsna consciousness, that you comply with what he says, even if it may be difficult for you to do so. Try to do so uncomplainingly and in this way try to gradually conquer his heart by your sweet service. In this regard there are some important statements by Srila Prabhupada:

> If any wife wants to be happy with her husband, she must try to understand her husband's temperament and please him. This is victory for a woman. Even in the dealings of Lord Krsna with His different queens, it has been seen that although the queens were the daughters of great kings, they placed themselves before Lord Krsna as His maidservants. However great a woman may be, she must place herself before her husband in this way; that is to say, she must be ready to carry out her husband's orders and please him in all circumstances. Then her life will be successful. (SB 9.3.10, purport)

The husband is a very intimate friend, therefore the wife must render service just like an intimate friend, and at the same time she must understand that the husband is superior in position, and thus she must offer him all respect. Even if there is some wrong on the part of the husband, the wife must tolerate it, and thus there will be no misunderstanding between husband and wife. (SB 3.23.2, purport)

1995

24 January 1995

Regarding marriage—I do not think your opinion to be more important than that of Srila Prabhupada and sastra.

9 April 1995

Family matters can be very complex and it's not possible to give any exact advice as the situation will always be changing; plus I'm quite removed from it. However, general advice is that family matters are usually best handled quite sensitively. I suggest that you try to keep as good relationships as you can with your brother and mother, and not say anything harsh to them, but more or less wait until your father's arrival to reveal your feelings to him and see if he can help build a bridge. It's interesting that in Guru Granth Sahib there are so many prayers to Krsna! Please also see the section in my Beginner's Guide to Krsna consciousness about dealing with near and dear ones.

3 October 1995

*** Prabhu tells me that you are distributing many books, but that you are suffering from health problems. Good news and bad news. Actually everyone has to suffer in this material world in one way or another, especially in the Kali-yuga. But somehow or other, if, despite all difficulties, we can go on serving Sri Krsna, that will be our pass for going back to Godhead. (See the verse beginning from "tat te 'nukampam" from Bhagavatam's Tenth canto, Lord Brahma's prayers; also quoted in Caitanya-caritamrita Madhya-lila in the chapter where Lord Caitanya converts Sarvabhauma Bhattacarya to Vaisnavism.

Bhaktivinoda Thakura's official diksa guru was Bipin Bihari Gosvami. I don't remember the name of Gaura Kisora Dasa Babaji's initiating guru just now, nor do I have the reference book (in Bengali) on hand. In the list of gurus given in our books, only the most outstanding acaryas in the parampara have been listed. Apart from them, there are many other gurus whose names have not been included in the list.

The name "Sri Varsabhanavi-dayita Dasa" of Srila Bhaktisiddhanta Sarasvati Thakura is not so well-known because after taking sannyasa, the sannyasa name is generally used. Just as the diksa-nama of Prabhupada, "Abhaya Caranaravinda" is not so well-known.

There are many details of knowledge of our parampara. When we meet, I can tell you more. The main thing is to serve the parampara through its present representatives, and pray for the mercy of the previous acaryas.

20 November 1995

We are also suffering from power cuts here. I go on reading and writing by candle light. You could do the same. Anyway, some way or other, do find time to read Srila Prabhupada's books. It is very important.

14 December 1995

The good news is that you have a potential translator for "Beginner's Guide to Krsna Consciousness." Is he a devotee? If not, the translation will have to be very carefully monitored as many misunderstandings may creep in. The language should be kept simple, or as it is in English, so that common people can easily understand it. Does this person want payment? If so, how much? Better to do it as a service, without payment. Let him do two or three pages as a sample, and have two or three devotees give their opinions about the quality of work. Translation is not such a simple task.

I am surprised at your determination not to get married as Srila Prabhupada repeatedly stresses in his books that all women must get married. This applies to devotee women also.

Hoping this finds you ever progressive in your determination to achieve love of God.

1996

25 January 1996

Thankyou for your COM letter. I am replying by post due to problems accessing COM. I remember that in Ljubljana you wrote a kind note and also presented me with a donation.

I thought I can become determined by my own efforts and then write to Your Divine Grace for mercy to accept me as Your disciple. But I was wrong....... I'm aware of the fact that I'm far away from the qualifications, required to become a bona fide disciple, but I still have faith and hope that You would be so merciful unto me to guide me in my spiritual life and, if that would be Your desire, accept me as Your eternal servant when I become at least a little bit qualified.

Yes, I will accept you as an aspiring disciple on the condition that you immediately and without fail chant 16 rounds daily and attend the temple morning program, whether you feel you like it or not. Without this, there is no question of spiritual advancement.

I lost taste for chanting, attending guru puja and morning lecture, visiting the temple in general.

Whether or not you have taste is irrelevant. Taste will come if you follow. If you don't follow, there is no hope.

Many times I hear that praying to Krsna is very important. Since now I've been neglecting that limb of devotional service, but now I have some desire to pray to Krsna. I've tried it and some questions appeared. Could You be so kind to give me some instructions about praying to Krsna? I feel that my prayers are not sincere, even when I pray to improve my sadhana. Sometimes I try to praise Krsna in my prayers, but I'm not very good at putting it together, many times it comes out very foolish. Please instruct me how to pray sincerely, what to pray for, how to form the prayer.

Your desire to pray is very nice. Actually, we should pray at every moment. It is best to pray as great devotees have prayed as in our neophyte stage we don't know what is pleasing to Krsna. "Reciting notable prayers" is described in the Nectar of Devotion, chapter 9. There it is recommended to select some prayers for recitation. Some of my favorites are Queen Kunti's prayers, Stotra-ratna, and Mukunda-mala-stotra.

I have a desire to correspond with one of Your disciples, but I couldn't find anyone. If You think there is someone I could correspond with, could You please give me her address so that I can write to her?

You could write to BK Devi Dasi, the wife of B Das.

The services you are engaged in are all very important. Please continue them with full enthusiasm.

4 March 1996

Thankyou for your letter of 27.2.96 and the nice picture of Srila Prabhupada. Good news of renewed endeavors in Krsna consciousness. Now remain steady. Don't slip back.

Immediately I started chanting 16 rounds and attending temple morning program—Srila Prabhupada guru-puja and Srimad-Bhagavatam class. As far as mangala-arati is concerned, I'd like to ask you for permission to have mangala-arati at home, because going out so early in the morning could irritate my parents. Sometimes I also get late to rest or I come late from the preaching program and then I have mangala-arati a little late.

Yes, have mangala-arati at home. If, due to circumstances, you have mangala-arati a little late, that is OK.

If I continue to follow everything in the future, when can I start reciting Your pranama-mantra?

Continue in this way, and when the local temple authorities feel that you are ready to take the pre-initiation test, you may start chanting my pranama-mantra upon passing the test.

The devotees have brought me Sri Sri Gaura-Nitai murtis. Please tell me whether or not I may put Them on the altar and offer Them some simple worship. If I may, could You then instruct me what worship should I offer Them to please Them?

According to Srila Prabhupada's direction, it is better for devotees living in the vicinity of an ISKCON temple to join in the worship there than to become absorbed in home Deity worship. Keep a simple altar of pictures only at home. You may daily offer mangala-arati and whatever food you offer at home.

Now learn some of those beautiful prayers.

17 March 1996

The best way to chant both the names of Radha and Krsna is as our acaryas have recommended, namely:

Hare Krsna Hare Krsna Krsna Krsna Hare Hare
Hare Rama Hare Rama Rama Rama Hare Hare

And the best way to chant the names of Lord Caitanya and Lord Nityananda is, "Sri Krsna Caitanya Prabhu Nityananda Sri Advaita Gadadhara Srivasadi Gaura-bhakta-vrinda." We may also chant Jaya Prabhupada. These are all transcendental, authorized chants that will help lift us to the stage of love of God. We should be careful to avoid speculative chanting. I have written an extensive section on this in my upcoming book, "Vaisnava Culture, Etiquette, and Behavior."

Srimati Radharani may or may not hear our prayers. We cannot force Her.

Now study Srila Prabhupada's books carefully, especially Bhagavad-gita As It Is.

8 August 1996

But don't overstrain yourself! Take time to read Srila Prabhupada's books. This is most important.

Of course I can never forget the devotee girls in D who received me so enthusiastically and affectionately. Her desire to help you in serving me is a spiritual desire (because I am attempting to serve my spiritual master who is serving Krsna). That desire will not go unfulfilled. Nothing material can stop Krsna consciousness; certainly not the death of the body. Na hi kalyana-krt kascid durgatim tata gacchati.

Might you be interested to write a few letters to devotees in different parts of the world? I have a few disciples and aspiring disciples in women's bodies scattered here and there who would benefit from your advice. You have a few years of experience of practicing Krsna consciousness at home which could help them. Please let me know in your next letter.

Hoping this meets you in good health, and that your book distribution is going on nicely.

26 August 1996

As I am quite sick I will not comment on every point. But I am very, very happy to hear of the preaching experience you are having. Anandambudhi vardhanam. By preaching we get practical realization of what we study. Everything becomes clear.

Your friend in Tamil Nadu who wants to join as a brahmachari may be directed towards me. Somehow or other, although I spend little time in Tamil Nadu, quite a few Tamil people are coming to me. Of course, we are not these bodies. Nevertheless, my temperament seems well in tune with that of the Tamil people.

At least, those who are devotionally inclined. For some of the bigger demons are also Tamils, is it not? Look at the present political scene.

Anyway, about this boy, I could suggest sending him to S in M. There are not many devotees there, but S is very good at looking after new men, and I will be spending six weeks there myself. It is a very nice preaching field, and one that is going to expand. Just two hours away, in U, is the school of *** Prabhu, the best teacher of philosophy in our movement. So although there may not be many devotees, the situation is on the whole quite good. Many devotees can sometimes mean many funny ideas, as you know from V. You survived the bhakta program without getting confused. Others might not be so fortunate.

Regarding, going to C. I already asked *** Prabhu about your studying temporarily with *** Prabhu, but he declined. Now that your service has expanded so much, it is even less likely that they will want you to go. If you were to go anywhere else, I would prefer to direct you to a project in which you could associate more with me, and I with you, so as to oversee your development. But anyway, travelling sankirtan itself is excellent training. Do you not feel that? One thing I suggest is that you join our travelling party here in Gujarat for some time to learn how to distribute sets of books. Our devotees here are concentrating on selling sets and are getting big results. You could come in Kartik when the V bus parties stop traveling because they think it is better to stay in V that time, although it is more in Srila Prabhupada's mood to go on preaching.

"Krsna did not speak Gita in Sanskrit." That is not what Vedavyasa says, or any of the great acharyas. Therefore it is nonsense. So many nonsense ideas are there. The BKs say that Lord Siva spoke the Gita, not Lord Krsna! Sanskrit is most common medium for imparting transcendental knowledge, but the knowledge and the language are quite different. Sanskrit language is ideal for philosophy and rasa, but mere knowledge of Sanskrit does not impart spiritual advancement. Spiritual knowledge is transmitted from a living source to a worthy recipient, and may be done through the most base of languages, such as English.

All of the nine processes of devotional service are fully potent for purification. In Kali-yuga, the essential practice is of chanting the holy names.

"Jaya Srila Prabhupada" may not be fully appreciable for those who have not developed firm faith in Srila Prabhupada. But it may help those whose faith is developing to become stronger. Three of the chapters, including "Inexplicable Srila Prabhupada" show how the pure devotee is not a stereotype. He is not like a mathematical equation. Understanding the total flow of devotion to Krsna that is the substance of Srila Prabhupada's personality, let your faith in him grow ever deeper.

Unknown Date

Regarding telling lies for Krsna—sometimes it may be done. Krsna Himself told Yudhisthira to lie. Anything may be done for Krsna, but generally devotees follow standard moral precepts. When selling anything, even for Krsna, some mark-up must be there. This is not exactly profit in the sense that a businessman thinks of profit, but it is laksmi to be used in Krsna's service. But everyone wants to get everything as cheap as possible, even unreasonably. So we may have to act like salesmen when selling for Krsna (cf. Gita As It Is 18.47, purport).

Srila Prabhupada wrote in a letter (30 Sept, 72), "The fact is that we have to adopt the same tactics as ordinary salesmen adopt, but the difference is we do it for the satisfaction of Krsna, they do it for sense gratification... Our policy is that his money which would have been used for purchasing cigarettes, liquor, sex literature, meat, will give him the opportunity to gradually become purified. So if by tactics we save that money from being spent on cigarettes, that is good. If we can take some money and give some literature that is a good service."

I always used to sell Krsna conscious paraphernalia when I was personally managing the bus parties. I made a good profit on it, but made it a point to give at least a small book with the more costly items. This way we supported selling the books at low prices. If anyone questioned the price of the paraphernalia, I would tell them frankly that our purpose is distribution of knowledge in the form of books. For that we sell the books cheap and make up the necessary balance from paraphernalia sales. I would tell them that this is not our profit because it is not a personal business. We live simply and whatever money we get we use for Krsna. "You spend so much for your family, maybe for cigarettes, why not give a donation to Krsna for your eternal benefit."

So we may lie for Krsna but it is best not to. Better to say something like, "We don't make very much profit" which is not exactly a lie, but ambiguous. Actually, I have seen that many of our devotees on our bus parties in India get into a kind of "business mentality" and they become more concerned to make a lot of sales rather than pushing the books which is the whole purpose of the bus party anyway. They push paraphernalia which is easy to sell, tell all kinds of stupid lies to sell it, and don't care whether or not books are sold. It is often this type of person who one day vanishes with the sankirtan collection.

Some devotees apart from yourself reported to me feeling shaken by reading my "Brahmacarya" book because they realized they are not up to the higher standard. Don't be discouraged. To perfectly follow brahmacarya is very difficult, especially in this age. That book is meant to encourage and guide devotees to come to the highest standard. But it may take time.

Your philosophical questions are very nice. I think the best thing is to keep a notebook with all your questions. Then when you meet me we can discuss. It takes much time to answer in writing. I don't begrudge that, but I have pressing services also, especially in writing books. Also, when we discuss I can answer more fully and satisfy each point in detail.

On January 3rd, probably in Baroda, my Vyasa-puja will be held. Immediately after that, I plan to spend 5–10 days with whichever disciples are gathered just so we can hear and chant together and all questions can be dealt with. So that would be the best time for you to come and we can discuss then. In the meantime, any pressing questions can be addressed to me.

Here are replies to your questions:

1) We sing "janme janme prabhu sei." When Srila Prabhupada was asked if he would come back to save disciples who returned to this material world, he replied, "Don't force me to come back and save you."

2) Regarding questions about the spiritual world, Srila Prabhupada would often answer, "You will find out when you get there." It is a different place of existence, not understandable by the measuring stick of our limited material experience. Surely the guru will know the disciple in the spiritual world. In one song Narottama Dasa Thakura expresses longing for the day when Lokanatha Gosvami (his guru) will offer him as a maidservant to Rupa Manjari in the spiritual world. This is a very exalted topic that we need not extensively discuss now, but it is seen how a guru may entrust his disciple to another leader in the spiritual world. That may be done in the material world also, that an initiating guru sends a disciple to someone else to study under.

3) Envy is the antithesis of Krsna consciousness and is not so much to be dovetailed in Krsna consciousness as purified and transformed into Krsna consciousness. In his Prema-bhakti-

candrika, Narottama Dasa Thakura suggests how the five enemies (kama, krodha etc.) may be dovetailed in Krsna's service, but gives no such prescription for envy. Nevertheless, we may feel, not exactly envy but almost hatred for very great rascals who pose themselves as God or deny the existence of God. Actually we hate the sin, not the sinner, but even Srila Prabhupada used to say, "I kick on their face with boots!"

4) Lord Nrsimhadeva is eternal and was certainly worshiped before his killing Hiranyakasipu. Nevertheless to make this lila more wonderful (adbhuta-rasa is prominent in this lila), His internal potency made even Laksmidevi as if unaware of His existence. You should consult SB 7.9.2, text and purport for clarification.

5) In the purport to SB 10.46.1 it is explained that Krsna did not call the Vrajavasis to Mathura as their feelings could not be properly reciprocated in that atmosphere and would clash with the feelings Devaki and Vasudeva had for Krsna. The beginning of the chapter, "Uddhava visits Vrndavana." in Krsna book also discusses this in some detail. A comparison is made with the lila-smarana of Lord Caitanya in Puri. Although Lord Caitanya was living close to Lord Jagannatha and daily went for his darsana, He spent more time in His own room feeling separation from Lord Jagannatha, for that is a more intense reciprocation.

6) I have not found any acaryas' comments on this but may make some suggestions. Nanda Maharaja and the cowherd men and boys are stated to have reached Mathura before Krsna, even though they started later, because they went on the main road, not along the Yamuna pathway. Topography may have changed in time.

Vrindavan at the time of Krsna's pastimes was big enough to accommodate millions and millions of cowherd boys and cows. How? Inconceivable. Plus taking bath in Yamuna (not an ordinary bath!) took some time. When Krsna wants His horses go in almost no time from Dvarka to Kundira. He can do, and does, whatever He likes. His lila is for His enjoyment. So maybe He liked to go slowly from Vrindavan to Mathura, maybe to enjoy seeing His dhama, to satisfy Akrura, or who knows what else happened along the way? It is all transcendental, inconceivable, and wonderful, and we bow down our heads to Lord Krsna and His beautiful pastimes.

7) Eternal Visnu-tattva forms such as Narasimha and Rama have Their eternal individual Vaikuntha planets. Matsyadeva and Varahadeva are also Visnu-tattva and have Their eternal planets. Lord Buddha is not Visnu-tattva directly. He is a saktyavesa-avatara and does not have His own personal Vaikuntha planet.

8) Mahavisnu sleeps on Sesanaga because He enjoys it, and that is why He smiles. His dreaming is manifest as the material cosmos. He is enjoying yoga-nidra, of which our sleeping is the perverted reflection. We also enjoy sleep, but that is perverted enjoyment which is actually only suffering. Mahavisnu's sleeping does not mean He becomes unaware. Again, we should understand that our understanding of God can only go so far. In this regard pleaseq consult CC, Madhya 21.25–28.

In a letter (22 Nov 74), Srila Prabhupada wrote, "In my books the philosophy of Krsna consciousness is explained fully so if there is anything you do not understand, then you simply have to read again and again. By reading daily the knowledge will be revealed to you and by this process your spiritual life will develop."

5 October 1996

You request my blessings for book distribution. Yes, be blessed! Be blessed a million times. Take my blessings, and, far more important, Srila Prabhupada's blessings, and distribute more and more books. One secret to increase book distribution is to enthuse others to distribute also. Spread the ecstasy.

13 December 1996

I have no personal power to bless anyone, but as much as I link up to Srila Prabhupada, by following and preaching his instructions, that much I get blessing from him. All glories to his divine lotus feet.

And all glories to your book distribution. Soon, the Srimad-Bhagavatam full set will be available in Kannada. That will be your next great challenge—to distribute full sets.

20 December 1996

Thankyou for your letters and kindly sent gifts. I got them all just a few days ago when I met GC Prabhu in Bombay. Now I am in Bahrain for a few days before going back to Bombay.

Very good news that you are also gradually moving into the field of preaching. Don't worry if you find it a little difficult at first. Slow but sure. Krsna will give you intelligence what to do and say.

I have one question regarding the group's name. When we were choosing it amongst the list of the names of Srimati Radharani, we chose Syama-sevika, which is a name of Radha that means 'she who uses everything in Krsna's service.' We thought it would be more familiar to us if we changed Syama with Krsna so that it becomes Krsna-sevika. But can we still say this is a name of Srimati Radharani, because such name wasn't on the list?

Syama means Krsna and Krsna means Syama. But why don't you get used to the name Syama? It is one of the best known and best loved names of Krsna in Vrndavana and all over India. So Syama-sevika is a good name.

Should I translate books or engage in preaching programs such as nama-hatta?

Meeting people and preaching to them is good, and translating is also good. Translating is also preaching. So do either or both; both are all-auspicious. But best, if the temple authorities have given you some specific guidance and service, is to stick to that.

For the end I have just one more question regarding standards. I'm becoming aware that now I offer all the food to You and I think I should raise my standards. But I would like to know, because my mother is very attached to preparing some food for me, if she prepares food which is offerable to Krsna (without garlic, vinegar, etc., and which was not tasted), but maybe in unclean dishes where previously meat was cooked, can I still offer it to You?

Can't you explain to your mother about the importance of keeping things in separate pots? Best is to buy separate pots, so that if she wants to cook for you, she should cook in those only. As your mother is so much attached to you, why not use that attachment to bring her to Krsna? Gently preach, and give her prasada.

In "A Beginner's Guide to Krsna Consciousness" you also write that we shouldn't take any food prepared by nondevotees. Does that include pasta and cheese, bought in the store?

Dear Guru Maharaja, please forgive me for asking such questions, not so important for spiritual life. However, different spiritual masters give different instruction regarding this so I thought the best way was to ask You personally.

You should learn to cook for Krsna also. Then you could feed her delicious Krsna prasada cooked by you. That is a good way to get the mercy of Srimati Radharani: to follow in Her footsteps by cooking for Krsna. Ask V to show you. And learn some Indian recipes! You can offer Krsna pasta, but Radharani doesn't.

In general, it is best to avoid food prepared by nondevotees. However, milk products are always pure. But then, karmi cheese often contains rennet and is therefore non-vegetarian, as are many items available in stores that you might think are purely vegetarian.

Yes, it will be very nice if you can come to the Gaura Purnima festival. Please try and come. And I'll also try to go to C, S etc. in summer '97. Man proposes but God disposes.

1997

Sometime in 1997

I was a pujari helper in Italy for Sri Sri Radha-Ramana Deities and Sri Sri Gaura-Nitai Deities. I am about to graduate from university. I am not sure whether to go back to Italy and continue to serve the Deities or to stay out of the temple and find a job in my profession. Please can you tell me what you think about this?

Serve the Deities. Such an opportunity comes after millions of births. Take it.

Staying in a house is not the same as staying in a temple. Be very careful not to slip into maya. Try to study Srila Prabhupada's books every day. That will help you immensely.

17 March 1997

To increase our service, strong desire is needed. Another idea is to engage others in service. For instance, you may want to distribute many books. If you can preach to others to distribute books, the book distribution will increase. Also, keep strong and pure by chanting japa clearly and attentively, reading Srila Prabhupada's books, praying to guru and Krsna for strength, and following all the other standard principles.

6 May 1997

Thankyou for your letter and the kind appreciation expressed therein.

There are also a few questions I wanted to ask You in India already but I didn't. In M Swami's book I read that Srila Prabhupada instructed everyone to bathe in Radhakund as often as possible, since we don't have the opportunity to associate with Radhakund often (I believe this is quoted from Caitanya Caritamrta). On the other hand some spiritual masters instructed their disciples not to bathe. What are Your instructions regarding this? And what about Radhakund tilaka? Is it acceptable to wear it on special occasions?

Regarding Radha-kund bath: This seems to be a vexed question as there are apparently contradictory instructions about it. In Nectar of Instruction Rupa Gosvami recommends bathing in Radha-kund as often as possible. However, this comes after many other instructions, beginning with controlling the tongue and other senses. Different instructions are applicable for different devotees on different levels of advancement. Bathing in Radha-kund does award the highest nectar to those who are qualified to accept it. We have seen that many devotees, even after bathing in Radha-kund, fell down into abominable activities. Therefore, it is more important for devotees who have not completely mastered the senses to concentrate on perfecting the primary instructions before they even dream of aspiring to a platform that is difficult to achieve even for Narada and others. Real bathing in Radha-kund is not simply a matter of immersing the body but of immersing the consciousness. A person whose consciousness is saturated with lust and greed can never get the real benefit of bathing in Radha-kund. Therefore, Srila Prabhupada warned us not to take it cheaply. If you dare, you may very respectfully bathe in Radha-kund, praying for the mercy to some day develop proper appreciation. But don't expect instant ecstasy. Or, you may sprinkle some drops of Her water on your head, and get back to doing what Srila Prabhupada showed us to do by example, that is, serving within the sankirtan movement.

There is no harm to wear Radha-kund tilak. Yellow gopicandan is the norm.

I also noticed that I don't appreciate properly things connected to the Deities, Srila Prabhupada, Your Divine Grace. This refers to garlands, pieces of cloth the deities or spiritual master were wearing, caranamrta (even books and pictures) … You also kindly gave me a present— Prabhupada's maha prasadam from Hyderabad. How to show proper respect to these items? What is the proper understanding, attitude? Thank You very much in advance for Your answers.

Appreciation develops by hearing and serving.

The Srila Prabhupada cloth prasad is best kept in a picture frame with a picture of Srila Prabhupada. You may put in a little typed note to explain what it is. That is what V in L did.

Regarding the Saranagati lectures: We are trying to send them separately—by regular post. Unfortunately, the files in which they are contained are too large to send them via COM. Please let us know when you get them.

2 July 1997

Thankyou very much for your letter that was sent on to me by e-mail. I am now in Germany and will go to America on 7th July. Hopefully Russia after that, and back to India probably in October. This is my plan; everything is in Krsna's hands.

I was just travelling in Croatia, Bosnia, and other parts of Europe. There are many devotees and quite a few centers in the ex-Soviet bloc. The response is overwhelming. The devotees are so happy to see a disciple of Srila Prabhupada. How great is Srila Prabhupada, that people are so eager to see those who saw him!

So now we should all try to become worthy representatives of Srila Prabhupada. That we can do by rigidly following the regulative principles, chanting at least 16 rounds daily without offenses, studying Srila Prabhupada's books very carefully, and seriously endeavoring to become pure devotees of Lord Krsna, the Supreme Personality of Godhead.

I am very happy that you are now happily situated in devotional service. I know you are a very serious devotee and I have great hopes of you developing into a first-class preacher and devotee. Everything is possible if we stop making offenses and surrender to Krsna.

Regarding your philosophical question, you wrote:

When we read the Tenth Canto of Srimad-Bhagavatam, in the story of the Syamantaka jewel Akrura is making a plan to kill the father of Rukmini. Then he went to Varanasi and was doing so many sacrifices. As a pure devotee of the Lord why he is doing like that? In the commentary it is said that because he had offended the gopis. Please explain.

Although this point is not explained more in the purport, I may venture the following explanation based on understanding culled from reading Srila Prabhupada's books.

That Akrura performed sacrifices is not suprising as most devotees in Dvaraka-lila perform activities concomitant with their varnasrama status, as does Krsna Himself. This is all to nourish Krsna's pastimes. If Krsna did not appear somewhat human, His pastimes would be less sweet. This is why Dvaraka is higher than Vaikuntha: because the opulence is mitigated by loving feelings of familiarity. The effect is even more pronounced in Vrindavan than Dvaraka. To augment this feeling of "ordinaryness," Krsna's associates may also act as if forgetting Krsna's supremacy. This pastime shows how the residents of Dvaraka were reminded of Krsna's supremacy, as some of them appeared to forget that, due to "familiarity breeds contempt." (cf. SB 10.57.30, purport)

Actually pure devotees of Krsna never forget Krsna and are never in a less than perfect position. But sometimes to facilitate Krsna's lila or to demonstrate some point, they may appear to be in maya, as did Arjuna to expedite the speaking of Bhagavad-gita. Similarly, Akrura's offense towards the gopis demonstrates that even advanced devotees have to be careful to avoid making offenses.

Please consider the following quotes from SB 2.7.15, purport: "A pure devotee of the Lord never commits any sinful acts, but because the whole world is full of the sinful atmosphere, even a pure devotee may commit a sin unconsciously, as a matter of course."

"The Lord descends on this earth and acts like others in connection with the activities of the world just to create subject matters for hearing about Him; otherwise the Lord has nothing to do in this world, nor has He any obligation to do anything."

And from Srila Kavi Karnapura's Sri Caitanya-candrodaya:

"When spiritual beings exhibit seemingly mundane qualities, their transcendental existence is in no way impaired."

These wonderful pastimes of Krsna are pleasing to hear and are full of many important instructions. Please go on relishing them and your life will be perfect.

May Giridhari bless you. My blessings to the devotees there. Please go on chanting Hare Krsna with full enthusiasm.

11 July 1997

Unfortunately, because of my stupidity I also have some bad news. Please, forgive me, Guru Maharaj, for offending Your lotus feet by breaking the vow I have given You and the deities in Mayapur. I have again watched television a few times. It HAS helped me a lot, because I feel less and less attracted to it and before I have watched it almost every day, but I also didn't succeed to fully keep my vow. Please forgive me. This has upset me a lot, because I started seriously thinking if I can't keep such a simple promise, how will I be able to keep the promise to chant 16 rounds every day and follow the four regulative principles for the rest of my life? But at the same time I have to accept initiation, because without it I am lost. Do I have to wait until I will be able to 'walk by myself' and stop falling down after every step I make? But this may take a lifetime.

Guru Maharaj, am I too ambitious and impatient and expect too much from myself or is it normal to make mistakes in spiritual life? I don't want to make cheap compromise saying that it's ok just to make me feel better. If this is very bad, I prefer feeling bad and guilty and better start making plans how to keep my promise in the future.

15% to the temple is ok.[2] The good news about preaching is good and the bad news about TV is bad. What can I say? You have to fly your own plane. Your solution is good: keep busy in Krsna's service.

18 July 1997

I finally got time to read "My Memories of Srila Prabhupada."

Generally I feel a certain intimacy in reading the works of authors I know. You wrote this book for those who asked you for your memories of Srila Prabhupada and therefore had a familiar audience in mind; of course, I wasn't one of those who asked you about your memories, but I happily shared in them and was touched by them.

The longest essay in the book is your article on strong speaking. Devotees have no objection to a sannyasi speaking strongly provided he practices what he preaches. And, especially in India, your strong speaking benefits your audiences.

In Western settings, it may be misunderstood or not comprehended. Anti-cultists who are a little sympathetic to devotees, in the sense of realizing that we are happy doing what we do, are still wary of the ability of cultists to strongly persuade young, unformed minds. Yet "preaching means fighting," you remind us. Indeed, ISKCON's public relations were stormy and difficult in the late seventies and early eighties, when we fought the anti-cultists.

---

2. This refers to the percentage taken by the L temple from the sale of my books.

Thanks for your critique of "My Memories." I really appreciate intelligent criticism, even if or especially if it is not all praise. It helps me to formulate and clarify ideas and responses and to feel how my writing is being received. Sometimes it moves me to shift my stance also (not in this case). Especially with subjects that could be controversial (and that constitutes quite a lot of my writing) I try to run it past some senior devotees before I print it. The problem is that everyone is so tied up they hardly have time to help. Jayadvaita Maharaja read the "strong preaching" essay before it was printed but just gave a one line response that he liked it. I am wary about adjusting our strong message to satisfy the public. This is already discussed in the essay. If anticultists are wary of strong persuasion, they are hypocrites. The educational system and mass media strongly persuade people that they are these bodies, that life comes from matter, and that the acquisition of money and sense gratification are the goal of life. They don't like us working on unformed minds because they want to form them in their own demoniac way.

Sometime in August 1997

Your letter has been a great relief for me. I have been very worried about you. I wish I could think of Krsna as spontaneously as I have been thinking of you.

Admittedly your present situation is not the best place to get inspired about pure devotional service. I pushed you to do TSKP because I wanted you to imbibe a strong service mood without which learning is useless or worse.

Some devotees talk about doing something significant, and read books and attend seminars on how to be a success. Others don't make a lot of fuss and bother but just get on with whatever needs to be done. They go on steadily with their service, even if it seems relatively inconsequential. But attention to duty and enthusiasm to serve gradually qualify a person and attract the attention of his superiors, who may then be pleased to give him responsibility. No one achieved anything worthwhile without much hard work and sacrifice. Success is not for dreamers. Hard work is a prerequisite to and symptom of surrender.

I want to see you happy, fulfilled and productive in devotional service, but I'm not convinced that your own ideas about how to come to that position are the best.

I recently got a letter from S Das who is on Padayatra in A.P. He wrote that it is austere but that he is very happy and is being nicely trained for the first time in how to serve Krsna. So I suggest to go on Padayatra in A.P. and maybe Braja Mandala Parikrama after which if J is coming you could join him. Otherwise in the meantime you could join A or B's padayatra. They are sincere devotees.

There is much to discuss for which we will have to wait until my return to India; it is not possible on email. But do not associate with B. His intelligent discussions cannot help you, only cause harm.

Doubts and complaints should be taken up (to more senior devotees) not down to juniors who will simply become confused. To dwell on the inevitable problems and anomalies within our society, without having a positive program for making improvements, is a particularly harmful form of prajalpa. Especially to expose newer devotees to such matters simply bewilders them and is one of the worst forms of violence to their tender creepers of devotion.

Go on chanting 64 for another 7 days or so. Take shelter of the holy name. And think positively! There is hope, tremendous hope in Krsna consciousness.

And do dance in kirtana. Dance for Krsna. He will be pleased.

Unknown date

I met your father. He is very nice, like a devotee. He gave $200 for you. You may take this laxmi from G Das and I will adjust it against the laxmi owed me by the party. I believe the rate is around 36, so you should get Rs. 7200. If this figure is incorrect, let me know. That's a lot of laxmi for a young brahmacari with all his basic needs met. What do you intend to do with it? Be careful. Laxmi can give a false sense of independence that is unfavorable for spiritual advancement. What is this problem with G Das? What do you intend to do? You need to work under a leader as you are not mature enough to work independently. My desire is that you continue to do sankirtana as that is best for you at this stage.

As Srila Prabhupada wrote:

"Please go on with your devotional service with all enthusiasm. Associate with devotees, chant attentively, read my books daily and distribute them also and surely advancement will be gradually there."

If you can't work with G Das that is unfortunate but not unusual. These kind of personality problems are there in sankirtana parties all over the world. It is maya's influence to try to stop our preaching. But you can also increase the preaching. Why don't you continue to use the A bus for A preaching and thus make another party?

02 October 1997

I have been thinking for some time to write to you but am afraid that you will not care what I say. Now I have come across a letter from Srila Prabhupada which better states anything that I could say.

"Try to convince them to return to our Society and work cooperatively. That they have gone away is not good thing and it is a deviation from our line of parampara. Rather, avoiding faultfinding and anarchy, they should keep our standards and work maturely and not cause factions and splitting. I am not at all pleased at what they have done, but if they return let us forget what has happened and go forward. We have got so much vital spiritual knowledge to distribute to the public and they are in desperate need of it. The whole world is going to hell and everyone is suffering. In light of this, how can we argue amongst one another and neglect our responsibility for reclaiming these fallen souls for going Back to Home, Back to Godhead."

I have much affection for you and had hoped that you had the same for me. So I appeal to you not to run off without even speaking to me. Is this the integrity that you so much value? It is very disturbing. Please try to meet me, either in Vrindaban in the first week of November, or in Vallabh Vidyanagar in the second week of November. In the meantime, it is best if you serve in any ISKCON temple or project.

16 November 1997

You should consider very seriously that what your guru wants you to do is best for you, not what you want to do. You should have faith that by following his instruction, even in the most unfavorable circumstances, you will be protected and nourished. Even if he has given you the choice to do as you like, you cannot make the same progress as you can by fully surrendering to his wishes.

Going to K to be alone with your mind is not at all a good idea. Better you go to Mayapur, chant and dance in the association of devotees, and take the time to think what to do in the intensely spiritual atmosphere of the dham. That is, if you do not follow the advice given in the para above.

17 November 1997

Due to what I don't know, several of my recent outgoing email letters vanished off my computer, and appear not to have reached their destinations either. So please excuse me if you are getting a late reply or if you are getting a similar letter twice.

So here's a little note again. It is very good news that you are chanting your 16 rounds with full faith and conviction again. It is a fact that without the shelter of Krsna's holy names, life is meaningless or worse. That is the sign of a pure devotee: that he feels uncomfortable without performing his devotional service. Much as we feel uncomfortable if we don't eat, we should feel the same way or worse if we don't hear and chant about Krsna.

Maybe your "big paper" could form the material for a BTG essay, or maybe for a paper in ***'s journal. Not that I'm much fond of artificial scholars or their honey-bottle-licking presentations, but if there is something in parampara line, written in a way that so-called scholars may appreciate, why not give it to them also? In either case, it would need some rewriting, which is good, because writing and rewriting is good meditation—when the subject is Krsna.

Keep up the fight against maya. It is a great credit to you that you are upholding your Krsna consciousness in one of the strongholds of the material energy, the slaughterhouse university for destroying spiritual consciousness. Now if you stick to your principles, you may gradually fulfill Canakya's proverb, that a single sandalwood tree can scent a whole forest. In other words, by being Krsna conscious, you can greatly benefit all the students and faculty members there by gradually introducing Krsna consciousness to them also.

1 December 1997

I was of course also hurt and shocked by ***'s (he probably has a new name now) going away. I wouldn't be so upset if I didn't love him but he doesn't believe in or care for that love. He always said he wanted to do something significant and now he has. He has significantly wounded my heart. To analyze all the reasons behind it might be very complex. He was not honest with me and I don't know exactly what he was thinking.

It seems he had his own ideas of what Krsna consciousness should be and what a guru should be. Instead of submitting himself to be molded by me, he rejected me as incompetent to guide him.

A few months ago he was supposed to clean my room one morning but instead just went to sleep. At that time I knew he was not sincere.

He is also callous about the feelings of others. Otherwise how could he kick me in the face like this when I have simply tried to help him? Why doesn't he contact his parents, even when he knows they are anxious about him? It is not that he is highly advanced in detachment; he simply doesn't care.

It is true that the circumstances he was staying in within ISKCON were not the most ideal or inspiring. But that was no justification for doing what he did. I could have arranged for him to serve elsewhere, but he has the same problem everywhere: he didn't like to serve.

Of course everyone comes to devotional service with so many disqualifications and we don't like to dwell on them. Rather we try to direct devotees so they may become purified. Those that leave ISKCON often blame the institution but ultimately the fault lies with them. We can either look for all the faults in ISKCON and blaspheme it and go away, or we can find all the tremendous good qualities, take advantage of them and become purified. At the same time we should be aware of discrepancies and try to rectify them.

Under the circumstances, I don't think you can consider him a godbrother. The question of him coming back is theoretical and at present doesn't seem likely. If he did come I would have to gauge his mood before accepting him. Changing a guru is not like changing a gamcha. Anyway, pray for him.

I am as always concerned about your continuing spiritual weakness but am very pleased by your practical commitment to service. The results speak for themselves. Whatever your frailties may be, the books are coming out. This concrete contribution to the sankirtan movement is far more valuable than volumes of high sounding philosophical abstrusities.

What to do? In a war there will be casualties, and there may be traitors also.

25 December 1997

*** Maharaja sent me a copy of your letter to him. I am shocked at how you could write to him like that. You are so fortunate to have a guru who cares for you enough to chastise you. He could have written, "ok, do whatever you like," but he perceived that you were not in good consciousness (as came out in your letter of reply) and took the trouble to give you the required medicine. He has praised and encouraged you so many times and presumed there was enough trust there that you could accept his chastisement, understanding that it is not the words of a cruel-hearted person out to smash you, but with genuine concern for your well-being.

The chastisement of the guru is a sign of his acceptance of the disciple. First, because he takes the trouble to correct him; and second, because he has faith that the disciple trusts the guru enough to accept the chastisement in the right spirit.

Try to understand—he knows better than you what you need. That's why you accept a guru. The guru is the personification of the personal interest and kindness of Krsna. That is why the devotee should surrender to the guru. Are you so superficial that you think kindness means simply smiling all the time?

I have seen that some devotees idolize their guru like the mundane hero worship of sports, cinema, and music stars. They collect photos of him, constantly talk of his exploits with great relish and reverence, and appear to be completely absorbed in thoughts of him. The real test of their devotion, however, comes when they are called upon to surrender to him. No amount of showy adulation is as important as this test: are you ready to follow his order?

If not, you are in VERY serious trouble. From the tone of your letter, it seems that you are on the verge of falling into the terrible pit of maha Vaisnava aparadha caused by rejecting your guru. Unless you pull yourself together right now, you are going to go on the path leading to hell. You may not like me saying this, but that is the fact.

If you want to save yourself from the worst of hells, immediately draft a letter of apology to your most merciful gurudeva. It has to be from the heart. Tell him that you are ready to do whatever he orders, even if it is against your personal desire and even if it means going to P. And then do just that—do whatever he says. Give your money, your camera, your computer, everything to him and start life again as a simple brahmacari, ready to do whatever you are told. That is the only way you can be happy.

27 December 1997

If you see B, please tell him that I do not like to think of him continuing in his misery and that I want him to come back to India immediately.

28 December 1997

When we, Your disciples, have some problems, do You know about them even though we haven't (yet) told them directly to You? Do You know something is wrong and pray for us to Krsna and try to help us? And if we pray to You in our daily life, do You know about it and help us, give us Your mercy, guide us in spiritual life in this way—indirectly?

I don't need a letter from you to know that you are struggling. You are always struggling! I am always thinking of my disciples and pray that the best wishes for them from this fallen soul may be favorably heard by Krsnacandra.

Thankyou for taking the interest to distribute my books, and for getting that book. Please bring whatever you can on disk to Mayapur.

Usually devotees here only offer respects in their mind to *** Prabhu, since he is not a sannyasi. But him being Srila Prabhupada's disciple, isn't the proper etiquette to offer him obeisances every day the first time we see him at least? I would also like to ask You for permission if it is OK if I sometimes consult *** Prabhu about my spiritual life (when I have difficulties), if I think he could help me in some way, since he is in L.

Yes, you are very lucky to get *** Prabhu's association. Take advantage of it as much as possible. Take advice from him, serve him, and offer obeisances to him. He is my old friend. We had some interesting times together in B.

It's good that you write articles. Writing is one of the best ways to focus on Krsna. But make sure the writing is actually Krsna conscious according to guru, sadhu, and sastra; not just some mental drivel.

Guru Maharaja, I have a question about the Vyasa-puja program. Some devotees in L have performed abhiseka in the guru's absence—they did it with a picture of His lotus feet. Is this bonafide? May we also include such abhiseka in the celebration?

Thankyou for your enthusiasm in arranging my Vyasa-puja celebration there. I never heard of abhisheka to a photo before.

Dear Guru Maharaja, I was thinking of sending a letter to COM free forum to devotees and Your godbrothers to write letters of appreciation of You and then read them on the Vyasa-puja celebration, and maybe make a little booklet if there will be more of them. May I do this?

Please don't write on free forum about my vyasa-puja or to godbrothers for appreciations.

My blessings to A, B, C, and all the devotees there, and to your prasada-loving father also.

Don't watch useless karmi TV ever.

29 December 1997

Thankyou for your letter and the kind sentiments expressed therein.

You have asked for my advice for your spiritual life. I advise that, although it will be difficult, you go ahead and find a job for a year and after that spend some time serving in our temples. This may seem to be strange advice. But I am seeing too many immature young people join our temples without really understanding what or why they are doing, and after some time going away disappointed because they did not get the phantasmagorial idea of spiritual life that they were hoping for. Some experience in the rough, tough world can help make you more sober and give some realization of what a precious gift Krsna consciousness is.

Of course, you must go on chanting Hare Krsna as much as possible. And read Srila Prabhupada's books primarily. There is no use to reading my books without reading Srila Prabhupada's books.

Unknown date

I was just travelling in Croatia, Bosnia and other parts of Europe. The response is overwhelming. The devotees are so happy to see a disciple of Srila Prabhupada. How great is Srila Prabhupada, that people are so eager to see those who saw him!

So now we should all try to become worthy representatives of Srila Prabhupada. That we can do by rigidly following the regulative principles, chanting at least 16 rounds daily without offenses, studying Srila Prabhupada's books very carefully, and seriously endeavoring to become pure devotees of Lord Krsna, the Supreme Personality of Godhead.

From Europe I will go to USA and hopefully Russia after that, and back to India probably in October. This is my plan; everything is in Krsna's hands.

I will be very happy if you can become happily situated in devotional service. I know you want to be a serious devotee and I have great hopes of you developing into a first-class preacher and devotee. Everything is possible if we stop making offenses and surrender to Krsna.

Please consider: accepting that there are problems within ISKCON, and in some cases severe problems, your perception of them is also not perfect as you are subject to illusion, mistakes, imperfect senses, and the cheating propensity. You have not stuck to the service given to you, namely book distribution, but have instead chosen to spend your time discussing all kinds of matters that cannot benefit you. You write to your spiritual master classifying him with idiots, rascals, and thieves. You use foul language in the same letter. And yet you want to be "a perfect brahmana by culture." You pontificate on the failings of others but do not properly follow the basic principles of spiritual life, like attending temple programs.

You write that you are fighting for life. If you at all value my advice, start chanting 64 rounds daily. Try hard to chant with attention and feeling, like a genuine cry of a child for his mother. Attend morning and evening programs without fail, even if you are tired and sick. DANCE IN KIRTANA. Any balance time, study Srila Prabhupada's books only. Do not at all waste time in idle talks. Pray to the most merciful Gaura Nitai for Their help, and resolve to surrender to Them. Totally refrain from criticising Vaisnavas or even thinking badly of them, even if it seems that there is ample ground to do so. Do not sleep excessively. Do this for at least 7 to 10 days, and then write to me again.

This is the medicine.

> *harer nama harer nama harer namaiva kevalam*
> *kalau nasty eva nasty eva nasty eva gatir anyatha*

Personally, I cannot give up this process of Krsna consciousness, no matter whatever anyone else may say or do. Nor can I dream of leaving ISKCON, whatever the problems may be. I cannot give up chanting Hare Krsna, and praying to Krsna to help me, despite my frailties and defects.

1998

Sometime in 1998

You have asked me to bless you so that you do not lose enthusiasm in devotional service. Please go on reading Srila Prabhupada's books and preaching this message to others. Do not concoct anything. Do not become proud, and do not become offensive to Krsna's devotees. If you follow this program of "dos" and "do nots," you will certainly remain enthusiastic in devotional service throughout your life.

You have referred to yourself as a "foolish mataji." It is nice that you maintain a humble mood, but you should know that birth in a woman's body is no bar to receiving the full mercy of Krsna, as Lord Krsna Himself clearly states in Bhagavad-gita 9.32.

You asked "How is it possible to know whether one has committed an offense to devotees and the Deities? What are the symptoms and how to counteract them?" First of all, we should be extremely cautious never to willingly commit offenses. However, we may commit offenses without our knowing them. For instance, we may say something to devotees which they misunderstand and take offense for. Or due to neglect, we fail to do something that we should have done. If we develop an offensive attitude, or are not careful to avoid offenses, that will be manifest by an increasing lack of enthusiasm for devotional service, and an increase in material desires. We may also guess that if devotees appear to be annoyed with us, that we may have offended them.

80

Daily we pray to the devotees to forgive all offenses, known or unknown, by offering them respectful obeisances: *vanca kalpa* ... And in Deity worship there is a prayer that is to be said at the end of puja, the purport of which is as follows: my dear Lord, I am always committing thousands of offenses. Please forgive me by Your causeless mercy. Better than counteracting offenses however, is being very careful not to commit them. It is good that you have asked this question, because offenses lead to obstruction in devotional advancement, and can even lead to falldown.

Next, you asked about preaching from the Bible or Koran to Christians and Muslims. Except for the few devotees who specialize in preaching to members of other faiths at the academic level, it is not necessary for devotees to deeply study the scriptures of others. Followers of other religious doctrines, if they are sincere, will appreciate actual love of God, in whatever form it appears. Those who are not sincere will not listen to us anyway, even if we quote all their scriptures inside out and upside down. Nevertheless, there may be no harm in quoting a few well known lines from these scriptures, as Srila Prabhupada sometimes did. For instance, there is the well known quote of Lord Jesus "Hallowed be thy name," which Srila Prabhupada also sometimes used to quote. On the whole however, it is better that we study Srila Prabhupada's books very deeply.

It is nice that when you think of Krsna's pastimes in Vrindavan, sometimes tears appear in your eyes, or the hairs on your arms stand on end. To develop such feelings for Krsna is our aim and our mission. However, you should know that as long as we are still infected by material desires, these natural feelings of ecstasy that arise when we think of Krsna have not yet become steady. We should not artificially try to induce such feelings in ourselves, and we should certainly not tell others if we are experiencing them. That becomes another type of sense gratification—to advertise oneself as an advanced devotee. Go on serving Krsna and praying to Him. When He blesses you with such feelings of ecstasy, take them as His mercy upon you, and go on serving, especially in the sankirtana mission, praying to become free from the material desires that hinder us from constantly experiencing such feelings of ecstasy, which are our natural birthright.

I look forward to meeting you and all my loving disciples in Russia in July.

January 1998

As this is the first contact I have had with you for several years, and it is anyway not very palatable, I will take the opportunity of expressing something that has peeved me since we last met. You probably remember that our last exchange … (matter deleted)

I don't hold any deep grudge against you for this, and do not discuss it with others. Although I feel that I was wronged, I take it that I must have wronged you—either in a previous life, or in this life—to be treated by you thus. I do not remember in this life having said or done anything to you that you appear to hold such a strong dislike for me, but if I have done so inadvertently, I apologize for my offenses, and beg to be forgiven. I have certainly done my share of mistreatment of devotees in this life, so I cannot complain. However, considering how events have developed, I would have thought it in order for you to apologize.

2 January 1998

Thankyou so much for your letter. I am always happy to hear from you. My instruction for preaching and book distribution is to keep on trying. Pray to Krsna, and He will surely help you. Even if we don't appear to be successful, Krsna is pleased with our endeavor.

You may worship Sri Sri Gaura Nitai at home. Please do so very carefully. I hope this meets you well and happy.

6 January 1998

I have just now received your letter dated 23 Nov 97. I am very happy to hear from you, and of the wonderful progress you are making in spiritual life. You may worship Tulasi devi in the way you have suggested. It is unusual, but you are living in unusual circumstances. Krsna and His devotees accept the sincere mood of service of those who wish to serve them. Your preaching endeavors are simply wonderful. This is a very good way to spread Krsna consciousness that Srila Prabhupada spoke and wrote about many times—going door to door.

You have met many sincere people. Now is a good time for preaching in Russia, so take advantage of the opportunity to bring more and more people to Krsna consciousness. Be gentle and kind with them. People are suffering so much in the material world. They are looking for the love that they have been missing in millions of lifetimes in this material world. So if the devotees of Krsna give that to them, they will respond to that. Please extend my heartfelt best wishes to your father and mother.

As far as your husband is concerned, I don't think you should unnecessarily agitate him. He's not opposed to your practicing Krsna consciousness, but it's understandable that he needs to get enough sleep, because he has to work hard all day. If possible, if he's agreed to it, you can get up early in the morning and chant very quietly without disturbing him, so that he can rest fully.

Otherwise, if you have to get up a little later, I think that under the circumstances that would be the best thing to do, so as not to agitate him.

Then if you are very understanding with him and caring for him, he will come to appreciate how Krsna consciousness makes you a better person, and he will gradually take more interest in it himself. However, if you agitate him before he has come to that level of understanding, he may go further away from Krsna consciousness. So the general rule is that we should try to rise before 4 a.m., but we may have to adjust rules according to the particular situation we are in.

6 January 1998

Thankyou very much for your letter and your kind appreciation. Please take up this proposal of marriage with Bhakta H very seriously. That means with full commitment to Krsna consciousness in family life and with full commitment to remain together in Krsna consciousness despite all difficulties.

6 January 1998

Thankyou so much for your nice Vyasa Puja offering. The news of the expanded preaching is very good. It is a fact that if we simply follow the program of sadhana and preaching, as Srila Prabhupada gave us, that the Krsna consciousness movement will expand more and more. It is an ever-increasing ocean of transcendental ecstasy. Let us all dive into it.

I hope to see you in the summer at the Suharevo festival, and I hope to visit Tambov also next summer. Please extend my blessings to all the devotees there.

8 January 1998

Thankyou so much for your nice Vyasa Puja offering. Your sentiments are appreciated by me. It is stated by Visvanatha Cakravarti Thakura that it is only by pleasing the spiritual master that one can be assured of pleasing Krsna. My request to my disciples is to go on cooperating with all of our ISKCON family members and to go on pushing on this movement with determination and sincerity, rigidly following the principles as received in disciplic succession from Srila Prabhupada.

On January 3rd I was at Vallabh Vidyanagar, a small college town in Gujarat, where we had a celebration with about a hundred devotees, before the exquisitely beautiful forms of Sri Sri Radha

Giridhari. At that time I accepted seven new disciples, and gave brahminical initiation to three other disciples. Our movement in this part of the world is spreading steadily and nicely, and signs are there that it will spread much more in the not too distant future.

This is a general request to all my disciples. Please send me copies of replies to your letters that I may have sent to you in the past—especially those with philosophical and practical advice. It will be valuable to collect this so as to instruct other disciples, because often the same questions are asked repeatedly. If you can send me the answers along with the original questions, that would be best, so as to see them in context.

8 January 1998

Thankyou so much for remembering me on my Vyasa Puja.

Srila Prabhupada used to quote the Bengali saying that if you go to Bengal, your forehead goes with you. In other words, what's destined for you will come to pass. It seems that, whatever your plans are, Krsna has some plans for you. It looks that at this point of life at least, you'll have to struggle in various ways. At the same time, Krsna is always giving the opportunity to serve Him in different ways. You are so fortunate.

8 January 1998

I hope you got the last letter I sent you. In that, I had stated that if you were not able to come to Gujarat and get verbal replies to your letters, that I would send them by post. The replies are below.

Regarding chanting pulling the beads in the wrong direction: just try to correct the wrong habit. If you go on trying, your habit will change.

Regarding yuga names, I wrote to *** Maharaja, who replied as follows.

"Someone asked me why there is a statement in the SB where it is suggested that there was a switching of theTreta and Dvapara yugas. I did research and found out that the names of the yugas are related to the names of the faces of the dice. Kali refers to a dice with one on it, Dvapara refers to the dice with two on it, Treta refers to the dice with three on it, and Krta (the usual name in the Vedas for what we usually call Satya yuga) refers to the dice with four on it. These yugas are always in that order and this is further confirmed by the numbering. In Vedic terminology sometimes things are listed from the top down and sometimes from the bottom up. It is not a quirk that the order manifested from the last to the first, it is simply another way of looking at the situation."

Should devotees offer obeisances in the temple room to sannyasis and other senior devotees other than their guru? Or even to their guru?

There are comments in the Caitanya-caritamrta in the Madhya-lila concerning a Vaisnava who washed and drank Mahaprabhu's foot water in Gundica. These indicate that only the Lord should be worshiped in the temple. The contradiction to this is that devotees began to do guru-puja to Srila Prabhupada in the temple room (this began before Caitanya-caritamrta came out), and Prabhupada accepted, so it has become a tradition. So worship or obeisances to Prabhupada is standard. Can this be extended to any Vaisnava? I would think not. We have to draw the line somewhere. That's my opinion. Others will differ. These things need to be standardized in our society. I would think that offering obeisances to any Vaisnava in the temple room, not directly in front of the Deities, could be acceptable.

SB 1.2.21 refers to seeing "the self as master." What does this mean?

By seeing the end of the purport, Srila Prabhupada mentions that by understanding our position in relationship to the Lord, the false ego is then removed by the Lord's grace and all doubts are then cleared. So this "self as master" could mean first understanding that the soul is superior to the material nature; and second that the soul is servant of the Supreme Soul. In Gita chapter 13 Lord Krsna also speaks of the soul as "ksetrajna," the knower of the body. He is superior to matter and should not be controlled by it. So to see the self as master means to see the atma as the ksetrajna, knower and master of the body.

I hope these answers are satisfactory.

My general request to all my disciples and aspiring disciples is to go on cooperating with all of our ISKCON family members and to go on pushing on this movement with determination and sincerity, rigidly following the principles as received in disciplic succession from Srila Prabhupada.

10 January 1998

Congratulations on taking up the service of manager in the *** temple. It is a great responsibility in Krsna's service. Please discharge it to the best of your ability in a mood of self-sacrifice and service to the devotees.

I heard that you had intimate sexual relationship with the person you have mentioned. If this is not true, please do not feel offended with me. It is only what I have heard, and I have to repeat this to you, as you have asked my advice. If it is true, or even if there is some inclination that way, then I would agree with +++ Prabhu—that it is better to politely break off the relationship. It is just too dangerous for both of your spiritual lives. Whatever the positive part of it may be, I don't think you should take the risk of falldown, especially as so many devotees will now be looking up to you.

As far as his parents are concerned, I suggest you introduce some other devotees to them, and let them cultivate them. Maybe that should be done by that devotee's future wife.

And if you do have this problem, the solution that Srila Prabhupada suggested is marriage.

Please don't take this advice as very harsh, even though it may be difficult for you to accept. It is offered in your best interest, with the long term view in mind.

If you come to India, I will also be happy to see you there.

11 January 1998

Yes, I did receive your Vyasa Puja offering, and I think that now you will have received my reply to you. If not, I'll state it again in brief: Thankyou.

Regarding your question about dilemma: I see very little point in your trying not to be attached to young men. It is the most common thing in the world. It is that which makes the world keep on running. Of course, as devotees, we're trying to get out of this world, but the reality is that most devotees will get married. Especially for women, it is recommended that they get married. The main thing is to go about it in as sane a manner as possible. For that, it would be better to consult your local congregational group leaders, and discuss this matter with them.

15 January 1998

Once, soon after Srila Prabhupada's departure, my husband was entrusted to deliver a cassette tape from India to Srila Satswarup Maharaj. On this tape were Prabhupada pastimes from Indians who had contact with Prabhupada. We listened to the tape before it was delivered. One story particularly impressed me. One Indian gentleman asked Srila Prabhupada how he always remembered Krsna. Prabhupada beckoned him close and told him to put his ear on his heart. In his heart the maha-mantra Hare Krsna Hare Krsna Krsna Krsna Hare Hare Hare Rama Hare Rama Rama Rama Hare Hare was always repeating. A miracle. I thought I'd share it because it never made it into Srila Satswarupa's books as far as I know.

It didn't make it because Satsvarupa Maharaja was very careful not to reproduce unauthenticated and quite likely spurious stories, *many* of which were collected in India. It is probably best that we also don't circulate such stories. Srila Prabhupada kept everything practical and based on sastra. He didn't fit the profile of a miracle maker, even though many people, especially in India, expect sadhus to be like that and even make up stories to "glorify" sadhus who don't have a repertoire of miracles.

15 January 1998

All glories to Sri Panca Tattva which is just about to come to L temple!

Jaya!

Is it possible that there will be a book of questions from Your disciples that You have answered?

I am thinking like that. Like everything else, it will take time.

In the future, should I also send You the copies of Your letters or will it be already done when You reply?

I intend to do it myself.

It would be nice if we would make a conference on COM.

Please contact your godbrother N dasa about this. He is on com and intends to do it.

Are there some rules which are necessary to be very very strict and with some others not so strict?

Of course. Four regulative principles essential, chanting 25 rounds on ekadasi flexible.

How can I take the middle path in everything I do?

It requires common sense, which isn't very common, but comes with advancement. Stick to the path, everything will come in due course of time.

Guru Maharaja, could You please give me blessings not to fall in maya.

Blessings, yes, but your own determination and sincere desire is also required. Always try to remember why you are doing it—for going to Mayapur.

15 January 1998

Please don't feel scared and blamed. The material world is a heavy place and we should feel scared of maya. But we have to take shelter of the Vaisnavas to overcome our anarthas, even if the process may be painful. I reiterate: if what I heard was not true, then please don't take offense. But if it was, then we must deal with the problem in an appropriate way.

15 January 1998

Thankyou for your Vyasa puja offering. You wrote:

Thus the more I preach the stronger I feel.

So preach! Do it and be blessed.

I hope to set up a conference for your disciples.

Better than hoping to do it is to do it. See attached file.

I am not in a position to make any monetary contribution now.

No problem.

With all best wishes in your preaching endeavors.

15 January 1998

In September 1997 I have received a nice letter from you where you expressed your interest for farms. Therefore I decided to write you again a more detailed letter about the project we are involved in here. Certainly you will have some advice for us.

In a condensed way I would like to describe to you how this project has started at all. You have certainly heard something about the civil war in ex Yugoslavia where the leading nations, Croatians and Serbs, conflicted. After the war there were some areas left uninhabited because the Serbs have escaped back to Serbia. Besides the war criminals, the refugees were mainly elderly people who are now partially coming back. The State has the appropriate legal procedure regarding the return of previous owners of the land and houses. These houses are mostly ruined, burned down and robbed, but some of them are to a certain degree adaptable for living.

One of such areas is Licka Jesenica.......

Thus we begun the colonization. There were many problems and difficulties: the houses had no windows, no doors, no bathrooms, no furniture, no water, or electricity. Even today we carry water from a nearby river. My husband and I came in the very beginning—July 1996, and made some provisory arrangements to make one room and a bathroom fit for living. Other devotees made similar arrangements because none of us have any laksmi.

In the beginning there were many disagreements between devotees, both personal and global, regarding the general directions of the development of the farm. Some of them wanted simple living, and others wanted to develop business, mass production of bio-food, and still others wanted both of that. This "quarrel" is still going on but in the meantime many devotees left the farm and gave up the project. Now there is just a few of us left, living in the four or five houses. The place is often visited by gurus as a part of their tours, and they encourage the devotees to go on. SR Prabhu is very enthusiastic about the project and propagates it everywhere, inviting devotees to move to the farm. However, devotees are until now just by-passers—nobody comes to stay. We regularly pray for new devotees to come. Gurus have given general directions for developing the farm in the sense of simple living, and some of the devotees who are currently here are still trying to make up their minds: to stay or to return to the city.

My husband and I have a strong desire to stay on the farm. Our inspiration is a devotee—S Das—a disciple of KK Prabhu. He is the only one who owns the cows given by the state to people who showed interest in breeding. His cows are called Lalita and Visakha, and there is also a calf, Bhima. They are all very beautiful. The cows give a lot of milk. S Das is nicely taking care of them. In the future, in one or two years, he wants to cultivate the land with oxen. We are medical doctors. My husband also wants (besides his job) to cultivate the land and grow vegetables, as well as to help the project financially, to host devotees and other visitors, and distribute prasadam (this is a poor country with many poverty-stricken families.) This is our current meditation, but Krsna has His own plans and we will submit to the will of the Supreme Controller. We are very satisfied with the life here. Previously we have been living a hard life of students with many obligations at the university, many more or less important contacts with people outside Krsna consciousness, and too little time for bhakti-yoga. Now we have considerably more time for reading, hearing the lectures and associating with devotees. We also preach a little to the village people.

In the last month S Das has been seriously ill, and so my husband and I are taking care of him, his household, and the cows. My husband takes care for the cows, firewood, and water, and I milk the cows, and cook. When S was in hospital we have been arranging prasadam for him daily. Krsna was very merciful engaging us in this service. The cows are so wonderful.

Now we are living from social aid money and we also sell products like marmalade, and winter-stock vegetables. By Krsna's mercy there are also sufficient donations we receive. These days we have two very respectable guests visiting us: Lord Caitanya and Lord Nityananda. A devotee has left us his Deities for fifteen days to take care of, and the atmosphere here is very exalted: the Deities in our home, regular programs with devotees, lots of snow, and so we are occupying ourselves with spiritual contents, cooking, sewing for the Deities ... The only problem is the job we are looking for since last August. The prospects are little although the country lacks doctors, but lacks money as well. Everybody expects from us to use our diplomas in the sankirtan mission. Some were amazed upon hearing that we are moving to the country, thinking that in the city we could contribute much more to the movement. We hope that by the mercy of Lord Caitanya we will manage to do this in the village as well, working and simultaneously preaching to the simple village people. It is still unclear what service is there waiting for us. Everything is mercy of the Lord anyway, and it will be as He desires.

I hope I did not make you tired with all this data and with my long narration, characteristic of women's nature. For the end I wanted to tell you about a very important thing for my spiritual life. I have great problems because I am not humble and have a controlling mentality, and I am afraid that is a great danger in association with devotees, and especially with my husband. I am skilled in practical dealings and am therefore inclined to give "smart" advice to everybody. This is sometimes very emphasized. I am endeavoring, but there is no change. Your Holiness would certainly have some solution which can be applied considering my capabilities, so please help me.

Thank you very much for your patience and forgive me for my imposing. I just want to tell you that devotees have presented me with a photograph of you, and I hope you will not object if I keep it as the source of my spiritual inspiration. If you do object, I will send it to your disciples.

Forgive me once more for taking so much of your time, so valuable for the sankirtan mission of Lord Caitanya.

Thankyou for your inspiring letter dated Dec. 20th 1997, which I only received two days ago. It is inspiring because you have realized the value of Krsna conscious farm projects, and even though you could apparently be doing much more in the city, you are determined to stay in the country and cultivate the land and spiritual life simultaneously. Thankyou very, very much for this decision. It is required that some if not most of our devotees are showing people how to live simply instead of just talking about it.

It is nice that you are fetching water from the river—just as in India. It is best to depend more upon nature and less upon government amenities. Fetching water, churning butter by hand—these are all womens' jobs that will keep you fit and heathly without any extra endeavor.

My husband and I have a strong desire to stay on the farm. We are very satisfied with the life here.

Very, very good.

I have great problems because I am not humble ...

Everyone has this problem to a greater or lesser extent. At least you recognize the problem and that is the first step in overcoming it. Everything takes time. We have to be steady and sincere. *Abhyasena tu kaunteya* (see the Gita).

... a great danger in association with devotees, and especially with my husband.

Be very careful not to alienate your husband. All your aspirations for Krsna conscious simple living will be frustrated if you don't learn to live peacefully with your husband. The secret is that the wife has to be submissive and serve her husband in Krsna consciousness. In this regard you should see the stories of Kardama Muni and Devahuti (SB3) and Cyavana Muni and Sukanya (SB9).

... a photograph of you, and I hope you will not object if I keep it.

No objection.

22 January 1998

These two weeks I have to work again at RS Prabhu's place because he is making some conditions regarding the payment of my journey to India. Anyhow, there I had opportunity to see that household life is not so charming as it can seem. As about my realizations about small children, I find them not much different from small animals. Srimad Bhagavatam is completely right saying that family life and children are the biggest attachment. The best thing is just to avoid all of it, but it is very hard because the senses and desires are so strong.

If Krsna wills, I am supposed to land in India on February 26th, and that is my main preoccupation right now. Do you already know what your schedule for March is going to be like? I am so happy to see you in Mayapur. I hope that this journey will help me to become more serious in spiritual life and strengthen my faith in Krsna and this process. I am also praying for your blessings to see India spiritually, not materially.

There is one more thing I would like to tell you. When I had really bad days at RS Prabhu's place I used to listen to seminars on "How to advance in Krsna consciousness" you gave last year in Mayapur. That is the best seminar I have heard since I joined this movement. It really kept me going on. At this moment I am a little bit fried with everything and I came to the point that I don't trust anybody except you. I feel very deeply that you are my well-wisher and that your desire is just to bring me closer to Krsna. This helps me to open my mind to you more and more because I realize that relationship with the spiritual master depends a lot on sincerity and trust of a disciple. It is strange in which ways Krsna is pushing me to open myself.

If there will be some major changes about India, I will let you know.

Please excuse the delay in reply. I was traveling in an area of India whose phone lines my modem couldn't negotiate.

Please make sure to come to India for the Mayapur festival. It is very inspiring, with many devotees from around the world, and many activities to participate in. I regularly give classes during the Mayapur festival and try to make myself available to my disciples, especially those who get to see me less. All in all, it is a great transcendental boost, which it appears that you need very much at the present time.

I don't trust anybody except you. I feel very deeply that you are my well-wisher.

Please don't think that I am your only well wisher. You should see all the devotees as your well wishers, which they certainly are—although in the course of ordinary dealings, we may not be able to see that. Actually, this "only my guru and me" mentality is very neophyte. Unless a devotee develops relationships with other devotees, he cannot advance properly, and will probably see so many apparent faults in other devotees, but never in himself. He will blame everybody, while maintaining a show of great love for the spiritual master. But his attitude is not at all pleasing to the spiritual master. Such a critical mentality sometimes turns into criticism of the spiritual master also, because the so-called love was based on sentiment only, and not proper understanding.

On the other hand, I do appreciate your expressing your difficulties to me. Sometimes disciples hide their difficulties from their gurus, and then go away blaming the guru for not helping them. I try to be straightforward with my disciples, and sometimes they might find my instructions and observations difficult to bear. But it is better to bear the weight of the guru's instructions than the crushing of material nature. This doesn't mean that you have to reveal every nonsense thought that comes in your mind. But if you're having genuine difficulties, they should be communicated to me.

Anyway, keep your spirits up, and don't fall into these useless mental depressions. Chant Hare Krsna and be happy. That may sound simplistic, but it is the essence of all our philosophy.

31 January 1998

I am writing to you for the first time. My name is M. My wife S contacted you several times already. My main problem is that I am sleeping too long. Since I know how much Your Holiness emphasizes proper sadhana and early rising, I decided to write You in particular.

Last year as a university student I slept for 9–10 or even 11 hours a day. Now my study is over and I live on the farm. Here I find it much easier to rise early because the mode of goodness is more prominent here than in the city. We (S and I) go to sleep at about 10 p.m., and we rise at 6 a.m. which makes about 8 hours of sleeping.

Many devotees I know have this problem with early rising. Many senior devotees sleep more than 6 hours a day and I see they are making compromises and extend Srila Prabhupada's limit of 6 hours of sleeping to at least 7 hours. Last year I complained to devotees that I could not study properly if I sleep only 7 hours and some of them openly said that I could sleep more than 7 hours during the intensive preparations for the exams.

On the last year's summer camp I slept 6 hours daily, but later when I was attending lectures I was tired and inattentive, thinking, "Oh if I could only sleep for another hour ..." So I felt I was not getting the most benefit from the lectures. Wouldn't it be better to omit mangala-arati and take a good sleep, being more concentrated on the lectures later in the day?

Here on the farm, when S das was ill, we had to take care of the cows for a month. At that time I was sleeping about 7 hours daily and there was no problem for me to rise, for I knew I must do it (because of the cows), but now it has become a problem again. My alarm clock rings at 5 or 5:30, but I rarely hear its sound, and even when I do, I continue to sleep 20–30 minutes more. Mostly S is the one who gets up first and after her toilet she calls me. I think I should get up first, however she is much stricter. She was very inspired by your lectures on the summer camp and when we came back, she was very enthusiastic to rise at 4 a.m., but later we failed to maintain this and she got very frustrated. I was saying to her how we used to sleep for 10 hours, and now only 7–8, so it is a considerable advancement.

My brother is a sankirtan devotee and he talks to me about the benefits of rising early, but I am not ready for this. I did not get through brahmacari life in the temple with morning programs and I can not feel the ecstasy like my brother. If I rise early then I sleep at least 1–2 hours during the day. If I feel nice due to early rising, later in the day I become frustrated because of tiredness. Six hours of sleeping seems an unattainable limit for me. Maybe for a short period, but too austere for the whole life. Are all devotees who sleep more than six hours insufficiently responsible in spiritual life? Why can I not be a devotee and sleep 7–8 hours? I know there are no unimportant things in Krsna consciousness, and that if Prabhupada has given this instruction, it is the best for us, but I still do not have a realization of this. In two weeks I must take service in the army force and I know that it would be best to rise one hour before others and chant, for I will not have any time for chanting later during the day, but I wonder how to do it?

The general principle is to reduce sleeping as much as possible, because it is a waste of time, and puts us more and more in the mode of ignorance. Better to sleep less, and serve Krsna more. In a purport in the Bhagavad-gita, Srila Prabhupada writes that anyone who sleeps more than 6 hours a day is influenced by the mode of ignorance. However, in other places in his writings, Srila Prabhupada says that devotees can sleep up to seven hours, or even eight hours.

Srila Prabhupada pushed his advanced disciples to sleep less than six hours. But it doesn't mean that if someone sleeps more than 6 hours, he can't be a devotee. All it means is that we are influenced by the mode of ignorance, which we all have to admit anyway. Nothing should be done artificially, and we should gradually try to reduce our sleep. The best way to reduce sleep is not so much by mechanically pushing our bodies, but by becoming more and more enthusiastic to serve Krsna, by which the desire to sleep is automatically overcome.

Another point is that what is required for one devotee will be different for another. Some people can get by with very little sleep, whereas others need more. If we are not able to concentrate on our sadhana or studies due to tiredness, then it indicates that we need extra sleep. It is simply a matter of common sense. However, rising early to utilize the hours of the brahma-muhurta for hearing and chanting about Krsna is very important. Here in India, which is a hot country, the tradition used to be that everyone would rise very early and engage in spiritual activities, but also take a mid afternoon nap.

Another important point for controlling sleep is controlling eating. If we eat too much, or if we eat too rich foods, or if we eat at night, our need to sleep will be increased. I have heard it said that an hour of sleep before midnight is worth two afterwards. So early resting, followed by early rising, is recommended. On the whole, devotees should try to reduce their eating and sleeping so as to concentrate more and more on the service of Krsna. Do not, however, be discouraged if you are not on as high a platform as you would like to be. Whatever platform we are on, we should engage in Krsna's service, and gradually make advancement. This we learn from Lord Krsna's instructions in Bhagavad-gita.

I hope that these thoughts are of some use to you. Below are a few more lines on the subject of anger, which bhn. S inquired about.

To S: Anger is due to excessive attachment. It must be overcome if you want to remain living in the association of devotees. Krsna does not tolerate it if one does not attempt to control his anger in his dealings with devotees. It's the neophyte tendency to blame others for difficulties confronted, vented as anger towards them. One who is Krsna conscious will never blame someone else, but will see whatever difficulty he faces as Krsna's mercy to help him take shelter at Krsna's lotus feet.

Sometime in February 1998

Congratulations on becoming a grandmother. That's what our movement needs: more grandmothers—oceans of compassion, and living shelters against the vicissitudes of the material world (manifested as nasty sannyasis, etc.).

I hope this meets you and your family members in the best of health, and that you are enjoying the pleasure of bringing up a new generation of Vaisnavas in America.

Sometime in February 1998

Lately I've read your book titled "Brahmacarya in Krsna Consciousness."

I decided to read this book although I'm not a devotee (... and you write this book cannot be understood by the common man). Anyway I risked and I think I learned some interesting things. Of course it's impossible for me to follow principles you recommend, but anyway... it's a fine book.

I have some questions for you.

1. Christian priests also live in celibacy. And they eat meat and sometimes drink wine (not only that). They do not have so many regulations about avoiding women. Could you explain how is it possible that they can practice celibacy?

2. I'd like to know how it is admissible that some ISKCON sannyasis are fat (decidedly overweight). I can understand that some young devotee is stout. He may have problems with controlling his tongue. But I cannot understand the fatness of swamis. Swami means master of the senses. If one has problems with overeating, he should wait with sannyasa vows. I saw some swamis who are decidedly too fat. What is your opinion on that subject? What about the first text of "The Nectar of Instruction"? I know it's an uncomfortable question, but it disturbs my mind. I want to understand the situation, because I don't want to insult anyone out of ignorance. Unfortunately I don't have so much courage to put this question to S Swami or any devotee from P Yatra I know. It's easier to write to someone who is far away ... so I'm writing.

3. One more inconvenient question. Some sannyasis (for instance A Goswami, B Swami) have many girl-servants. How does it correspond to the principles of sannyasa? What is your private opinion?

4. There is a psychological theory that when a married couple has a child then the man and the woman are less agitated sexually (and, what makes me laugh, it's a problem for many couples. In newspapers you

can read such letters: "After bearing my child I lost appetite for sex. Is something wrong? Please, help me."). What do the Vedas say about it?

5. You may treat this question as a joke, but I'm really serious. What does it mean: "to beat the mind with a broom"? Or "to beat the mind with shoes"? Of course it's nice poetry, but what is the benefit from such advice?

6. This is a personal question. I think I couldn't ask it if I were a devotee. I suppose it could be treated as an offense. But … anyway … it torments my mind …

How do you feel being a guru? Is it a nice position? Isn't it a reason for becoming proud? You write that a guru should accept service of disciples for their benefit. Is it so natural and simple? Didn't you ever think: "Oh! I'm a guru, I'm a really advanced devotee. I won't fall down," or "I'm better than all these grihastha men, let alone the karmis! I'm BETTER!"

(Please, write about your experience. Not about theory. I know the sastras' point of view.)

7. Are you convinced that "material life is no better than a ditch into which people pass stool"? (see page 83)

Are you not?

So you want to say that all the people except you and your friends are passing stools? Everything in the world is one big defecation? Yes?

There is another point. All right, I agree with you. But what is the problem? Stool is also a creation of Krsna. And only the senses order us to think that stool is something unpleasant. From the higher point of view stool is as nice as flowers or halawa and so on.

What do you think? (You, mister guru, not the Bhagavatam!)

That's the last question. I know the Hare Krsna movement since February '94. I tried to become a devotee, but … unfortunately I failed. There were many reasons of my falling down. Now I'm studying resocialisation. I don't feel happy in life. I feel some kind of emptiness in my heart (or mind) from time to time. I think I'll come back to Hare Krsna, but first I must understand some things outside of ISKCON.

Anyway I respect and like devotees.

All right. Hare Krsna. Have a nice new devotional year!

I hope you understood my letter. Please forgive me for mistakes. They are caused only by my insufficient education in English.

Thankyou for your appreciation of my book, Brahmacarya in Krsna Consciousness. You have written that it is impossible for you to follow the principles recommended therein. In one sense that is true, and in another sense untrue.

Most of the members of the Krsna consciousness movement who follow these principles are from a background similar to yours, so if they can follow the principles, there is no reason why you cannot also. The reason that you supposedly cannot is because you have not understood the purpose of life and dedicated yourself to understanding Krsna. Unless and until you do that, following these principles will be impossible for you.

You also quoted me as writing that "This book cannot be understood by the common man." This principle is relevant in considering the nature of your questions, which border on the dangerous. They are dangerous because they call into question the behavior of advanced devotees, which is not understandable by those who are not devotees. There are higher laws at work here that nondevotees cannot appreciate. One of the most important—if not the most important—transcendental principles is that Krsna, the Supreme Controller, does not like His devotees to be maligned or considered ordinary people.

You are also a devotee because you like devotees and like to chant Hare Krsna. You are also applying your analytical intelligence to try to understand that which, in your experience, does not seem to tally with what the scriptures state, or what would be expected of devotees. Such attempts are not to be denied. Indeed, the scriptures encourage us to use our discrimination and intelligence to make sure that those we accept as spiritual guides are actually qualified according to the standard given by scriptures. However, overly skeptical analysis can be dangerous if it leads one to see apparent faults in those who are dear to Krsna.

For instance, you have asked about ISKCON sannyasis who are decidedly overweight. You consider it to be an uncomfortable question and it disturbs your mind. I, of course, am also aware of the bodily structure of the sannyasis you have mentioned, but it has not disturbed my mind. I have hardly even noticed it. What I have noticed is their tremendous dedication to the preaching mission in which they undergo difficulties, accept the burden of many disciples, travel, preach, and in so many other ways, give themselves to others, and have been doing so for so many years.

As you have mentioned, if a young devotee is stout, he may have problems controlling his tongue. But if senior devotees who are otherwise exhibiting symptoms of being highly advanced and dedicated in Krsna consciousness are overweight, I would come to the conclusion that they are not having problems in controlling their senses, but that there must be another cause for their stoutness.

To tell you the truth, I never really thought about it before, but now that you have brought up the subject, I could volunteer some explanations. According to Ayurveda, or even modern medical science, there are different types of bodily constitutions. Some people by bodily constitution have strong appetites and even if they eat little, easily put on weight—whereas others, like me, can eat all day, and will remain as skinny as a rake. So it may be a question of metabolism. In regard to one of the sannyasis you have mentioned: I remember a devotee who is a qualified Ayurvedic doctor telling me that, according to his analysis, an operation that this sannyasi had in his childhood affected his metabolism in such a way that he very easily puts on weight.

Another consideration is that one of the most pleasant forms of Vaishnava exchange, which Srila Prabhupada also vigorously propagated, is the offering of prasada to devotees. Disciples especially like to prepare many nice items to offer to their guru as an offering of love. And in the spirit of loving exchange, the guru will not want to disappoint his disciples, and will happily take what they offer. For those who do not have such a relationship of love, this may be difficult to understand, but my poor digestive system knows well that I have many times overloaded it, even though I would rather not have, just to please devotees who had gone to so much trouble to prepare various items.

There is a story of Sripada Madhvacarya who, being an incarnation of Bhima, was well-known for taking large quantities of prasada. One day he had honored a large feast when one of his disciples brought a bunch of 50 huge bananas which he had been keeping for the arrival of his guru. Madhvacarya finished them all off on the spot. Bhaktivinoda Thakura was also quite portly, and if you see photos of Srila Bhaktisiddhanta Sarasvati Thakura or Srila Prabhupada from the side with their shirts off, you will also see that they had quite round bellies.

Undoubtedly, the tongue should be controlled, and it is an important principle for Krsna consciousness, which should be emphasized among those eager to advance in the principles of brahmacarya. So controlling the senses by not taking excessive prasada is an important principle in Vaisnavism, but pleasing the devotees who offer prasada by honoring it is also an important principle (cf: Nectar of Instruction, verse 4). I would suggest that for neophyte devotees who are struggling to control their senses, the first injunction is more important—although, as Srila Prabhupada once said, his disciples are all devotees of prasadam. And we would rather expound the glories of prasadam and how it has made and kept so many devotees rather than dwell too much on self-denial. So both sides are there, and those with transcendental vision can understand this apparent contradiction.

If you're not satisfied by this analysis, please go ahead and write to those who you feel are too fat. I'm sure that if you present your doubt in a humble and respectful manner, they will not feel offended, and may be able to give you more insight than I have.

Regarding your next inconvenient question about those sannyasis who have many girl servants: I do not know what the situation is in this regard with A Maharaja, because I have not personally seen or heard about how he lives. I think that if there were any slightest hint of grounds for a rumor in this regard, it would have already been well circulated and exaggerated throughout ISKCON, because unfortunately there are certain people around the fringes of our society who are very enthusiastic and expert in propagating rumors, especially about the supposed misdeeds of our leaders.

Regarding B Maharaja: I have seen how he conducts his programs and I am a great admirer of him. It is true that he has many young lady disciples, which could maybe be attributed to the glamorous style he brings to presenting Krsna consciousness to the masses, and also to his caring and fatherly nature, all of which are attractive to young ladies. At the same time, Maharaja is very strict about dealings between the sexes, not only in his own personal dealings, but between the members of his festival programs also.

Maharaja is an experienced enough devotee and preacher to know that, if dealings between members of a Krsna conscious group become sexually loose, then everything goes to pieces, no effective preaching can be done, and—on the contrary— whatever preaching is done becomes spoiled by the poor reputation that becomes ascribed to the party. So I don't see any cause for concern there. On the contrary, Maharaja deserves all praise for his exemplary service.

You have asked about Christian priests also living in celibacy. How do they do it? Those who have a taste for God realization may get the mercy of God, who appreciates their sincerity at the level they are on, and gives them strength from within to make advancement within that situation.

Unfortunately, at least in the modern age, such priests may not be many. Srila Prabhupada noted having heard a report about a hospital for alcoholic priests in America with several hundred beds (I forget the exact number just now). As soon as it was opened, every bed was taken. So it may be that the priests are suppressing their frustration in intoxication.

I know that one of the reasons for my disenchantment with the Catholic Church in which I was brought up, was seeing so many priests who were alcoholics, chain smokers, TV addicts, and in general talking, acting, and apparently thinking in a manner little different from ordinary people. They had little sign of the God realization that might be hoped for in a person who has supposedly dedicated his life to God. Although they may have been celibate, they were not brahmacaris in the true sense (brahme carati iti brahmacarya) of being absorbed in God consciousness. For further analysis on this topic, please read "Celibacy: Exquisite Torture or a Yes to God?" by Ravindra Svarupa Prabhu, published in his book *Endless Love*, available from BBT Bombay.

You have asked what the Vedas say about a modern psychological theory about sexual agitation. I have no idea what the Vedas say about it. There are so many modern theories. The Vedas do not address every speculation that comes in the minds of deluded people. They generally reject the knowledge proffered by conditioned souls as imperfect, due to the four defects of being illusioned, making mistakes, cheating others, and imperfect senses. There are devotees in our movement who have gone deeply into studies of psychology, both Vedic and modern, and I suggest if you want a more thorough answer to this question, you write and ask them. One of them is Suhotra Swami.

You have asked what it means to beat the mind with a broom. As the mind is subtle, and a broom gross, this is obviously allegorical. A person who is wicked and deceitful by nature, and who is expert in offering arguments to delude and misguide others is not worthy of being given a hearing. He should just be beaten. When he understands that he won't be listened to, but simply has to do what he is told, then he may start to be tamed. Of course, we don't generally recommend such treatment in ordinary life, but the allegory is there. The mind is very wicked, and should not be indulged. When the mind offers various schemes for material enjoyment, we should just kick them out. Judging by the nature of your questions, I feel that this would be valuable advice to apply in your own life.

You have asked how I ("mister guru"—are you envious or uncomfortable that anyone should be a guru?) feel about being a guru. What I feel about it is not very important. It is my service and duty, that's all. You ask: "Is it a nice position?" No. It is the antithesis of Vaisnavism to accept worship from others. Therefore a Vaisnava should not accept worship, but offer it up to his own guru, who again offers it up in the parampara system to Krsna. What is nice is to see our spiritual master's mission being fulfilled by so many people coming to Krsna consciousness. It would not be nice if they were denied the guidance and shelter that gurus are supposed to give, as they themselves received it from their own spiritual master. I think this answers the second part of this question also.

You asked me to write according to my experience and not theory, according to the sastra's point of view. But as my life is guided by sastra, my experience is concomitant with sastra.

You asked, "Are you convinced that material life is no better than a ditch into which people pass stool?"

Yes.

If you think stool is as nice as halawa, try eating some. Or do you have to come to a higher realization to do that?

Thankyou for wishing me a nice Gaura Purnima. The Mayapur festival this year, as usual, was transcendentally hectic and blissful. More than 2,000 devotees attended. It is really a wonderful spiritual experience, despite the concomitant austerities, and one that I pray to be able to take part in every year for as long as I remain in this body.

2 February 1998

I have received your letters dated 9.1.98 and 16.1.98, for which I thank you. It seems that in the first letter you are feeling much disturbed at the difficulties in balancing your academic duties with your devotional practices, but by the time of writing the second letter, you seem to have reconciled this somewhat in your mind.

Now that you have taken up this path of study, you should follow it through, at the same time not neglecting your spiritual practices. It can be difficult, but it is quite possible. Not only you, but many thousands of devotees all over the world have faced a similar dilemma, and are able to adjust within their lives. That is to say, there are many devotees who are busy in secular occupations, or are students or housewives, who have to balance their spiritual obligations with their familial, social, and occupational ones. Even many, if not most, of the devotees living in the asramas of ISKCON around the world have so much service to do that they do not have as much time for sadhana as they would like to. But somehow or other, most of us are coping and going on, and you should try to do so also, especially now that you've taken the solemn vow of initiation. You are lucky in that you have association with like-minded students, and also one lecturer (*** Prabhu). Without their association, it would be even more difficult for you.

As far as not getting good results in your studies, we learn from the Bhagavad-gita to try our best in all our endeavors, but realize that the result is not in our hands. Of course, the modern society is extremely competitive, and people tend to be judged by results only, which is very unfair, and leads to much distress and mental disturbance. However, as a devotee of Krsna, please try to be fixed in the understanding of trying your best and not being attached to the results.

Regarding the translation of Brahmacarya in Krsna Consciousness, I don't think you should begin it now, as you are already under so much pressure of study. In the long holidays and the summer, you could take up this work. I understand that you have a week holiday in the first week of March. I expect to be in Baroda at the beginning of March, but by the second or third, I'll be going towards Mayapur to attend the festival there. However, G Prabhu will be doing many college programs at that time in V, and he has expressed that he would be very happy to have you present at that time. So if you can, please do come, and avail of the association of your godbrothers at V.

Regarding my visiting P, I wrote the following to R Maharaja:

"I changed my mind about going to P. One reason is that I'm overextended, and thought it better not to add more engagements, however transcendentally exciting they may be. Another reason is that, as you are going there regularly, the place is being serviced already, so it may not be so necessary for me to go there. There's a huge ocean of preaching all over the world, and it's just a matter of deciding which part we dive into."

I would like to be everywhere in the world at once, but it is not possible. So I am thinking to concentrate more on writing books, which can go all over the world, at least to those who are interested to read them. I hope to bring out at least three new books during 1998, but to do so I have to concentrate on this work, and not travel too much. I hope that you can understand this, and that this doesn't disappoint you too much. However, I hope your disappointment will be at least somewhat mitigated when my new books come into your hands. I very much appreciate your loving sentiments. My visit to Russia this year will commence from late June or early July.

Regarding your questions:

1. "If I see a senior Vaisnava committing an offense what should I do? It so happened that, one devotee used to wear his socks and then take his bead bag or chant his rounds. Also, sometimes he used to touch his feet and then take Caitanya Caritamrta or Gita and read. Though I understand that the devotee is a great person, and the sastric principle that one should never find fault with a Vaisnava, I feel that should I oversee this, or what should I do?"

Many mistakes in points of Vaisnava behavior are made even by senior devotees, due to negligence or ignorance. This is because the Vedic culture of proper behavior, which was previously handed down generation to generation in India, has broken down, and outside India, it has not yet been properly established. To help to rectify this situation, I am compiling an extensive book on Vaisnava etiquette that covers all these points in great detail. I hope that this will go a long way to increasing the awareness and practice of proper Vaisnava behavior.

Exactly what you should do in this situation is difficult for me to say, because I am not aware of the relationship you have with this devotee. If you feel that he would be ready to hear it from you, you could approach him in an extremely humble and respectful mood, and politely point out the discrepancy. Another way to do it might be by sending him a letter. This might be especially effective if the letter is sent when you're not in his direct association and may not see him for some weeks. That way, if there is any displeasure on his part at having his discrepancies pointed out by a junior, they may subside before you meet again, and he may be thankful that you brought this to his attention. But if you feel that, under any circumstances, he would not be willing to accept instruction from you, then it is better not to try to give it. Let him read the book when it comes out.

2. "One senior devotee said that whatever you buy in Vrndavana (non prasadam) can also be taken, i.e. you can buy some milk sweets, and mix them with prasadam to distribute. He also said the Srila Prabhupada had said that in Vrndavan, all foodstuffs are prasadam. I didn't agree with that, and maintained taking prasadam in Krsna Balarama Mandir. How far is this true?"

Obviously it is better to take prasada that has been offered to the Deities. It is a devotee's natural tendency to offer everything he takes to Krsna first, and that should be more so in Vrndavan, rather than less so. The standard practice in Vrndavan is to purchase sweets from the shop and then offer them in the temple. What is the difficulty to offer, and why shouldn't we want to? Even if we consider that everything in Vrndavana is transcendental, why should we avoid offering bhoga to Krsna? It doesn't make any sense to me.

Please go on with your devotional sevice with all enthusiasm. Associate with devotees, chant attentively, read Srila Prabhupada's books daily and if possible distribute them also and surely advancement will be gradually there.

3 February 1998

I have received your letter dated 10th January 1998, and noted the contents carefully. During Kartika, you approached me in Vrndavana and asked about entering into a disciple-guru relationship with me. You told me that previously you had been aspiring for the shelter of S Maharaja.

When I asked you why you were changing your mind, you could not very clearly say why. But nonetheless, you tentatively started taking my shelter. Now you have decided you do not want to do that. I have no objection, and I understand your point, that you want to be sure "who is the person who you're willing to serve life after life."

There is no harm in taking time to make sure who is that person you want to request for shelter. But please don't approach any other guru until you are absolutely sure of what you want. It is not good to go to one guru after another, requesting shelter, and then later tell them that you don't want it.

You wrote, "I'm sure that anytime I need someone to talk with, I can find a qualified Vaisnava." Please don't take the association of devotees so cheaply. Association with devotees is a gift which is attained after many lifetimes. Even if we have the opportunity to avail of that gift, if we don't have the right attitude, we will not be able to take advantage of it.

Just see how Srila Prabhupada's family members lived on intimate terms with the most outstanding Vaisnava in the universe, yet they were not able to recognize him. If you are actually serious about spiritual life, I advise that you do not put off the matter of surrendering to a guru for too long. Otherwise, your own mind will be your guru, and I cannot think of a worse guru for you than that.

5 February 1998

That you sold 30 sets of Bhagavatams as well as many other books in December is astounding, especially considering that all the devotees there have jobs and other commitments. ISKCON H ki jaya! *** Prabhu ki jaya! Srila Prabhupada's transcendental book distribution ki jaya!

You ask for my blessings to distribute books but considering these results it should be me who is asking you for blessings.

Thank you for your appreciation of my writing. In 1998, I want to concentrate more on writing. I will cut down on travelling and write more. Please pray to Krsna, and with His blessings and those of the Vaisnavas, I hope to bring out three new books this year.

As the number of my disciples is increasing, I wish to collect old letters I have written, because many valuable instructions contained therein may be shared with others. If you have kept the letters that I have sent to you, please send photocopies of them to me.

Distribute Books!
Distribute Books!
Distribute Books!
And read them also!

10 February 1998

I also look forward to seeing the other offerings—not that I'm fit for any glorification, but it is a pleasing exchange of transcendental affection, and it is gratifying that at least a few drops of the ocean of affection that Srila Prabhupada showered on me is reaching through to my disciples also.

18 February 1998

Thankyou for your letter. You ask how to find a balance in your life. That will be different for each devotee. But basically everyone should follow the programs of sadhana as given to us by Srila Prabhupada, and remain fully engaged in Krsna's service all the balance time, minimizing (but not fanatically reducing) eating and sleeping.

Regarding staying unmarried: The best thing is just to make a decision not to do so and stick to it. If you're really not interested in the opposite sex, then they will also not be interested in you. At least, that was my experience as a brahmacari.

20 February 1998

I understand that you are upset with me for not recommending you for simultaneous first and second initiation. Please do not be upset with me. That will not benefit you in any way.

I suggested that you follow the usual procedure of taking first initiation, and then after some time, after becoming more qualified, to take second initiation, as and when you are recommended for it. But instead you decided not even to take a recommendation for first initiation, and not to go to Mayapur, where you were hoping to be initiated. You told me that, "There is no point in taking first initiation, because my service situation would be the same, whereas if I had taken second initiation, I could have done Deity worship."

This suggests to me that you do not properly understand the meaning of initiation. It is not simply a formality which bestows upon a devotee the right to perform special services. Rather, one is allowed to perform such services because he has satisfied the spiritual master with his submissive and steady service. That is why second initiation is only very rarely given at the same time as first initiation.

You asked me for a recommendation for second initiation, but I am not obliged to give that simply because you want it. As giving initiation is not a formality, giving a recommendation for initiation is also not a formality. The condition of the prospective disciple, and what will be best for his spiritual advancement, has to be considered. To give recommendations for initiation simply as a formality would also not be fair to the spiritual master being approached. My personal experience is that those who are more insistent and demanding about taking initiation are often those who go away soonest.

These may seem like harsh words to you. I have on several occasions spoken to you strongly, and it is to your credit that you have not taken them in the wrong way. I don't know if you are aware of it, but from the point of view of other devotees, you are considered a difficult case. From this latest episode, it has become even more apparent that, despite your good theoretical grasp of the philosophy, you still have serious misunderstandings of very basic points.

I don't know if you'll be able to understand or digest what I am trying to relate to you. Generally, you try to understand everything through your own intelligence, which by the grace of God is more than that of others; unfortunately, it is materially contaminated, and therefore you cannot understand anything properly through it. Lord Krsna states that the mind can be one's best friend, or one's worst enemy. In your case, you have made friends with a mind who you take to be your best advisor. But as the saying goes, one who takes himself as his own guru has a fool for a disciple.

This is why I always recommended that you spend at least two years doing the most menial services, such as washing pots—just to help you understand the most basic point of our philosophy: that we are all the servants of the servants of Krsna, a thousand times removed. Within Vaisnava society, there is a hierarchy, but those who rise in it without this basic understanding simply disturb themselves and others.

It is very nice that you aspire to be initiated as a Vaisnava brahmana, and to serve the Deity form of the Lord. However, it would not be conducive to your spiritual advancement to do that until you have imbibed the proper basic attitude. You may think that it would be good for your spiritual advancement to take up such a service, but that again is symptomatic of your disease: that you have "worked out" your own program for advancing, rather than engaging in service as is given to you by the descending system from competent authorities. Under the circumstances, it would not be conducive for you to accept brahmana initiation at this stage.

Therefore I reiterate my advice: take it step by step. First take harinama initiation (if you are so fortunate to have it bestowed upon you). Then, when the relevant authorities are satisfied with your service attitude, aspire for brahminical initiation. After millions of births you are now so fortunate to be able to associate with devotees and engage in devotional service. Can't you wait a few extra months before accepting brahminical initiation?

24 February 1998

Certainly I remember you from India. My congratulations to you. It is excellent news that you are on your way to being published. Did you tell your teachers at the gurukula also?

Writing for Krsna is a very important service. The world is polluted by concocted ideas, that are communicated to the world by deluded intellectuals. Writing is a powerful medium to counteract this mental pollution and establish reality: Krsnas tu bhagavan svayam.

What are your writing subjects? I remember your father telling me that you were mostly interested in stories. Maybe I could interest you in some story work I am doing. I have been giving classes on great devotees by reading and translating from Bengali books. The materials are transcribed but need putting into presentable English for reading. It needs a lot of work on it. If the idea of working on this appeals to you, please let me know and I will send the material across.

May Krsna bless you to lead a long and productive life in His service. Please convey my obeisances to your father.

13 March 1998, Gaura Purnima

Regarding the question about Ganga and Yamuna, there is no clear reason given why the Yamuna is referred to as the Ganga. Here in Mayapur and in other areas of Bengal the branches of the Ganga, such as Bhagirathi, Jalangi and Hooghly, are known both by their individual names and also as "Ganga." As the Yamuna is also a tributary of the Ganga, the local usage may have been to refer to her as "Ganga." Even today some people claim that Yamunotri (the source of the Yamuna) is actually the main source of the Ganga. Other explanations may be found in commentaries by the acaryas. Or maybe not. Generally we accept the acaryas' statements as good as or more important than those of sastra. "More important" in that they clarify sastra, as in this case.

15 March 1998

Please excuse the delay in reply. I have not logged in, or even hardly looked on my computer in the last few days, since I was in Bangladesh and Mayapur.

I understand that you are experiencing difficulties in personal relationships with other devotees. This is symptomatic of Kali yuga—the age of quarrel and is therefore not very surprising. It appears that in R in particular this problem is chronic within our movement probably because of the rapid expansion of the movement there, and the concomitant lack of trained leaders.

I think, under the circumstances, the best thing you can do is to tolerate the difficulties as much as possible, at the same time not giving up the association of devotees because all devotees, whether they be neophyte or advanced, are all great souls.

If you can set a better example for others by your own ideal behavior, that will in the long run probably be the best contribution you can make towards rectifying this problem. In this regard, the advice of Lord Caitanya is most relevant: trinad api sunicena taror api sahisnuna/ amanina manadena kirtaniyah sada harih.

I hope this meets you well and happy, and look forward to meeting you at the Suharevo festival in July.

16 March 1998

I am writing from Mayapur. The Mayapur festival this year, as usual, was transcendentally hectic and blissful, and about 2,000 devotees attended. It is really a wonderful spiritual experience, despite the concomitant austerities, and one that I pray to be able to take part in every year for as long as I remain in this body. Please make a special effort to come whenever it may be possible for you to do so.

Thankyou for your letter. It is nice to hear from you after a long time, and to hear of your renewed commitment to Krsna consciousness. That you are again chanting 16 rounds is especially good news, as is that of your preaching engagement. You have had quite a few ups and downs in your Krsna consciousness, so now please try to remain steady and keep up this standard.

Of course, as you accurately suspected, the news of your splitting up with M is not so pleasing. It seems that in the modern age, for a husband and wife to stay together throughout their life is becoming an exception, rather than the norm. Although you have had difficulties living with him, I'm sure you would also agree that M is not a bad person by any means. He is also a devotee, although maybe his devotional aspirations are not as strong as yours. Then again, you yourself have not been very strong or steady. You have expressed terror at the thought of my advising you to go back to M, so I shall not do so.

But please bear it in mind that the way of this material world is that—except for those who are exceptionally spiritually advanced—a man needs a woman, and a woman needs a man to live with. Perfect matches are rarely or never found. Still, the religious rule in all civilized societies is that marriage, once entered into, should be maintained throughout life, or at least until the couple are elderly. Although married life is fraught with difficulties, even more difficulties ensue in societies that condone the breaking of marriage, except in the most exceptional circumstances.

Anyway, whatever circumstances we are in, we should all try to become worthy representatives of Srila Prabhupada. That we can do by rigidly following the regulative principles, chanting at least 16 rounds daily without offenses, studying Srila Prabhupada's books very carefully, and seriously endeavoring to become pure devotees of Lord Krsna, the Supreme Personality of Godhead.

I thank you very much for your generous donation of 20 pounds. I know that you must be struggling financially, and therefore appreciate it further. I hope to be able to send you more books as I publish them, and in this way reciprocate with the kind sentiments of yourself and others who are sending me donations.

16 March 1998

Please bless me so that I may improve in my sadhana.

Blessings are there but you must do your part also.

Please pray to Sri Chaitanya Mahaprabhu that I should become a true devotee and be of service to you as you deem best.

I am always praying for the welfare of my disciples and hope that they will be kind upon me also.

17 March 1998

Don't believe these rascal scientists who now say they have found water on the moon. If they actually went to the moon, they would have found a heavenly planet. But they cannot go there because they are not qualified. It is all bluffing.

24 March 1998

Hare Krsna. I am writing from a single room farmhouse just outside the city of Baroda. There is a 2.5 meter snakeskin draped on the banister of the stairs leading to the roof, where I sleep at night in my mosquito tent.

It is peaceful here. There is no hubbub of traffic or parping of horns, nor people coming to me every moment with their problems and concerns. The birds sweetly chirp in different varieties of trills and tunes. Sometimes the monkeys, who live in an adjacent banyan tree, start hooting. There is also the sound of water constantly pouring from a deep well to irrigate the surrounding tobacco fields. At night jackals on and off join the dogs in howling.

Here I see peacocks and hens everyday as I walk up and down, fingering my beads and chanting "Hare Krsna Hare Krsna, Krsna Krsna Hare Hare, Hare Rama Hare Rama, Rama Rama Hare Hare." Occasionally I see a mongoose, and once I saw a group of sheeny blue and brown wild asses, who quickly ran away when they saw me. But I have not seen the snake who lives around here and who donates a snakeskin every year.

Now the winter is over. The nights are still cool, but yesterday the temperature reached 37 degrees Celsius (almost 100 degrees Fahrenheit), and the worst of the heat is yet to come. We tolerate it. What else can we do?

I have come here to write. Although I am trying to make writing the central focus of my life, involvement with ever more people and projects makes it necessary to go for retreats if at all any work is to be done. I haven't brought out any new books in the last two years but hope to complete at least two this year. Please pray that God blesses my endeavors.

My tentative travel plans for this summer include short visits to Russia, Germany, Croatia, and Serbia, with maybe brief stops at countries in between. I do not plan going to Britain or Ireland. I need to get back to India and to writing, so something has to go.

So there's my news. Of birds chirping and the sun shining. And writing. Not much to astound anyone, but whatever it is, it is. Please convey my affectionate regards to Mary and whomsoever of the family members you are in contact with. And I'll look forward to hearing from you in a few months and seeing you in 1999. When you've passed so many summers, an extra one doesn't seem like so much.

26 March 1998

I admire your determination to preach in America, but if you think that makes you better than others, that is arrogance.

If you think that all devotees in India are bums and thieves who never read Srila Prabhupada's books, that is not only arrogance, but also ignorance.

Your nature is certainly fiery. Fire is the color of renunciation, white of peaceful swans and also of surrender. If you get married, I hope your future wife can absorb the heat. Otherwise, your marriage may end in a ball of fire.

And before taking a firm decision on it, please read "The Forest of Material Enjoyment" again more carefully than ever before.

2 April 1998

I just want to inform you that in this moment I am OK and that devotees here are accepting me very nicely. I am trying to engage myself in the service in the temple and I am going to help in the Deity department. As you know I am entering the new asrama now, and also I have a few questions about that and I want to know answers before I make any step.

I want to know is it OK to live with her in a flat at least or minimum 6 months before I decide to live with her all my life, because I am not 100% sure that she is the right girl for me, and maybe she will see that I am not for her? Also what will happen if after these 6 months I will not be sure?

Is this a sign that she is not for me? I am very sorry because I am disturbing you with all these things, but you must understand that I am very scared about all this because I don't want to make a mistake and then suffer all my life. Dear Guru Maharaja, please understand me and help me to make the right decision.

Very good news that you are engaged in service in the temple, and that the devotees are accepting you nicely.

Regarding living with your future proposed wife before marriage, this idea may appear to be suitable to modern conditions, but it was never recommended by Srila Prabhupada. Even if you live with her for six months, you can't be sure that she will be the right person.

The actual fact is that any relationships except those which are 100% based on serving Krsna must have so many discrepancies in them. How this applies to marriage is that there is no perfect marriage, unless maybe you take examples like those of Kardama and Devahuti. (Even then, Kardama left home at a certain time.) But to make marriage as conducive as possible, Vedavyasa has compiled the story of Kardama, Devahuti, and others, and Srila Prabhupada has given his purports to describe the basic principles of civilized family life, which can be followed even today. The basic principle is one of responsibility. As Srila Prabhupada once said, a man needs a woman, and a woman needs a man. You have to get married to somebody. So if you enter into marriage with the consciousness that, "Whatever happens, I'm going to take the responsibility to maintain this woman, and the children that I give her, until there is a son old enough to take care of her," then somehow or other things will work out. Or even if they don't, you will have to live with it. That consciousness is required. For the woman, submissiveness to the husband and chastity are the most important principles.

And over and above these social and psychological considerations, there is service to guru and Krsna as the center of Krsna conscious married life.

Without the proper sense of commitment, when problems come—as they inevitably will—you may consider leaving your wife after having entered into the bond of marriage. This is not at all wanted. The civilized system is to check beforehand by astrological and other means whether the couple will be compatible, but after marriage if somehow or other they're not, divorce and remarriage is not an option. It is with this understanding and consciousness that marriage should be entered into. Otherwise, it is too much likely to end up as yet another unhappy statistic.

N Prabhu was based in S up until recently, and was helping devotees with these kind of questions. Please contact him. He is my godbrother and old friend. He was with me in B for some time. At least you could contact him on COM. I am referring you to him because he has much experience in these matters.

2 April 1998

Please accept my blessings, if that's what you want. Actually, sannyasis usually offer blessings. But because most devotees seem to think that only their own guru should offer them blessings, I generally offer them greetings, which is a way of opening letters that Srila Prabhupada sometimes used. All glories to Srila Prabhupada.

You may remember that I told you several times in the past to keep more connection with your initiating spiritual master. I'm glad that you've now understood the point, and the consequences of not doing so, and that you're going to rectify the situation.

As far as your broken promises to me are concerned, don't worry too much about them. Life in the material world is like an ocean with many tossing waves. Circumstances change, and commitments made may not always be possible to fulfill. I understand this completely, and have never felt bad about you because of this. It is only you who are feeling bad about it, which, as you know, may be because you are your own worst enemy. But then again, you are friend to yourself inasmuch as, whatever happens, you keep on holding on to the association of devotees.

Whatever else you may do, or fail to do, if we can somehow or other get the mercy of devotees, that will help us. Srila Prabhupada once related how the crocodile who attacked Gajendra was saved because somehow he was in contact with the lotus foot of a devotee. Of course, being in contact in such a hostile way is not recommended, nor are you doing that.

I'm not thinking of writing fiction. I'm more interested in writing truth.

Thankyou for the news from Taiwan. It is inspiring to hear of devotees in different parts of the world struggling to make the dreams of Lord Caitanya and our predecessor acaryas come true.

Keep in touch from time to time.

Unknown date
[to the recipient of the letter featured immediately above]

When referring to one's spiritual master in the presence of others, you can always say "my Guru Maharaja." Honorific titles, such as "Srila XXX" are, strictly speaking, meant to be used among the disciples and in direct address to the guru only—although if you know others feel comfortable with you using such a title, then you may of course do so. According to Hari Bhakti Vilasa, such honorific titles are awarded to spiritual masters. But in the fallout after the zonal acarya system, many devotees think that the only honorific title in our movement should be that of Srila Prabhupada.

I'm sure you're well aware of these things now that you're back in America. And there's no harm to be sensitive, as there are people with hurt feelings out there. At the same time, if you can convince others about the reality of your feelings towards your spiritual master that will be very nice. Reverential and loving feelings towards the spiritual master are not optional for spiritual advancement. Unfortunately, recent unhappy history has created much confusion.

8 April 1998

Even saintly people appreciate some practical help when they need it.

8 April 1998

*** Prabhu has asked me to intercede on his behalf, as he is very much anxious to get the Bengali verses of Preyo-bhakti-rasarnava, and you are exhibiting your pastime of not being merciful to him. I suggested to *** Prabhu that in this circumstance some charity given to a poor brahmana would be in order, as even the most saintly of people have practical needs that are not easy to meet in present day circumstances.

I don't know if he just wants a photocopy of the Bengali original or if he expects you to write them out in English script, but I request you (for all that I am, a meaningless personality) that if it is not too much difficulty, to kindly oblige him. *** Prabhu has an insatiable thirst for memorizing verses. It is an excellent sadhana and one that deserves to be encouraged. Whether or not he can correctly pronounce the Bengali is another question.

I hope that you received my books, which were sent to you. It might be too much to expect you to be happy and healthy in Krsna's service, but there is no harm in hoping so.

8 April 1998

You have asked me which of two services you should take up. Both are directly involved in preaching. Preaching is the life of this movement so either of them will be good for you. You have mentioned financial difficulties, but that is the usual situation, especially in R. If you struggle to serve Krsna, that will help to make you strong. Both options are good, so you may choose either of them. If you think you can do it, best to choose the service at S because it seems as if you would be taking up more responsibility in that service, with many devotees serving under you. It is good to take responsibilty in Krsna's service, if we do it with a purely service-oriented motive. As this movement spreads more and more, some devotees have to come forward to take up leadership roles. If you cannot decide which of the two offers to choose, think which leader you think you could best serve under and make your choice based on that. If you are still unsure, better stay at S, because that is where you have been based for quite some time. Unless there is a good reason to change, better continue to work with devotees you know, rather than having to enter into a whole new set of relationships. I hope this advice is helpful to you. Please let me know of your decision.

9 April 1998

It seems that there is a kind of fundamentalist vs. liberal struggle going on within ISKCON, and that the fundamentalists, who were previously dominant, are being steamrollered by the liberals. As an apparent fundamentalist, I fear that the liberals may be so illiberal as to not allow me to speak. I also fear that if certain trends continue, the time may come when there will be a move to edit Srila Prabhupada's books to make them more in line with modern ways of thinking.

10 April 1998

In Bg 3.20, why is Janaka given as an example?

There could be many people cited as examples but one is enough to make the point. As Ram-lila was well known to all, giving the example of Janaka is immediately and clearly understood.

Don't get hung up on minor abstruse points. Stick to the essence.

24 April 1998

Thankyou for your letter. I was also happy with my stay at P, and I hope to spend more time there in future. Please convey my regards to *** Prabhu and all the devotees there and thank them for receiving me so nicely.

Regarding your questions:

It is true that Krsna is not happy with the conditioned souls' being in the material world. Yet He also takes pleasure in creating, maintaining, and annihilating it. The material world is a place of reformation for the fallen souls, yet it is also a playground for the Supreme Lord where He performs many pastimes, some of which are not possible in the spiritual world, such as killing the demons. The material world is also a source of pleasure for the Supreme Lord, for it is a pleasure for Him that the devotees preach. He takes pleasure in seeing them deliver others, and He takes pleasure in seeing conditioned souls become purified and come out from the material world. Apart from that, there is the pleasure of creation itself—just as a child takes pleasure in creating some sand castles on the beach.

It is best that you become fixed in the knowledge in Srila Prabhupada's books. The visistadvaita philosophy is, in essence, the same as Gaudiya Vaisnava philosophy, but there are differences also. For instance, in our Gaudiya Vaisnava line, we understand that the position of Radharani is supreme; but the

Sri Vaisnavas concentrate on Narayana, and some even take Laxmi to be a jiva. There are many subtle philosophical differences also. Even among the Sri Vaisnavas themselves, there are major philosophical disagreements.

Therefore, it is best for you to try to clearly understand the philosophy as given in Srila Prabhupada's books and be fixed in that. This advice is not for you only, but for the whole world. Srila Prabhupada is the essence of all the acaryas because he is presenting, in a manner suitable for modern man, the teachings of all the previous acaryas. This is not to denigrate the position of the Sri Vaisnavas in any way, for I hold them in the highest respect. I am simply recommending what is best for your own spiritual development, so that you do not become confused.

Regarding serving prasada to the spiritual master: Srila Prabhupada usually had meals served to him which were not offered to the Deities, but were brought to him directly from the kitchen. He also, on occasion, did amazing things like eating unoffered sweets in the Deity kitchen while he was showing devotees how to cook them.

Srila Prabhupada is a maha-bhagavata. For him, everything is prasadam, because he has the vision of seeing everything as nondifferent from Krsna. The behavior of the maha-bhagavata is not to be imitated.

30 April 1998

I was wondering if there are any restrictions concerning using artificial flowers on the altar that you know of? Is it acceptable to use them if the temple is hurting financially and cannot afford nice fresh flowers? Is it acceptable for the Deities to hold them in their hands?

There is a Prabhupada letter which was published in the Prabhupada Nectar series, in which Prabhupada said not to use silk flowers. Plastic and paper are certainly out if silk is.

I remember when I first joined at Bhaktivedanta Manor that the devotees were stringing garlands of flowers and leaves, because of a difficult financial situation. The devotees had asked Prabhupada, who had given his permission.

My feeling is that somehow or other, some effort must be made to give Krsna a garland, even if it means cutting back in other areas. After all, we have invited Krsna, and He is Krsna.

Do you remember the story of the female disciple willing to give up her chastity so that the grocer would give nice foods for her to serve Ramanuja properly? This is the ideal for a devotee—to make all kinds of sacrifices to please Krsna. And I'm sure if we do that, then Adi Laksmi Radharani will reciprocate.

Is there no one in the whole city of Denver who will reciprocate to preaching about giving some donation, either of cash or flowers, to the Supreme Lord?

30 April 1998

You wrote that it is normal in the modern age to live for some time with one's future wife before the ceremony of marriage. That is true, but it has not added to the stability of marriage. You want to try to live with your proposed future wife to see if everything is going to be all right. I can assure you now that everything will never be all right. That is just the illusion of maya—to think that everything could possibly be all right in married life. Nevertheless, it is required for most people to undertake the responsibility of marriage, as it is more suitable for them to prosecute their spiritual advancement within the grhastha asrama.

But there is no allowance within the Vedic tradition for pre-marital companionship. We should try to comprehend and implement the principle behind such restraints, rather than acting upon our own notions. Nevertheless, if you feel it is essential to live with your proposed wife for some time before marriage, and would be extremely disturbed if you could not do that, I could give my begrudging consent. But you should know (have you not seen?) that the relationship and behavior of the spouses alters almost completely after marriage, when the courtship is over. So what is to be deduced from this experiment?

I'm glad that you accept this to be a lifetime commitment. This understanding is the crux of successful marriage. As is said in the Christian marriage ceremony, "I promise to live with this woman in happiness or distress, sickness or health, etc." This commitment will make the marriage work one way or another, despite all other obstacles. Nevertheless, you should have an astrological compatibility check, as I had previously advised you.

Thankyou for taking up the service of coordinating with my aspiring disciples there. Bhakin I is probably in V, finishing up her art school studies. Her mother is in R. Maybe you could encourage M to, if possible, come to India. Even if he could not stay very long or get absorbed in service here, at least he could visit the holy dhamas. As you know, that is a great boost to one's Krsna consciousness, and a wonderful experience, the impression of which will remain throughout life, even for those who subsequently do not practice Krsna consciousness at a very high level.

2 May 1998

My own standard is to accept only uncut fruit in the homes of people who are not vegetarians. This was the standard I imbibed from your guru maharaja from the days when I was preaching in Bengal. Otherwise, if people are at least vegetarians, I may take milk, milk products, and fruit in their homes, and sometimes whole meals, even if they are not chanting. Srila Prabhupada sometimes did this, and I do also. If I have to go on a long journey—for instance, a 24 hour train ride—I bring some cooked prasada with me. Even twenty years ago in India, people from respectable families used to do that, because they were very careful about what they ate and who they took it from. Considering Caitanya Mahaprabhu's warning about taking food from nondevotees, I think it's an area that it's better not to become lax in.

You have asked whether it is offensive to eat food from nondevotees. The answer, according to the Nectar of Devotion, is yes. That we may sometimes relax that rule, as Srila Prabhupada sometimes did, doesn't mean that it should become the norm. I personally wouldn't consider eating potato chips and the like. And you probably wouldn't want to either if you had seen the way they're prepared.

5 May 1998

Yes, disciples are a burden for the spiritual master, but it is a burden of love. Just as the child is a burden for the parents, but they take pleasure in it—in seeing their children struggle, make mistakes, and gradually grow up to become responsible citizens, and have their own children also. Disciples should try not to be a bad burden by misbehaving.

15 May 1998

Thanks for your letter and appreciation. You asked me to shed some light on the hatha and ashtanga yogas and their effectiveness in controlling the sex desire. I do not know in detail what Patanjali has to say about it. I have not studied his works in detail. I only know what Srila Prabhupada has stated about him. I am confident that for my purposes, and for anyone else's, that is enough. For more details, please read "The Path of Perfection" by Srila Prabhupada.

The hatha yoga system is a mechanical means to attempt to subdue the senses. Although some effect may be produced by it, it is extremely difficult to follow all the practices in the correct manner, especially in the modern age. For instance, the first rule in hatha yoga is to go to an undisturbed place. If someone tries to control the senses by the hatha yoga system without following this first rule, whatever incremental advancement he may make by imperfectly practising breathing and asanas will surely be washed away by the gross sexual propaganda that is everywhere in the modern age.

Therefore harer nama eva kevalam—in this age, even more so than in others, the only way to make spiritual progress is to take shelter of Hrishikesha, the controller of the senses, by chanting His holy names.

18 May 1998

I am sorry I can not fully perform devotional service. But the little I do I hope Krsna, Prabhupada and you are pleased ... If you could kindly give me any advice on obtaining Krsna-prema, I would be very much indebted.

I feel the same way about not being fully able to perform devotional service. How much can we tiny limited beings serve the unlimited Supreme Lord? But we have to try. I am trying to serve Srila Prabhupada by connecting others to his teachings, so I can only recommend you to go on following them and thus get Srila Prabhupada's mercy.

Then, gradually, development will be there, up to the point of Krsna-prema, as outlined in Bhagavad-gita As It Is 4.10 purport. It takes time to reach the goal, and guidance is required. As you are approaching me for guidance, I shall do my best to impart it, as I have understood by hearing from and serving Srila Prabhupada.

I am trying to go on book distribution. But my scores are extremely low, which shows my devotion.

It is not necessarily true that low scores indicate low devotion. I used to go on book distribution with a godbrother whose scores were for months very low. But he really wanted to do well because he wanted to please Srila Prabhupada by this service. So he kept on praying and kept on trying. After about two years of struggling like this, Krsna suddenly blessed him and he became one of the top distributors, and maintained that standard for several years, until he changed to another service. So please keep trying, and go on praying. There is no saying what wonderful things Krsna can do through us if we are simply sincere to serve Him.

Hope to see you very soon.

Srila Prabhupada used to recommend seeing a sadhu by hearing his instructions. If possible, you may contact S dasa on COM. He is organizing a tape ministry of my lectures.

Hoping this meets you well and happy serving the sankirtana mission in the most important city in the world.

19 May 1998

These days I'm in a really strange mood and I have problems with my mind.

Please read Srila Prabhupada's books, especially Gita, very carefully for at least an hour daily. This will help you tremendously.

24 May 1998

I am very happy that you are very happy in Krsna consciousness. Actually Krsna consciousness means to be happy. By doing everything for Krsna's pleasure, we also become happy. So if you're happy in your present service, please continue with that, and that will make me most happy. Don't cut yourself off completely from preaching though, because that is the life of our movement, and the mission of Sri Sri Gaura Nitai.

I am also very happy that you became very happy in the holy dhamas. Both C and K have written expressing the same thing. I wanted you all to come to the holy dhamas. I knew that you would not understand how wonderful it would be until you came, and that you would be very enthused by doing so. So yes, please do try to come to Mayapur and Vrindavan year after year, and I will be happy to see you there also.

Actually I was invited to come to the summer camp in Croatia, but because the date was put back to the beginning of September, I wrote and said that I probably wouldn't be able to attend, as I would probably be back in India by then. However, my plans may change. Let's see what happens. Even if I turn up at the last minute without much prior arrangement, then probably the organizers could still find a few minutes to speak, and there might be a few hearers also.

24 May 1998

At the end of a class in V, you stated that Srila Prabhupada had said not to use Gita Press Gitas, even though it is known to everyone that I regularly do so. I felt a little peeved about this, and thought about mentioning it to you. But I considered that, as you were leaving anyway, and it wasn't such a big issue, it wasn't worth doing so. I had mentioned this in passing to *** Prabhu, but did not intend that he should broadcast it.

Thankyou for bringing this to my attention. I will ask *** Prabhu to be more discreet in the future. You may also learn from this incident about how to speak with proper consideration of time, place, and circumstance. I certainly don't hate you, and I wish you all success in your ongoing endeavors to reach the lotus feet of Krsna. You are young and brash. I was also once young and brash. Now that I am older, and a little less brash, I have taken it upon myself to try to help upcoming devotees not to make the same mistakes that I have. Please don't feel bad for that.

24 May 1998

Book distribution in India is going on in pretty much the same way it has for many years—that is, it's not super organized, nor is it strongly pushed, but still a lot of it goes on. You are right about the lack of communication and cooperation between the centers. Somehow or other, that's the way things are in ISKCON in India, and there's no sign of things changing soon … which brings me to your question about my plans and vision for book distribution in India.

I'm basically doing what I can to develop it in the small sphere of influence that I have, which is basically in G, working out of ISKCON B and V. I have a few brahmacaris, both from India and the West, who are working under me. We have a mini padayatra which is concentrating on book distribution, one bus party fully dedicated to book distribution, and another party that concentrates on college preaching, but also does a substantial amount of book distribution. I'm always stressing to the men that here cultivation of devotees and book distribution must go on side by side. There's a huge field that cannot be covered by the few brahmacaris that we make. We have to cultivate an interest in people and make them devotees and naturally when they get inspired, they will want to go out and distribute Srila Prabhupada's books. This is the major factor in Mayapur running up such massive scores. Because they've been cultivating devotees in Nama hattas for so many years, they have a huge army of preachers, who all contribute to the sankirtana effort. Of course, there is a similar system in the West, with contact sankirtana. With France, Italy, and other areas, B dasa, the ex-GBC was developing this systematically and very successfully, until he unfortunately left his service.

I don't know what the situation is in other parts of the world, but I feel that Congregational Preaching and book distribution could in all areas move much closer together, as there is tremendous potential to make devotees all over the world. The effect of distributing Srila Prabhupada's books for more than twenty five years has created a situation in which devotees can be made anywhere, among all classes of people. You must remember the almost-forgotten GBC resolution of a few years ago, encouraging ISKCON leaders to inspire their followers for book distribution. In that, it is stated that leaders should stress the importance of making devotees, because making more devotees means making more book distributors. There is a lot of emphasis in India now on developing congregational preaching, and literally hundreds of people are coming up to the level of initiation. ISKCON C is famous for its congregational program, and that was also the basis of their recent debut success in book distribution. They got hundreds of congregational members out distributing books. I'm sure you're aware of all things, but I just thought to share my realizations about them with you.

26 May 1998

Generally it is understood that the maha mantra is praying to Krsna and His internal potency for engagement in Their service. Lord Caitanya, in the mood of a devotee, also chanted this mantra. Of course, Krsna and Lord Caitanya are not different, so chanting the name of Krsna also refers to Sri Krsna Caitanya. The Supreme Lord is always present with His energies, and is to be approached through His internal potency. Lord Caitanya is the Supreme Lord and His internal potency, Krsna with Radha combined. However, in Lord Caitanya's lila, Radharani also appears separately as Gadadhara Pandita. Some devotees worship Gaura-Gadadhara. This is a very confidential form of worship, in which Gadadhara Pandita is assisting Lord Caitanya to relish the mellows of devotion to Himself. These are all highly esoteric subjects, but the basic understanding is that the Supreme Lord is to be approached through His devotees. This could actually form the subject of an essay, but only devotees advanced enough in understanding of Gaura-tattva and rasa-tattva would be able to appreciate it. In the meantime, we can all go on chanting the Hare Krsna mantra before the Deities of Sri Sri Gaura Nitai, knowing that they are pleased with this chanting, and understanding that they are non different from the mantra that they also chant.

You asked, "Is praying to the guru the way to remove all anarthas from the heart?" It is an important part of the all-inclusive process of devotional service. Our regular hearing and chanting and other services must simultaneously continue. But you are right, that the mercy of the guru is essential, otherwise other processes will not be effective. And praying to the guru helps to invoke that mercy. It is not that the guru is more powerful than Krsna, but that Krsna is pleased with those who take shelter of His devotees and favors them accordingly. And because I am taking shelter of Srila Prabhupada, you may also take shelter of remembering and serving me, seeing me always in my position of service to Srila Prabhupada, who is himself in service to his guru. This is the parampara system.

4 June 1998

The news of your preaching activities there are most inspiring. I feel as if I should immediately run down there to be with you all. But I have other commitments, and indeed increasing commitments throughout the world.

Most important is that you are steadily fixed in service and in an ashram best suited to your present position. Where you serve and the exact nature of your service is a detail.

27 June 1998

You have written that the best way to get an answer to your personal problems is to ask the local devotees, try to get the solution in my or Prabhupada's books, or to ask me personally. But you think that asking me personally is best, because I "cooperate perfectly with the Paramatma."

It is always auspicious and best to follow the advice of the spiritual master, and in making major decisions for one's personal life—even though one may consult with others—they should be confirmed by the spiritual master. But inversely proportionate to the increase in the number of my disciples is my capacity to become intimately involved in their personal problems. It is therefore incumbent on the disciples to form relationships and trust with those around them, so that they may be guided.

In general problems of a local nature are best sorted out by consulting with devotees in the local vicinity, who can better judge the situation than I, who am unfamiliar with the circumstances. You should also consider carefully the gravity of the problem before bringing it to me. It is the specific duty of the spiritual master to instruct the disciple how to go beyond all problems by becoming Krsna conscious, but it is not his duty to get involved in the temporal affairs of his disciples, although he may give advice about them also just to help his disciples advance. The disciple should not bring every little personal problem before the spiritual master. Nor is it proper for the disciple to neglect to inform him of a major problem that could markedly influence the disciple's life or impede his spiritual progress.

Often disciples approach their spiritual master to get a definitive solution to their personal problems—for instance, "Should I marry or should I not, and if so who to?" Devotees expect that by doing so, all their problems will be solved. This is not necessarily true. Even if the disciple perfectly follows the guru, he should not think that all his problems will be finished by doing so. As long as we live in this material world, there will be problems. For instance, by following the advice to marry, a disciple enters a situation of multiple problems. And even if the advice is not to marry, still there will be problems. The spiritual master should be approached with the understanding that he can ultimately solve all problems by giving advice on how to get out of this material world by surrendering to Krsna. He may also give advice on personal problems to direct the disciple so that his material situation may be more favorable for advancing in the surrendering process.

The spiritual master is not omniscient like the Paramatma. He cannot predict how others will behave in future, or what exactly the result of following his advice will be. Many spiritual masters in our movement who previously engaged in arranging their disciples' marriages have stopped doing so, seeing that quite often the marriages did not work out, and the disciples blamed the spiritual master for the arrangement. In such a case it is not actually the fault of the guru that the marriage did not work out, but that of the disciples for not following the guidelines in Srila Prabhupada's books for successful Krsna conscious family life.

I have elaborated on the marriage question in this text because most personal problems center around this issue. It certainly is a difficult one, especially in the modern age, and especially in the Western countries. I am very concerned about my young unmarried disciples, especially in the West, and of their future marital status. From the Vedic cultural viewpoint, it is an anomaly that young ladies remain unmarried after puberty. There should be at least one person whom they fully trust and can turn to at all times, and that is their husband. We live in a society far deviated from the Vedic ideal. But it is that ideal that we have to work to establish. In Vedic culture, spiritual masters instruct the men, who then instruct their wives. Within the joint family unit, young women would be guided by the elders of the family, particularly her mother-in-law.

Modern society is unnecessarily complex, and has caused a great increase in the physical and mental problems of its members. An important part of the mission of the Krsna consciousness movement is to establish a civilization in which people can live more simply and be close to God, and thus giving people the opportunity to live far less compromising lives. My upcoming book, Glimpses of Traditional Indian Life, is meant to give an idea of such a civilization.

Although I don't have many disciples compared to other gurus in our movement, I am on the whole very happy with the level of seriousness and dedication of my disciples. I pray to Srila Prabhupada and Krsna to always guide you properly, and thus reciprocate the trust you have placed in me.

As for your ongoing spiritual crisis, I can give instructions and advice, pray for you, and plead that you make the determination to overcome the lower self with the higher. But ultimately it is up to you—to surrender to maya or to Krsna. Please deliberate carefully and decide to do that which is for your eternal self-interest. It is only after many lifetimes that we get the chance to associate with devotees and serve Krsna. Please do not waste this opportunity simply for the sake of some hoggish sense gratification.

I can see even now that trying to go for sense gratification instead of becoming more Krsna conscious is actually bringing me closer to Krsna consciousness, because finally I will get some realization that there is no happiness in leading karmi or material life. I will probably just get more attached to Krsna consciousness.

Please don't try to justify your nonsense by saying that it will make you more Krsna conscious. If you want to be Krsna conscious, follow the process and stop all this nonsense. Initiation means commitment. Please don't take Krsna so cheaply and think that you can take Him or leave Him at whim, as you can a boyfriend.

24 July 1998

I agree with the great majority of senior devotees in our movement, that guru issues in our movement need careful looking at. There are a number of serious theological and ecclesiastical issues that need addressing, especially in the light of the falldowns of several ISKCON gurus.

My position is this. I know who I am and I am not a maha bhagavat. I hope I have never been perceived as trying to convey such an impression. I am a follower of Srila Prabhupada, who is a maha maha bhagavat, and thus my duty is to guide my disciples to follow as Srila Prabhupada taught us. I am confident that if I am sincere in doing so, Prabhupada and Paramatma will give me the intelligence how to properly do so.

It appears that *** Prabhu favors a system whereby ritvik-gurus initiate but have very little responsibility to guide or uplift the disciple. I find this overly impersonal. It is clear that Srila Prabhupada wanted his disciples to initiate. With initiation goes a commitment to the disciple.

I consider it my personal responsibility to guide my disciples and be involved with their ongoing spiritual progress. In doing so, however, I do not demand exclusivity and encourage my disciples to also hear from and serve other properly situated disciples of Srila Prabhupada.

I heard from +++ Prabhu that in the Sri sampradaya there is a pranama mantra as follows:

"I offer my respects to my spiritual master, who is worshipable because he is a faithful follower of Sripada Ramanujacarya."

I would feel comfortable with such an understanding vis-a-vis Srila Prabhupada. Personally, I am nothing. *Yogyata vicare, kichu nahi pai, tomara karuna sara.* But because I am representing Srila Prabhupada, I must instruct as I have heard from him and may receive respect up to the level of worship (as is the etiquette), but only with the understanding that all honor is to be offered up to Srila Prabhupada. Srila Prabhupada is a guru, and on his order I am also a guru. Garuda is a bird; a sparrow is a bird. Not all birds are on the same level, nor all gurus.

Much discussion about this is going on now in our society. Please do not become confused. Go on with your hearing, chanting, preaching and other services. Let us see what the outcome is. I am confident that it will all be for the best. Lord Caitanya wants Krsna consciousness spread to every town and village and ISKCON is His medium for doing so. Our society has been through upheavals before and will no doubt go through more in future also. So stick to the basics and don't be discouraged.

7 August 1998

The best news therein is your continued enthusiasm for book distribution. Srila Prabhupada wrote one letter to a disciple in which he said to make "lifetime plans for book distribution." In other words this is something which we have to do throughout our lives. If we try, Krsna will give us the intelligence to increase our book distribution more and more. Already the effect is there—your book distribution is widely known among the upper classes in H. Now see how to increase more and more.

Good news also that so many devotees are giving you association and that preaching is going on nicely in so many ways in H because you are sincere, Krsna is sending you devotees to associate with.

Both in the matter of Back to Godhead and BBT you are having difficulties. It is an unfortunate fact that our society is often lax in such areas. Despite our external display of togetherness, we are actually disorganized in many ways. What is the problem? Lack of Krsna consciousness? Lack of intelligence? Laziness? I'm not sure, but it is something we are all living with. All I can suggest is to remain patient and keep up the pressure until you get what you need. I discovered that with Bombay BBT, to place an order usually was not sufficient. I would have to go personally to get the books. So you are not the only one suffering in this way.

I'm planning a South India trip this winter. I suggest you write all your questions down in a notebook, then we can sit together for some time and go through them all. Sometimes I'm more busy and sometimes less so, but hopefully I'll never be so busy that I can't go round to answering your letters.

Thanks for your "book distribution" card. Just find out the ways and means to bring people to Krsna consciousness, Prabhupada and Krsna will bless you. You are asking for my blessings, whatever I have to convey, let you be blessed. I have no strength of my own but if I can form a channel to the ocean of Prabhupada's and Krsna's mercy, that is my only chance to help others.

9 September 1998

It is not true that listening to karmi music, watching karmi sports etc. are necessary so that our minds do not flip out from the pressure of trying to be Krsna conscious (?). Rather, if we actually want to be Krsna conscious, we should strive to perform only activities that are favorable for the cultivation of Krsna consciousness, and should reject those that are unfavorable. Do you really want to be Krsna conscious? If so, follow the advice of the acaryas, not that of foolish neophytes.

Rupa Gosvami has outlined the whole process of development in Krsna consciousness in his Nectar of Instruction and Nectar of Devotion. Nowhere does he recommend indulging in karmi music or sports. Rather, he enjoins that we give up such things and replace them with hearing and chanting about Krsna. Even if we feel no taste for hearing and chanting, we should go on with it, and it will act, just as sugar candy acts to cure jaundice.

You state that you have an inclination towards philosophy. This should be developed in a systematic way. If you take up a study program of Srila Prabhupada's books (for instance by following the Bhakti sastri study guide or by taking a correspondence course) this should regulate your study, give you a fixed goal, and save you from nonsense karmi music.

21 September 1998

I have heard from several devotees that to eat such prasadam (which was cooked by a mataji) is not auspicious for a brahmachari.

Srila Prabhupada never said that. It has always been standard in ISKCON that all devotees take prasada without consideration of whether it was cooked by a woman or not. Who is introducing these speculations? Let them starve.

Please answer what the Vedas say about it?

In Vedic culture, brahmacaris beg door to door and receive food from housewives. They are trained to see all women as their mothers.

21 September 1998

Dear Gurudev, I want to ask Your permission to perform agni-hotras.

Actually Gaura-Nitai are more satisfied with preaching and sankirtan. I would think that especially in a small temple it is best to concentrate on these essential activities rather than peripheral ones.

25 September 1998

During the last visit of X Swami in Belgrade, bhn. G wanted to have a darsan with him. I was there as encouragement and help. So he wanted me to write this letter, explain the situation, and ask you for advice. She has a restaurant where they serve chicken, fish and alcohol. She has a partner so they run the restaurant together and they divide money earned from it. She is also ordering for last two years some kind of bread from the temple for that restaurant.

She knows devotees for three years, she is helping them mostly with money and other ways too. Now she wants to advance more in spiritual life and her question is how much karma she gets from that restaurant? Does this prasadam distribution help, or makes her karma less? Do you have some advice for her what to do? She has old parents—she has to take care of them; she is forty, difficult to start something new, but she has to maintain herself. X Swami suggested to separate money earned from meat and alcohol and give to partner and keep the rest for herself, but that could not be enough for living. Do you have some suggestion, advice?

A difficult situation. I can offer two examples of how Srila Prabhupada responded to similar situations.

In Fiji, when Vasudeva Prabhu became a devotee, he said to Srila Prabhupada that he would now have to stop selling canned meat in his shop. Apparently Srila Prabhupada replied that nothing had to change.

The next story I heard directly from the devotee involved. He had just become a life member in Hyderabad and asked Srila Prabhupada about whether or not he should continue his business of date tree cultivation for producing toddy (cheap alcohol). Srila Prabhupada thought about it, then said, "You have to maintain your family." That man therefore continued his business, and eventually retired and is now initiated by Jayapataka Maharaja.

Considering this, I would say that if there is no other way around it, she may just have to continue, pray to Krsna for forgiveness, and look forward to the day when she no longer has to maintain her parents and could then maybe give up the business and join full time.

According to fate, some people taking to Krsna consciousness find themselves in situations that are contradictory to the principles, and, despite their unwillingness, cannot extract themselves. There are, for example, many instances of prostitutes who were devotees.

This should not be taken as a general example for others to follow, or for devotees in general to use as an excuse for not following the principles.

Her question is how much karma she gets from that restaurant?

As Krsna states in the Gita, the ways of karma are difficult to ascertain. Karma is burned away by bhakti. According to the level of her sincerity, Krsna will reciprocate. I suggest that she use money thus earned only for maintaining her parents, giving donations, and maintaining herself at the minimum standard. No luxuries. Any sense gratification indulged in from such earnings will certainly invite karmic reactions.

Another point to consider is that even most devotees who earn money by relatively "clean" means do so by serving grossly sinful people. For instance, a bank worker serves those who finance wars, slaughterhouses etc.

Does this prasadam distribution help, or makes her karma less?

I don't like the idea of prasada bread being mixed with fish and chicken.

8 October 1998

One significant piece of news is that most of the foreign devotees in the area are getting anxious about a possible upcoming war between India and Pakistan. (You may know that in April 4, 1975 Mayapur conversation, Prabhupada indicates that the next world war will start between India and Pakistan. And various happenings in the news, and the general mood of the public suggest that it may be imminent.)

Of course, we all aspire to be fully surrendered like you and just go on preaching without being distracted—but personally I don't want to be a foreigner caught in war-torn India. And once it starts, it may be difficult to get out. So I have been seriously considering moving to New Zealand in the near future. A, B, C, and D are thinking along similar lines.

I know it may all sound like utter craziness, but still, I am afraid to be caught unprepared. I also thought that you should be kept posted about the consciousness of the devotees here, even if (especially if) we are crazy.

Now I'm working on filing some of the miscellaneous references for the etiquette book, including that file you gave containing many references from com. When you asked me to send you some files, I could not immediately because I wanted to add these miscellaneous references to any file that I might send. When BGP returns I will send something (b/c I have to send it through WinCOM).

Actually Y is no longer living in the temple, so he doesn't have time to do that work. Also we don't have an extra computer, what with A traveling here and there (we tried to get yours from Delhi, but were not successful).

I never heard from F Prabhu, except immediately after sending him the book 3 months ago, to say that he received it.

I will be glad if we can get this etiquette book in print soon and distributed. I am anxious that something may happen and we may not get to complete it.

Your return will be a much needed spiritual boost, as many of the devotees here are lacking in enthusiasm and not so much engaged.

During much of the 1980's there was much war fever generated in the press and it just seemed a matter of time before Indo-Pak war broke out, which it didn't. This is all propaganda produced for political purposes. If there was really a serious threat of immediate war in India, it would certainly be big news in the West, but it isn't even an issue. Nothing about it in the papers. I've been inviting devotees to come travel with me in the winter in South India and no one has expressed such fears.

During the 1980's, many people were convinced that America-Russia nuclear war was inevitable. *** M. even made elaborate arrangements, wasting hundreds of thousands of dollars, to stock food and illegal arms and ammo.

There may indeed be an upcoming war, but it is not so certain that we should base our life plans on it and thus spoil valuable time and energy that should be focused in the service of Krsna.

So please don't buy your tickets for NZ yet. At least wait till I come, then we can all discuss together. If need be, I will go with you. If not, better you stay with me.

I will be glad if we can get this etiquette book in print soon and distributed.

Me too.

Your return will be a much needed spiritual boost, as many of the devotees here are lacking in enthusiasm and not so much engaged.

Why? Are they all dreaming of NZ and all the beautiful young girls there who will relieve them from all distress? "Not so much engaged" is very dangerous. They should immediately start daily Harinam for at least as many hours as they are unengaged. Even if they go round and round the same bazaars three times a day, it's better than sleeping and dreaming of maya.

9 October 1998

Trust no future however pleasant (or unpleasant).

13 October 1998

The local hospitals pay Dhs. 200 (US$ 54) for those who donate blood. Blood can be donated once in 3 months. I may be able to muster up quite a number of people to donate blood (around 50 or so). All the laxmi earned by the individuals can be donated for spreading KC. I have heard of some Christian missionaries who organise blood camps and collect the laxmi for social work. Even if I am able to muster up around 50 devotees only once in 6 months, (out of our congregation of over 200), we can easily earn Dhs. 20000 or US$ 5400. These funds can be used for many purposes: donations to Guru Maharaja/temples, donation/subsidy of Gitas in India, organise conventions for satsangis like the one being organised at KL, Audio Cassette/Video Cassette library from Tape Ministries, welfare of satsangis in trouble/in case of emergency etc.

In addition the recepients of the blood get Krsna conscious blood—chanting and prasad (I have heard before that Sheikh R whenever he had to have blood transfusion would go to Pakistan specially to have Muslim blood).

Kindly advise if this would be okay and not go against any scriptural injunctions.

According to G Prabhu, it's not so good. According to X Swami, it's not so bad. According to BV Swami: yathecchasi tatha kuru. But the same time could be spent in preaching to others, who if convinced will "give their blood" (as well as their laxmi) to Krsna. It is better to give your mercy to others in the form of Krsna katha than in the form of blood, even if your blood is prasada enriched.

Nevertheless, if you can raise substantial funds without much entanglement, and use it all in directly Krsna conscious ways, it's not such a bad idea.

29 October 1998

You have asked how devotees can develop self-confidence and self-esteem. But we do not find such terms anywhere in Srila Prabhupada's books or throughout the Vedic literatures. That we should develop self-confidence and self-esteem is an idea borrowed from karmi books. Modern culture promotes the idea of the rugged individual who makes his own way in life without depending upon others. A person with such a concept of life is described by Lord Krsna in the Bhagavad-gita as a very great fool and rascal.

prakṛteḥ kriyamāṇāni
guṇaiḥ karmāṇi sarvaśaḥ
ahaṅkāra-vimūḍhātmā
kartāham iti manyate

A devotee is not self-confident, because he knows that individually he has no power. Materialists who delight in apparently manipulating and controlling the material energy are actually manipulated and controlled by the material energy. Even if a person wants to desist from the vain effort to control material nature, he is so much accustomed to interfacing his senses with the sense objects of the material world, that he cannot get free from the clutches of maya by his own efforts.

daivī hy eṣā guṇa-mayī
mama māyā duratyayā
mām eva ye prapadyante
māyām etāṁ taranti te

"This divine energy of Mine, consisting of the three modes of material nature, is difficult to overcome. But those who have surrendered unto Me can easily cross beyond it."

The only solution is to surrender to Krsna. This entails taking shelter of Krsna and His representatives through the process of devotional service. A devotee is not so foolish to think that he can cross over maya by his own efforts alone. He does not, therefore, cultivate self-confidence, but confidence in the mercy of Krsna and the Vaisnavas. Although thinking himself very small and insignificant, he is so much confident of the good wishes of Krsna and the Vaisnavas, that he can move freely in this world, executing his devotional service without fear or discouragement. A devotee is certainly confident, but his confidence does not spring from a foolish sense of self-esteem, as does the misplaced confidence of the materialist. Indeed, a devotee does not cultivate self-esteem at all. Rather, the opposite. A devotee thinks himself the lowest, meanest, and most sinful person within the fourteen worlds. Krsnadasa Kaviraja Gosvami, the author of Sri Caitanya-caritamrta, was certainly one of the greatest devotees of all time, yet he wrote: *jagai madhai haite muni se papistha purisera kita haite muni se laghistha*—"I am more sinful than Jagai and Madhai and even lower than the worms in the stool." (Cc. Adi 5.205) Vaisnavas are certainly the greatest people in the world, but their greatness does not spring from a foolishly inflated false sense of prestige. Their greatness springs from their utter humility, submission to and dependence upon higher authorities. Materialistic people desire to develop self-confidence and self-esteem, so as to become a "success" in terms of material achievements. It is those, however, whose consciousness is most far removed from such ambitions, whose only desire is to please the previous acaryas, who have no motivation for their own prestige or glorification, who embody the humility, tolerance, and pridelessness of Caitanya Mahaprabhu's *trnad api* verse, who are empowered by Krsna and the Vaisnavas to make the most extraordinary achievements. For instance, a composition of Sri Caitanya-caritamrta is far more important and notable than the conquering of many empires. Materialistic people will not recognize this. But for all their self-confidence and self-esteem, they have to end up being reborn as cats and rats. Whereas the humble devotee, by his utter submission and dependence upon the mercy of Vaisnavas, ultimately conquers Krsna and captures Him within his heart.

10 November 1998

Srila Prabhupada sometimes encouraged devotees who had already started courses to finish them. A diploma is some kind of an asset that may come in useful at some point. At least we can say that some of our devotees are educationally qualified. To stop your course now would, it seems, cause too much disturbance from your father. I suggest that, especially as you have already started the course and it's only 2 years, you might as well finish it.

In the meantime, you can tell your parents that, after you finish the course and before taking up a job, you would like to join a temple for 3 months. You don't have to insist on it or reply to their objections, simply prepare them for the idea.

I know this will be difficult for you, but your proposed alternative of defying your parents would not necessarily be better. Sri Sri Gaura Nitai have come to you, so take solace in Their service. Remember Raghunatha dasa Goswami, who wanted to run away from home to join Lord Caitanya but was told by Him to wait until the time was right. Read the pastime in Caitanya Caritamrita. It will help you.

From a letter from Srila Prabhupada:

Regarding your manner of behavior with your parents who are not in Krsna Consciousness; I may inform you that you should treat four different classes of men in four different ways. A devotee should love God and God's devotees. A devotee should make friendship with devotees. A devotee should try to enlighten innocent persons, and a devotee should reject opposite elements. As father and mother they should be offered proper respect according to social custom, but you cannot accept their non-Godly instructions. Best thing is, to avoid misunderstanding, to remain silent without any affirmation or negation of their instructions. We should try to keep our friendship with everyone in the world, but we cannot sacrifice the principles of Krsna Consciousness on being employed by some relative of this world. Don't let them know that you do not approve your parents' instructions, but at the same time you should be very careful in dealing with them. If you object to their instruction and let them know it, then they will feel sorry, sad.

10 November 1998

Thankyou for the good news. As Lord Nrsingha has come to you, it means He wants to be worshiped by you. Do it as nicely as you can, but remember that whatever standard you worship Him to should never decrease.

If there will be a distinct advantage to your moving out to live with other devotees, you may do so. But if so, don't neglect to visit your parents and help them increase whatever appreciation of Krsna they may have developed.

She had gone to India (this is more than 1.5 month ago) and she will be there for about two more weeks.

So she's probably fixed in her ways, in which case better not to disturb her.

I don't want to do anything artificially.

Not being KC is artificial. The rules and regulations are to bring out our true nature.

I want to be myself.

Good. You are a servant of Krsna.

I can't pretend I'm something that I'm not.

So why pretend to be an enjoyer of this material world?

I think this is the latest fashion in ISKCON.

Read: "the latest excuse for insincerity." The old fashion is best: rise early, chant 16 rounds, follow the 4 regulative principles, read Srila Prabhupada's books, etc.

11 November 1998

I visited B this summer and loved it. The devotees are great—simple, old style brahmacaris.[3]

I am staying in B now, they are a great bunch. Willing to learn not puffed up and fun. Mostly they are from Ireland so have a different

---

3. These two sentences are from a previous letter by Bhakti Vikāsa Swami.

outlook and upbringing to the Brits. Not everyone agrees with their way of perceiving and doing things though. How to preserve it?

That's up to individuals. You might be labeled a dinosaur. I am, by some.

What to do about the Gujarati "takeover"? Is it inevitable? It seems to be their nature, virtually to walk over everything and everyone and corrupt and control with money? One very nice doctor from Delhi recently told me: 'they are just bunyas' and are not generally held in high esteem in Indian society.[4] It is very easy to sell out Srila Prabhupada's society and ways in exchange for a comfortable existence and a handful of money to do your perceived projects which often has a hidden price tag attached? The brahmacaries want to divorce themselves from getting overly entangled with the Hindus. When abroad they are only looking for personal profit and gain.

Yes, Gujaratis are business minded by nature, but they are devotees also. Many of them are very serious devotees (Have you visited Nottingham Nama Hatta? Please do. The driving force is P Prabhu and his wife. She is Gujarati); others are still developing towards that platform. It doesn't all happen in one life for everybody.

The Pandava Sena are better than most young Gujaratis. They have more touch with Krsna and less with gross sinful life. Not everyone is prepared to be a fully surrendered devotee, so we could take the attitude of appreciating and encouraging those who make at least some moves towards Krsna. Who knows, when they face difficulties in life, they may turn to Krsna more. *Catur vidha bhajante mam* ... Maybe we were on that platform in a previous life.

I suggest you contact Sruti and respectfully tell him of the problems you are feeling. If it's presented to them properly, can't the Pandava Sena be more considerate if landing on top of a small group of brahmacaris?

---

4. *Bunya/baniya* (Hindi)—merchant.

Developing good congregations is a long term effort.

Yes. Most if not all of the gurus in ISKCON are involved in building up congregations and individuals by keeping in contact and regularly visiting them.

15 November 1998

Dear Gurudeva, I don't know why but I feel like I did something wrong. I feel that your letters are a little bit impersonal to me. I know that in relationship between guru and disciple, guru gives instruction and disciple follows, but I know also that in that relationship there are a lot of personal exchanges. I have seen your relationship with other godbrothers and godsisters and I can feel that your relationship with them is more personal. I would like to ask you humbly if I can somehow deserve to have a personal relationship with you. I would like to excuse myself if I have done something wrong or offended you somehow. Please forgive me because I am just a fool. I am writing you this because I feel like that so if there is something wrong in that please let me know.

No, you haven't done anything wrong that I can think of that you deserve to be treated impersonally, and I am very sorry if you are getting this impression from me.

The real relationship between guru and disciple is established on the platform of service. I am trying to serve my guru and you are trying to help me in that. If that relationship is established, it will give eternal and complete satisfaction. So strive for that. It takes time.

About relationships—different people relate in different ways. Generally I try to be friendly to all I come in contact with but am slow to really get to know people.

As far as letters are concerned, please try to understand that I get a lot of them and often try to answer them as briefly as possible. Otherwise, on some days I could spend all day just answering letters, but I have other services to perform also.

I asked you to stay in Ireland and get fixed in your service of distributing books. This is not because I don't want you to come to India, but (as I told you previously in Ireland) because I feel it is better for you at this stage of your spiritual development. As you have yourself noted, you have a somewhat wild nature. So getting steadily fixed in a service is important for you. Especially this book distribution will be suitable for your nature and a great benediction to all those who get books from you.

So please do it with all enthusiasm and don't feel discouraged. Please have faith that I am advising you for your own best interest. Without such faith, no proper guru-disciple relationship can develop.

17 November 1998

I am not sure if I ever met you or how you thought to write to me, but as you have inquired, I shall try to answer.

There is no one fixed standard for Deity worship, either at home or in established temples. In his books, Srila Prabhupada stresses that grhasthas should perform Deity worship at home; he especially stresses Radha Krsna worship. Yet in his personal instructions to devotees, he sometimes gave other directions. Thus you can understand how differences of opinion about this may arise.

Devotional service should be performed under the direction of a guru. This is especially so in the matter of Deity worship. Different gurus will have differing approaches and levels of strictness in instructing their disciples about Deity worship.

Actually, Deity worship can only be properly performed after initiation, for Krsna is to be worshiped with permission, blessings and mantras received from one's guru. The real way to receive Krsna is from one's guru; to receive Him as a wedding gift is unconventional. So the real answer to your quandary is: "Ask your guru."

In the meantime, as you have asked me, I think it is very nice that you are attached to the worship of Radha and Krsna, for this is the perfection of life. But again, proper guidance is required so as to know how to look after and please Krsna in the best way.

I have referred your letter to the Arcana conference to seek the learned input of the devotees thereon.

17 November 1998

I'm very glad that your relationship with your parents has improved. Although you haven't directly stated thus, it appears that this is because you started to respect them more, after reading my "Glimpses" book.

I'm convinced that traditional family values are the best. I'm often misunderstood or disliked for stressing on them, especially the point that women should be subservient to and serve their husbands, but I'm sure this is right because sastra says so, Srila Prabhupada stressed on it, and I've seen how it works. Independent women cannot be happy.

The "Glimpses" book portrays this and other messages in an oblique way, and gradually I hope to write other books stressing these points in a systematic manner.

Don't worry if you don't have enough laxmi for India. We can do a "communist" project—those who have more can help those who have less.

There is a new cow in our village—Bhumi. Soon we will have a whole herd. Devotees are happy.

This is very good. Look after the cows very nicely; then only can the devotees be happy. This is a secret of human civilization that we are to teach in these farm communities.

18 November 1998

If we were sure for anyone never to fall down, it was H Maharaja.

That's probably because so much hype was built around him, which didn't help him or anyone else.

So now I keep thinking that it might happen to others also and I think we exaggerate if we call them pure devotees etc. And then I am not so eager to get their mercy, which I used to run after.

Mercy is required for our spiritual advancement and mercy comes down, so we have to take it from those who are connected with the flow of mercy. Connections may be disrupted due to offenses etc. but that doesn't mean that we should make offenses and get our supply cut off.

However, we should understand that mercy comes principally by hearing and serving. Beware of dreamy mysticism. What did Srila Prabhupada emphasize to his disciples again and again?

"Please do not fail to chant 16 rounds, rise early, read my books carefully and follow all the regulative principles."

1999

19 February 1999

I am very sorry to hear of your recent falldown. But I am not very surprised as I know that you have a lot of struggles in spiritual life, and this is not the first time you have got yourself in such a mess. But I am happy that you are honest enough to admit your difficulty and to look for help, and that you are going on trying to get established in Krsna consciousness.

Now that you have your visa for I, and you feel inspired in C, I suggest you stay there at least for the duration of your visa. After that you could maybe join *** Prabhu in Vrindavan. Please write to him on COM and ask him about that. If you can take shelter of the dham, and resolve to give up this nonsense forever, that will be best for you.

I can't comment too much about your boyfriend as I haven't met him. Somehow or other if he comes to Krsna, that would be very nice. But you have to see how serious he becomes about Krsna. Don't become exploited for sense gratification and don't get bewildered by mundane "love."

14 March 1999

When I was in V, I spoke to *** about his engagement. He told me that he was getting on fine with +++ now and that as assistant head pujari he was trying to tighten up the Deity department. I applaud his efforts to systemize and standardize a department that had been so loose for so long that everyone takes that as the norm. In doing so, it is inevitable that he will tread on a few toes. If he could do so sweetly, that would be best, but few are the managers who are so expert to be both efficient and simultaneously pleasing to all.

*** told me how many devotees take bhoga that is meant for worshiping the temple Deities and that he wanted to stop that, and had done so beginning with M. Even if devotees pay for the bhoga they take, it means so much less will be offered to the temple Deities. Don't you think it better that devotees doing their own private Deity worship arrange their own bhoga?

From what I gathered from ***, A was welcome to dress the Deities, but that at least on the altar he should follow the standard dress code. I don't find this unreasonable.

It is true that *** is strong minded and independent and doesn't easily put his trust in others. Such qualities may sometimes lead to his being brusque, and also makes it difficult to get points across to. In other words, he is not so easy to train. On the other hand, such qualities may also help him survive in the Vrindavan smorgasbord of weird attitudes and ideas, which to date he has done well, without any sahajiya or other deviant tendencies which are lamentably common in Vrindavan. At least he is fully and meaningfully engaged, which is more than can be said for many devotees more senior to him who live in the dham with more time on their hands than is good for them.

It is true that *** hardly reads and I always mention this to him. He told me that he listens to the classes and to cassettes. When I asked him this time in Vrindavan to recall points from that morning's class he did so surprisingly well.

I don't find Vrindavan a good place for writing as so many people talk to me and I can't get the concentration needed. It is not my policy to remain aloof from the temple while there as other sannyasis do.

No doubt I am lacking in many ways in my duties as guru but I also have my priorities and limitations. You might understand more about this if you took up such a service yourself which I very much encourage you to, as Srila Prabhupada wanted all his disciples to be initiating gurus.

As you noted, it would be better if *** went through +++ while dealing with senior men. Similarly, it would be better if you had +++ deal with this problem between you and ***. Report it to +++ and let him take action as necessary. If this is done, I will be glad to give input in this matter if required or requested. But to go directly to the guru every time there is a problem with a disciple circumvents proper management procedures and perpetuates the "diksa guru as all in all" syndrome. If, every time I was snubbed by a godnephew, I was to write to their guru, I would be even more drowned in email than at present.

I will write to *** about this and caution him to be careful in how he goes about his service. For whether he is right or wrong, if Vaisnavas feel offended, it is very dangerous, especially in the dham.

18 March 1999

I am very glad to hear from you. I inquired from devotees from C visiting India about you, only to hear that after leaving for studies you had given up association with devotees. I was hoping that you would again become attracted to Krsna and am so happy that you have done so, soon.

You have asked me to help and I want to. But I can only help you if you are willing to follow my directions. There is nothing difficult to follow, and by doing so, you will become very happy. But you will have to take up this advice seriously.

One of your main problems is lack of devotee association. You must again try to find out devotees in P and associate with them. If possible, shift your residence to P so that you can associate more with them. Do not at all get involved with Sai Baba followers. However "nice" they may seem to be, they cannot help you in spiritual life; rather, the opposite.

You may also associate with devotees by letters and phone calls. I am sure there are many devotees who will be willing to help you if you are sincere to reciprocate with them. I can suggest keeping contact with S d.d. from L.

One pure devotee who you can always serve and take shelter of is Tulasi devi. You already started service to her by translating a book about her. I suggest you keep her nicely in your apartment, water her and (important) chant your rounds in her presence. You could learn different prayers in her glorification and recite them regularly. Tulasi devi will help you. And Srila Prabhupada will help you. Read his books daily and pray to His Divine Grace.

And I will help you. And the Vaisnavas will help you. And then surely Krsna will help you. There is no shortage of help if we are sincere to take it.

20 March 1999

It may be unrealistic to try to change strong-headed people who are fixed in their ways. Sometimes we may have to adjust ourselves towards them. Canakya recommends that proud people be assuaged by humility.

At a temple I regularly visit, a pujari used to deal with me roughly. It was as if he wanted to show that, although junior to me, he was the authority in the Deity department and I had to follow him. I didn't protest or complain to anyone about him. I considered that Krsna had been accepting his service for many years and hadn't rejected him, so He couldn't be too discontent with him, even if I had cause to be. I respected his authority, accepted his often unreasonable chastisements, and deferently took his permission to do any Deity service.

After some time, when he understood I respected his position, he softened up towards me. Now, whenever I go to that temple, he invites me to do aratis and arranges maha-prasada for me.

27 April 1999

Advancement in devotional service depends to a major extent on our taste for meditating on more and more aspects of Krsna's personality, His name, form, qualities, and pastimes.

This is true, and it is very nice that you have such an inclination. Actually, there are many factors influencing our advancement, such as proper chanting, service to Vaisnavas etc.

The most important literature in this regard is Srimad Bhagavatam. By studying Bhagavatam carefully again and again, simultaneously chanting carefully, serving Vaisnavas etc., gradually many realizations will come by the grace of guru and Krsna.

The Bhagavatam contains many descriptions of the various incarnations such as Kapila, Nrsimha etc., which are important for us to hear. Actually, before we can enter deeply into pastimes, we have to properly understand philosophy. Bhagavatam, especially with Srila Prabhupada's purports, gives a delightful and balanced blend of lila and philosophy.

I suggest you read Bhagavatam again and again, as I have done and am doing. Be careful not to try to enter too soon into esoteria that you are not prepared for. Srila Prabhupada said that we should first try to understand how the Supreme Lord creates the world; understanding of Vraja-lila comes later. Therefore study of Gita and the early cantos of the Bhagavatam should come first. Of course, you can also read Krsna book as much as you like, but do not neglect to study more "basic" texts.

There are those who mostly speak only of Vraja-lila, but Srila Prabhupada didn't, as he knew what we needed. What we think we need, or what we like, may be different to what we actually need. Narottama dasa sings that when our hearts are fully purified, then only can we understand Vrindavan. Therefore we should take guidance in these matters from those who are properly following Srila Prabhupada, as you have done in writing to me. Then we can be safe.

So be slow and careful and gradually everything will be revealed. I hope that at some point in time you can come and spend some time in Bharata varsha and visit the holy dhamas that are manifest here.

I will not be at the Suharevo festival this year as it coincides with the Baroda ISKCON temple opening. I therefore expect to visit Russia and Europe later, probably around Janmastami. I get much inspiration from seeing how the devotees in Russia carry on with their services despite all difficulties, so I look forward to seeing you and so many other wonderful devotees at that time.

1 May 1999

Another point: dramas are excellent for becoming absorbed in the Lord's lilas and for helping to communicate the mood of those lilas to others. Last time I was in Russia you performed some nice dramas, so please go on doing these. You can do them with your Nama-hatta members also.

6 May 1999

Thankyou for your letter. Now, in the midst of great difficulties, you have a very good opportunity for remembering Krsna. Please do so by chanting His names with great attention, and also by studying Srila Prabhupada's books very carefully. You have discovered that you are a person, not a machine. Now re-inforce that realization by carefully studying Srila Prabhupada's books, and thus realize your position as the servant of the Supreme Person, Sri Krsna.

I hope to see you later this year in Serbia—Krsna willing.

In the meantime, enjoy chanting Hare Krsna. Go on chanting, develop your faith in the holy name, and make this your last birth in the material world.

10 May 1999

… the bhakti-sanga met: almost no Krsna katha, and it was impossible for me to reverse this flow.

Then it is not bhakti-sanga but maya-sanga. If the members can't talk Krsna katha, better you all just read from Srila Prabhupada's books than waste time talking nonsense.

Hopefully there must be someone there who is interested in Krsna katha. You could maybe put up a notice asking others to informally join you for meetings purely dedicated only to Krsna katha.

As I see this is that I'm lacking in Krsna consciousnes, because I'm just a neophyte, and there is not much support at the moment, so it's quite a dangerous position for me. Where to take shelter?

Presumably things should improve by S Maharaj's presence. If for some reason it doesn't, best is to take shelter in the holy name and Srila Prabhupada's books. I went through several years of little or poor association in Bangladesh, Burma, and Thailand, during which Srila Prabhupada's books especially kept me spiritually alive.

So what to do when one is destroying that faith by criticizing Srila Prabhupada?

Anyone who criticizes Srila Prabhupada is a fool and a rascal. Don't have anything to do with such people. If there is a syndrome of such faithlessness developing there, due to the blasphemous utterances of useless people, then please request S Maharaj to hold isthagosthis and blast away this bhakti-destroying nonsense.

Anyone who carefully reads Srila Prabhupada's books can understand that faith in him and in Krsna is not fanatical or dogmatic. Srila Prabhupada's books systematically and reasonably present the science of Krsna-bhakti, and are internationally respected even by mundane scholars.

11 May 1999

I accept that it is quite possible that certain people of sinister motives may be trying to destabilize our ISKCON. What I cannot accept is that the leadership of our movement is infiltrated by such people. The leaders of ISKCON, in R and elsewhere, have all been chanting Hare Krsna for many years. A gross materialist cannot do that. Even if, for subversive reasons, a gross materialist started to follow all our principles and chant, then he would become purified. However powerful a nondevotee may be, Krsna is more powerful than he.

I appreciate your concern for ISKCON, which is certainly going through a very difficult time. However, purity is the force, and the best thing you can do to offset all negative elements is to yourself become a pure devotee by chanting very carefully and attentively.

As individuals, the members of ISKCON are not very prominent people in society. We cannot overcome the forces of evil by any material means. But if we fully take shelter of Krsna, then even if Ravana himself were to attempt to overcome us, we would emerge succesful.

So please have faith in Krsna and His holy names as your only recourse. Go on chanting, develop your faith in the holy name, and make this your last birth in the material world.

11 May 1999

Please forgive me if my previous letter was insensitive. You have been and are going through a very difficult trial. I cannot imagine how shattering it must be to you to have your spiritual master leave ISKCON and act and speak as he is now doing.

For years, *** Maharaja was a great pillar of ISKCON. I don't have to tell you this as you know it better than me.

However, the reality is that now *** Maharaja is not the person we knew before. He no longer even wants to be known by that name. He is not only breaking the principles, but is blaspheming Srila Prabhupada and blaming him in so many ways. We all pray that this is a temporary phase that he is going through, but as time goes on and more offenses are made, the hopes of him reverting to his devotional mood appear to be increasingly dim.

Fortunately, we are advised to depend not only upon guru, but upon sadhu and sastra also. Please see SB 8.20.1 in this regard. Therefore I have recommended you to carefully study Srila Prabhupada's books. Also, please take shelter of the sadhus—those who are not deviated from the line. Do not depend upon sentiments and emotions only. Important as they are, they are, until we reach the perfect stage, to be tempered by sastric understanding.

You can still achieve all perfection in Krsna consciousness and be blissful eternally. You are not without help. You just have to have enough faith to reach out and get it. Having had your faith broken, it may be difficult to re-build it, but if you are at all to progress in bhakti, then faith must be there, for that is the essential basis on which Krsna consciousness stands.

I hope this is somewhat digestible for you.

25 May 1999

In my own case, my unique offering to Srila Prabhupada is my books, and I don't expect all my disciples to help with that. But I'm happy to see and oversee them engage in Krsna consciousness in the various ways that they do. I'm already feeling a little overloaded with the 120 or so diksa disciples I have (and many other devotees who I know and interact with in a siksa role) and wonder how to personally reciprocate as the numbers increase—as presumably they will do.

4 June 1999

It's very nice here although many devotees are not satisfied with the authorities. I'm trying not to get very much into devotees' discussions about authorities. I feel that these discussions are dangerous.

If anyone has any problem, better they take it to the concerned authority. Just to discuss won't do any good and can be a form of detrimental sense gratificatory prajalpa. So better you go on with sankirtan and tulasi-seva. Remember you went to L to serve Krsna, so do that and you will be happy. Maya comes in many forms.

15 June 1999

At this time in my life, I find that after 13 years of being associated with ISKCON, I find that I have made little progress in the matter of advancing spiritually.

At this time in my life, I find that after 24 years of being associated with ISKCON, I find that I have made little progress in the matter of advancing spiritually. Really. I can hardly dream of getting Krsna prema. But I have to do some service. That is my only hope.

"Anyone discharging his entrusted duties in disciplic succession from Brahma is sure to gain fame in this life and salvation in the next." (SB 3.13.8)

At this time, I generally don't rise before 7 a.m. (in spite of all attempts), sometimes, on the plea of work, or writing something for the current ritvik controversy, or whatever, my rounds don't get finished. I try to make them up the next day, but many times even this doesn't work out.

This is not good. You have to make some changes in your life, as you are suggesting. You are right inasmuch as basics should not be neglected.

In my mind, I am trying to discover the cause of my laziness, my reluctance to accept spiritual life in full inspite of all the good instruction and all the chances given to me.

Good. Introspectiveness is the first step in improvement.

When I try to understand what could be the possible hindrances, I speculate that these may be the major stumbling blocks:

1) Offenses commited against devotees, either in this life or in past lives;

2) reluctance to accept the guidance of a spiritual master in toto;

3) prarabdha karma—I have some serious mental deficiencies which may be partially responsible for the continuation of (1) and (2). For example, I have a propensity to overeat—ever since I was a child. And other things you know about as well.

Yes, these are all possible causes. If you can't control overeating, I wouldn't worry about it too much, as long as you eat prasad only. In course of time nature will force you to eat less by making you sick.

Once while I was travelling with *** Swami, after my attempted suicide in 1990, we discussed this issue, and he commented as follows: Sometimes we see people in the kirtan play karatalas in a very fancy way. But when the time comes to play a simple rythm, they cannot do it, and thus spoil a sweet bhajana. He compared my devotional practices to such karatala players, that I learned some fancy things in Krsna consciousness, but neglected the basics.

Good analogy. Maybe just recently you were getting a little proud in showing your knowledge and intelligence and Krsna reminded you where you were at.

Not long after I came back to America, +++ told me that I should not involve myself with any of these controversies. I didn't do that, did I?

I think, perhaps, I'm begining to understand the consequences of being whimsical.

You lost your logical skills here. +++ later congratulated you for your rebuttals of ritvikism. Obviously he didn't want you to get on the wrong side of any controversy, and maybe not even to become fanatical on the right side, but he is pleased with the intelligent participation you have shown.

Perhaps someone like you or Srila Prabhupada can do many things at once, but then you all are in control of your mind and senses—I am not.

You sound frustrated, as if your attempts to control your mind and senses are all in vain. They are not. Krsna appreciates the struggle. Don't give up faith that Krsna will help you.

"There is every chance of failure on the yogic path; even a great sage like Visvamitra Muni can fall down due to material allurement. Although the muni fell for the time being, he again resolved to go on with the yoga process, and this should be our resolve. Krsna informs us that such failures should not be cause for despair. There is the famous proverb that "failure is the pillar of success." In the spiritual life especially, failure is not discouraging. Krsna very clearly states that even if there is failure, there is no loss either in this world or in the next. One who takes to this auspicious line of spiritual culture is never completely vanquished." (The Path of Yoga, Chapter 6: The Fate of the Unsuccessful Yogi)

"As in the material world sometimes failure is considered as a pillar of success, similarly in the spiritual order also the same principle can be applied. So don't be disappointed. Maybe Krsna's desire is something higher in this connection." (Srila Prabhupada's letter to Gurudasa—Los Angeles, 31 July 1969)

Remember Robert the Bruce and the spider.[5]

---

5. Robert the Bruce was the king of Scots in the early fourteenth century and was fighting with England for Scottish independence. According to legend, at some point while he was on the run during the winter of 1305–06, after having

You all are in control of your mind and senses—I am not.

Do I detect a tinge of envy here? Be careful. Anyway, how do you know what goes on in my mind? I don't have manic depressive tendencies like you, but I'm a product of Kali-yuga as much as you are. By Krsna's grace it seems I've found my niche in life, which is a great help in making the mind peaceful and thus controlling the senses. It gives an inner satisfaction to have a steady service and feel that guru and Krsna approve of it.

You have been trying to make your niche but it hasn't worked, at least so far. You were supposed to be helping me but decided to be an independent businessman. You were confident of success but ran up debts and couldn't pay them off. You went to USA to study but ended up in a similar situation to the one you left in India, as a struggling independent dissatisfied businessman, wondering how to get your life together, making little progress either materially or spiritually.

And you know that that is just how I work, I am unable to "multi-task." After considering all these things, I am thinking that the best thing for me will be to just keep my life simple.

Not a bad idea, if you can do it. Even a man of knowledge acts according to his nature.

I wish to permanently withdraw from our activities in the anti-ritvik think-tank as well as the anti-feminist think-tank. Anyway, everything goes on by the will of Krsna, with or without me, so it will be no loss if I do not participate as I have been doing.

Also, I wish to retire from any more writing activities, since I am not spiritually fit. The qualification to write about Krsna-consciousness

---

been defeated several times by the English, Bruce hid himself in a cave on Rathlin Island (off the north coast of Ireland) and therein observed a spider attempting to spin a web from one point of the roof of the cave to another. Each time that the spider failed, it simply started over again, until finally it succeeded. Inspired by this example, Bruce returned to inflict a series of defeats on the English, thus winning him more supporters and eventual victory.

is that one must be on the Vaishnava platform, then he must take permission from his spritual master to write. Surely, I'm not at all a Vaishnava—perhaps superficially, but certainly not up to the standard required for someone to write books.

Maybe you misunderstood when I suggested you write for me. The idea was to write under my direction, putting together my notes and giving shape to ideas, using your God-given skills in His service. Something like a craftsman's job. The question of permission comes when one undertakes to personally start an original work. Assisting someone else is different, especially when requested to do so.

Our process is not to give up activities, but to rise up to the challenge of employing our abilities in Krsna's service. Come on, this is ABC stuff. You know it as well as me.

Maharaj, I don't think I will be of any more use to you in this life. I wish to take your leave. Perhaps some smaller, more realistic goals would be better for me. All I want to do now is maintain my wife and household, worship Gaura-Nitai and read Srila Prabhupada's books 10 more times before I die, and just pray that my next life may not somehow or other be in a lower species. For me, I feel, taking birth again is a certainty, it is just a question of how.

You don't need to reply to this if you don't want to—it probably isn't necessary.

Every so often I get some crazy letter like this from you. Just prior to sending it you were writing lucid, assured letters on ritvikism. Then something happened and you flipped.

Do what you can do nicely for Krsna. Don't spin into some imagined martyrdom. Mr. Spock, it's just not logical. Why do you think I should suddenly cut all ties with you just because you feel like it? Did you ever check out if you need some chemicals, like G?

Signed: An idiot who is his own worst enemy, *** das

P.S. BTW, I owe you money. We might as well settle that up too. As soon as a payment owed to me clears (about 1 week), I can send you a cheque.

I won't complain if you do. I'm also not against the concept of you worshiping Gaura-Nitai and reading Srila Prabhupada's books 10 more times. It is an excellent idea. But do it happily, peacefully. And remember you also have to serve and please the Vaisnavas.

Even if you cannot be of "any use to me," does that mean you should slam the door on me? Do you think I am so mercenary that after all this time I only care what you can "do for me"? Don't you know that I spend much time writing letters to and speaking to many people who are not of "any use to me"? Why do you think I am attempting to write these books, anyway?

I don't hold it against you 'cos I know you were in a mental twist when you wrote that, but I'm a little disappointed at the insinuation therein.

Anyway, Hare Krsna. Chant Hare Krsna and be happy.

18 June 1999

I just keep thinking to myself "Is there some switch that needs to be turned on? Something I'm not doing? What is my fundamental problem?" and I find that it is just beyond my comprehension.

As you note, patience is also required. Your resolve to stick to the process, even if it takes millions of lives, is the determination that sits side by side with patience.

But then, if you are already proud, how can you constantly chant Hare Krsna? Without some sort of causeless mercy, some kripa, I don't see how it is possible.

With the instruction comes the mercy to fulfill it. It requires faith to see the helping hand of guru and Krsna in the midst of difficulties. We may not even clearly see it, but if with faith that it is there—"surely they will help me in my greatest need"—we reach out, surely that hand will be there to pull us up. The mercy comes down, but we still have to constantly reach up to get it. Pride, laziness, complacency, offenses etc. block the flow of mercy. Out of mercy our protectors may let us experience how miserable everything is without their mercy so that we again reach out to get it.

Krsna's grace? How did you get it? (If you don't mind my asking.)

Whether or not I actually have Krsna's grace is debatable. More likely it is false pride masquerading as some kind of advancement. However, the process to get Krsna's mercy is no secret. We sing it every morning in Gurvastaka.

Better you don't mention my name to your wife. I agree with you that it is better that when you get into a downward spin (as occasioned in your letter under discussion), you speak to her. She in many ways is a very practical woman—at least that is the impression I got.

Good news that your business is picking up. I hope you get rich and spend it all for Krsna.

Every so often I get some crazy letter like this from you.[6]

It's becoming a regular thing, huh?

About 3 times total now.

… including all the times you chastised me.

Just see—I can't remember chastising you even once. Not that there's anything intrinsically wrong with chastisement, but I thought I had become more mild. Probably I don't know how heavy I am. It would be good for someone to give me a neutral character analysis so I can work on improving myself.

---

6. This sentence is from a previous letter by Bhakti Vikāsa Swami.

I really do miss you—please believe me on this one thing, even if everything else I say is false.

And of course I miss you also. Don't tell your wife that. And of course I don't think you are a mithya-bhasi.

"If you want peace of mind, don't come to Krsna, because He won't give it to you. But if you want Krsna's service then come to Krsna."

That's a good quote. When did I say that?

Does this mean I should be happy with the misery allotted to me, chant Hare Krsna, and be happy—I mean be miserable . . . I mean be happy? :-)

Stop thinking about being happy or miserable, chant Hare Krsna, and you'll be happy.

sukhe duhkhe bhulo na'ko, vadane hari-nam koro re

"Do not forget this chanting, whether you are in a happy condition or a distressful one. Just fill your lips with the hari-nama."

Sarasvati Thakura said that three of the ten offenses that can be committed while chanting the holy name were very difficult to give up: lack of full surrender to the guru (third), committing sins on the strength of the holy name (seventh), and giving up the concept of "I" and "mine" (tenth). "These are possible to be given up only by guru-kripa," he said.

11 July 1999

You asked if it is all right to read the books of a certain sannyasi. I find that his books tend to emphasize esoteric aspects of Krsna consciousness much more than Srila Prabhupada did, and without the same level of caution that Srila Prabhupada exercised with presenting these topics. Srila Prabhupada certainly had a reason for such caution, and the reason is that such topics can rarely be understood by ordinary devotees and are generally misunderstood. It is better therefore, that ordinary devotees approach the pastimes of Krsna very carefully and also continue to plentifully hear the basic philosophy of Krsna consciousness as presented in Bhagavad-gita As It Is and other books. To come to the topic at hand, I do not very much recommend reading the books of the sannyasi in question. You may keep this advice to yourself, as I do not want it to be a point of misunderstanding between Maharaja and myself.

Regarding the Ekadasi book, I believe the stories in there are from sastric sources. Not everything in sastra, however, is meant for pure devotees. Much is to bring people to the point of pure devotion. The stories in the Ekadasi book are of this category. They promise material benefits for observing Ekadasi vows. Ekadasi is so spiritually powerful that even if observed for material gain, by doing so attraction to Krsna will gradually be awakened. For devotees whose attraction to Krsna is already awakened, such stories have no meaning. Devotees observe Ekadasi for the real purpose of satisfying Him and increasing their attraction for Him.

Therefore the Ekadasi book is of little or no use to practicing devotees.

15 July 1999

You have asked me about the obstacles coming in your path of surrender to Krsna. You are confused by fighting among the followers of Srila Prabhupada. You want to get the mercy of saintly persons, but your faith is diminished due to hearing of falldowns.

Actually, there is no need for confusion at any time for those who adhere to the path of guru, sadhu, and sastra. All disputes and misgivings can be settled by those who have faith in and strictly follow these invincible authorities.

You have asked why it is that gurus and sannyasis have fallen down. The answer is simple: maya. Of course, it is not expected that gurus and sannyasis fall down, but that they may do is recognized in sastra, e.g. in Srila Prabhupada's purports to S.B. 2.6.20, 6.18.41, 9.18.40 etc., as also in the text and purport of S.B. 11.27.29 (this purport is culled from those of the previous acaryas). See also Nectar of Devotion, Ch. 7 for a note on how gurus may fall down.

Narahari Sarkara, an associate of Lord Caitanya, wrote in his "Krsna Bhajanamrta" that there had been many cases of gurus deviating after the departure of Lord Caitanya, and advised disciples what to do in such circumstances. A similar phenomenon has occurred in our society at present. Due to inexperience, imitation of paramahamsas, lack of caution in dealing with women, living artificially opulent lifestyles, inattention in sadhana, or whatever, several sannyasis and gurus have fallen from their exalted positions.

These falldowns have been widely publicized in a most disparaging way by those who wish to "prove" by such circumstantial "evidence" that Srila Prabhupada did not want his disciples to be gurus. However, it was not Srila Prabhupada's policy to publicize falldowns. Even in Srila Prabhupada's personal presence, quite a few sannyasis and other leaders fell down. Srila Prabhupada's general attitude was to forgive, encourage them to come back, and appreciate the service they had rendered rather than condemn them. This is the Vaisnava mood.

Indeed, those who vilify even fallen Vaisnavas lose their taste for bhakti and instead take hellish pleasure in mocking Vaisnavas. For even a fallen devotee is dear to Krsna (cf. SB 1.5.19).

Better than castigating fallen Vaisnavas is to pray for them and learn from their unfortunate example. Falldown shows, not that Krsna consciousness does not work, but that it does work. This can be understood by seeing that those who practice it properly remain protected, but even exalted or highly placed devotees are susceptible to fall if they do not carefully follow sadhana, do not properly associate with devotees, become proud, develop materialistic tendencies, become complacent, etc. The example is there of Jada Bharata (SB Canto 5).

The falldown of sannyasis in ISKCON is most unfortunate and suggests the need of reform. Such reform can be best effected at the individual level, by sincere introspection, and as much as possible also institutionally.

However, neither guru, nor sadhu, nor sastra support the ritvik speculation, which would not be true even if every sannyasi in ISKCON fell down. It is indeed a great concoction that is not at all supported in Srila Prabhupada's teachings, nor by Vaisnava tradition, nor by sastra. When asked about initiations after his departure, Srila Prabhupada clearly referred to "disciple of my disciple" and "granddisciple." Much debate has gone on about this, but these words are clear enough, what to mention the many times that Srila Prabhupada said and wrote that he wanted his disciples to initiate in future.

Ritvikites have been empowered by the material energy to interpret Srila Prabhupada's statements out of context, ignore his clear instructions on the matter, fabricate a supposed "Final Order," blaspheme Vaisnavas and publicize difficulties within ISKCON in a most biased and derogatory way. However, they do not have the slightest shred of proof that Srila Prabhupada wanted such a system of initiation after his departure, nor will they ever have any, because Srila Prabhupada was a follower of parampara and wanted it to continue.

I had asked for the book "Ritvik-maya-vada-sata-dusani" to be sent to you. I hope you have received it by now. That may clarify some of your doubts. It is not possible for me to cover so many points simply in a letter.

I know you are a sincere devotee and have deep faith in Vaisnavas. Unfortunately, there are those who, for their own less than ideal motives, have made it their business to shatter the faith of others in Vaisnavas. Those who become afflicted with the disease of anti-Vaisnavism may apparently be practicing bhakti, and may have rendered sincere service previously, but they cannot be pleasing to Krsna. This is clear from sastra. There is no neutral stand on this issue. Those who do not keep faith in guru may not be able to be convinced otherwise, due to their offensive mentality, but such persons should not be intimately associated with.

Lack of association is certainly a problem in ***. Many good souls there have taken to Krsna Consciousness, but have received very little in the way of experienced guidance and training. Indeed, the same could be said of ISKCON B, which has for years not allowed its members to interact with the greater world of ISKCON.

Which brings up other questions. How is it that ISKCON B temple was built up on faith in guru, but that now most of the devotees who worked hard to build it have become discouraged and are leaving?

If at all possible please spend some time in Mayapur and try to discuss with Vidvan Gauranga, Hari Sauri, or Bhadra Balaram Prabhus, who are intimately familiar with the multiple abstruse arguments of ritvikites and who can expose their multiple blunders. Otherwise you could write to any of them with specific doubts.

I am going overseas soon and plan to be back for the temple opening for Sri Sri Gaura Nitai, Sri Sri Radha Syamasundara, and Sri Sri Sri Jagannatha, Subhadra, and Baladeva, in Baroda on Janmastami. So please write to me around that time or better still, attend the function in Baroda.

Somehow, by Krsna's arrangement, you have been writing me for several years and I have been advising you according to my knowledge and realization of guru, sadhu, and sastra. I feel concern and responsibility for your spiritual progress and would be very unhappy to see you flounder now. So please keep in contact, especially during this difficult period of yours, and pray to Krsna to help you understand matters clearly. If you are sincere, which I know you are, then surely He will help you.

P.S. Chant attentively.

26 July 1999

Please bless me to get Krsna-bhakti!

Officially as a sannyasi I give blessings but in reality I'm far from qualified to do so. By meditating on Srila Prabhupada's lotus feet I try to follow in his divine footsteps.

28 July 1999

Thankyou very much for writing to me with your queries. Please try to see everything from the platform of eternity. On this platform we can see that even if some devotees are losing their faith or becoming discouraged, or even skeptical or critical, the basic facts of Krsna consciousness have not changed and never will change—although due to maya, the perception of those who have not fully committed themselves to Krsna consciousness may change. Our determination should be that even if every devotee in the world falls into maya (which will not happen), we will continue with our service to Krsna.

In some ways it is good, and even inevitable, that devotees there are facing these problems. Difficulties should be seen by devotees as tests from Krsna. When everything is going on nicely, it is relatively easy to practice Krsna consciousness. Difficulties are Krsna's test. Do we actually want to serve Krsna, or do we want to enjoy Krsna. Krsna does not accept the advances of conditioned souls who approach Him in an enjoying mood, and instead sends them back to the realm of illusory enjoyment.

Due to your irresponsibility, several devotees were almost killed. This can hardly be ascribed to Krsna's wish. He certainly does not want that His mission be stopped, but He may be testing to see how serious you are to execute it, and teaching you to be more careful with His property and with His devotees.

Anyway, now that you are in the hospital, take the opportunity to read and chant constantly.

You wrote that sankirtana Laksmi just goes for some "bills and walls." But they are not ordinary bills and walls. They are the bills and the walls of Krsna's temple, by which so many people have been benefited in Krsna consciousness, and can continue to be benefited. Even if, as often happens, there is some mismanagement or misspending, that does not mean that we should just "see to ourselves." It is good that you see how the book distribution mission goes on, but it is not good to become inimical to the temple.

Krsna has given you a stern warning. Because you are His sincere and determined servant, I am sure you will understand it in the proper way. If we consider how much Srila Prabhupada had to struggle to bring Krsna consciousness to us, we shall not give up our service to him under any circumstances, but rather see all obstacles and challenges to inspire us to become more enthusiastic.

You might want to consider your chanting of Nrsimha Kavaca in the light of the following quote from Srila Prabhupada, who did not seem very enthusiastic about such chanting:

"Regarding the Narayana Kavaca mantra, the Hare Krsna mantra is everything." (Letter to Jayapataka, 4th December, 1976)

5 August 1999

"16 is enough?" 16,000 rounds a day of the sweet maha mantra could never be "enough"! In one sense, yes, because Srila Prabhupada said minimum 16, so that is "enough" to get Srila Prabhupada's mercy. But minimum does not mean maximum.

Chanting Hare Krsna is the yuga dharma so it is your good fortune if you feel inclined to chant more.

It is good to cultivate taste for chanting in association with devotees, both in kirtana and japa. Public chanting is very purifying.

9 September 1999

I don't recommend that you take up complex Deity worship. It's not the mood of our sampradaya, nor are you capable of following all the intricate details. Nor, even in the Sri sampradaya, are intricate details observed for home Deities.

Do not take up something you cannot maintain. It may well be in future that job or family responsibilities will leave you little time even for basic sadhana, what to speak of elaborate pujas.

You want to know the mood of your Deities. In this age Lord Nrsimha has appeared as Lord Caitanya. His mood is to deliver the conditioned souls by sankirtana. By His arrangement, you have taken birth in a female body in Slovenia, which is probably more favorable for getting His mercy than birth as a rigid brahmana in India. Take advantage of His mercy and don't be distracted into that which is not meant for you.

Of course, Lord Nrsimha also has a mood different from that of Lord Caitanya, but you should not try to understand Him separately from Lord Caitanya. These are deep topics. I wonder how much you have studied Bhagavad-gita. Deity worship is meant for brahmanas, those who are learned in sastra and approach the Lord in knowledge, not sentimentality.

Regarding your question about service, yes of course we should try to please the Lord as much as possible.

Chant Hare Krsna intensely and depend on Sri Krsna. That is our only hope.

6 October 1999

I hope by now you will have settled into whatever situation Krsna has arranged for you.

Living here, I'm just remembering all days we were with you. IR Mataji said that perfect life for us will be if we could always be together and serve you. We all share her opinion.

I feel the same way, but as Srila Prabhupada wrote:

I wish to remain with all my disciples together, but we have to do preaching work and therefore have to remain separate. But actually there is no question of separation for one engaged in Lord Krsna's service. (Srila Prabhupada's letter to Hrdayananda, 4 January 1976)

I consider myself as very fortunate soul because you all accepted me so kindly in your wonderful godfamily.

I am also basically happy with my nice family of disciples.

The following quote from Srila Prabhupada's letter is relevant in this regard.

Now you have got the golden opportunity of this human form of life, and it is not by accident that you have met your spiritual master, so if you are actually intelligent you will stick very tightly to your position of Krsna Consciousness and go back to home, back to Godhead. The essential point to remember is that you should try always to please your spiritual master under every condition. That means to follow his orders and instructions very carefully. My first instruction to all of my disciples is that they should help me spread this Krsna Consciousness movement all over the world, utilizing their energy as best they are able to do it. In this way, keeping yourselves always engaged in Krsna's business 24 hours, you will become free from all attachment to maya by Krsna's grace. Just as when the darkness and the light come together, the darkness cannot stand before the light, so maya cannot remain in the presence of Krsna. Always remember therefore to chant Hare Krsna and that will save you in all circumstances without any doubt. (Srila Prabhupada's letter of 9 January, 1973)

I just hope that I will have more oportunities to be with you, to serve you and learn.

As far as my duty to instruct you, that I am much aware of, and am trying to fulfill this need by writing many books. I have much work to do so please pray to Krsna to give me long life, clear intelligence, and the help needed to perform this service to Srila Prabhupada.

I will be very happy if my disciples can take up Krsna consciousness seriously, studying Srila Prabhupada's books carefully and with conviction, assiduously practicing sadhana, and preaching to the best of their abilities.

I have also one question: how much energy should I put in my studying? Sometimes I think that I should do minimum and use the time for reading, etc. And sometimes I think that I should do more, because in the future I can serve devotees and you in this way?

As you have taken up this course, you might as well do it properly. At the same time, sufficient time must be kept for devotional life. Academic studies can be very demanding but somehow you have to try and keep a balance.

I don't advise my young lady disciples to be career oriented. Nature has given you a body for bearing children and it is a mother's duty to spend time with and properly look after her offspring. Big preaching at grassroots level will be if our grhastha devotees take up the responsibility of showing an ideal example to the world.

11 October 1999

It is good that you are now introspective. It's true that often devotees reject you and I've previously advised you to examine yourself to find out why.

Good relationships are founded on trying to give to others more than you take from them. "Giving" includes giving respect and consideration of others' needs as well as physical and monetary help. A main distinction between a child and a mature adult is that the child expects to be given to, but a responsible adult, at least as a sense of duty, gives at least as much to society as he receives. Now you are no longer a child so please consider these points and remember, "failure is the pillar of success."

"Thus there is every chance of failure on the yogic path; even a great sage like Visvamitra Muni can fall down due to material allurement. Although the muni fell for the time being, he again resolved to go on with the yoga process, and this should be our resolve. Krsna informs us that such failures should not be cause for despair. There is the famous proverb that "failure is the pillar of success." In the spiritual life especially, failure is not discouraging. Krsna very clearly states that even if there is failure, there is no loss either in this world or in the next. One who takes to this auspicious line of spiritual culture is never completely vanquished." (The Path of Yoga, chapter 6: The Fate of the Unsuccessful Yogi)

You have not fallen, but you are struggling. Take your difficulties as a sign from Krsna that you should improve, and go forward from here.

23 October 1999

It is by your causeless mercy that you accepted me. Instead of wholeheartedly accepting that mercy, I'm more and more sinking into maya's quicksand. At present my mind is very much perturbed because of many material desires, which are haunting me. Though I'm intelligent enough to understand that they are material desires, I'm not strong enough to purify them. And of this I'm not happy.

This weekend I'll be going to Vrindavan (Oct 25th) and I'd spend a few days in the Holy Dhama. Srila Guru Maharaja, please instruct me how to properly submit myself to the Holy Dhama so that I'll get the Dhama's mercy. Please instruct me how to make best use of this journey to the Dhama. I have been going to Vrindavan for the past two years and still I think I didn't properly utilize my intelligence in properly worshiping the Dhama.

There are many things you could do in Vrndavan but most important is to go with a mood of service. That is the basis of Krsna bhakti. So go and do all the regular things such as chanting extra rounds, visiting the Goswami temples, Yamuna snana etc., but remember to pray always for the mercy to always remember our constitutional position as servant. I find that Srila Prabhupada's room in Vrndavana is most intense and is the best place for prayerful meditation on future service and purification.

1 November 1999

Very nice to hear from you. I'm often thinking of you and very happy and proud that you are so determined to carry on the sankirtan party mission, especially at a time when others have retired or faded away.

As for my qualifications for being a guru, I don't have any except Srila Prabhupada's order to his disciples to carry on the great work he began. As Bhaktivinoda Thakura prays to his guru, *yogyata-vicare kichu nahi paya tomara karuna-sara*—"If you examine me, you will find no good qualities; your mercy is all that I'm made of."

However, despite my lack of inherent qualification, I'm sure that Srila Prabhupada is so great that if I simply stick to what he has given us, I will get sufficient energy, intelligence and everything else needed to help guide others on the path back to Krsna.

It's true that there are all kinds of crazy ideas floating in and around our movement these days. Best stick to the basics. Read Srila Prabhupada's books, follow what is in them, and distribute them to others. Krsna consciousness is simple for the straightforward but complex for the wicked.

I appreciate your frank revealing of your mind to me and hope these words help to make things clearer. I could have written much more but trust that you will be able to catch the essence from these few words.

6 November 1999

It certainly seems to be a strange situation there, with *** Prabhu in disagreement with the B team and with ISKCON in general. Does he have his own personal understanding of Krsna that surpasses that of everyone else on the planet?

This is the danger when someone, with no training or association, becomes a leader. Even with little understanding or actual surrender, he becomes the de facto guru and it goes to his head. Maya has her ways, which are inscrutable.

Anyway, please try to keep yourself strong, and keep association with those devotees (if any) in the locality whose notions of spiritual understanding are not trained by any modern, newly imagined ideas.

In the meantime, you can get strength from reading Srila Prabhupada's books and chanting Hare Krsna mahamantra clearly and attentively.

Remember—whatever form Maya may come in, Krsna is always stronger. And certainly sweeter. There is no taste but despicable bitterness in defying Krsna and His devotees.

18 November 1999

Your tone should be as strong as is needed to do the job. You should certainly know by now that I'm not at all beyond goofing up. If I were, I wouldn't need an editor. As I do, it is his (i.e. your) job to see that the goofs don't get printed. It is the tendency of every writer to consider everything he writes to be wonderful. If the editor has to scream at the writer to convince him that he is goofing, then failure to scream would be dereliction of duty.

3 December 1999

I survived some time in sankirtan, but I had big problems all the time. I felt so unhappy and my mind was completely destroyed. I just felt that I don't have enough strength to be on the street and trying to stop all the busy people who don't have time for anything. People are much different and more impersonal than in Croatia, and that is my problem in general here in London. *** tried to inspire me and +++ Prabhu also. We are so lucky to have him here, he is taking care of everyone. Finally, I decided and he agreed that I will again do my service in the kitchen and back-up pujari. I feel better now. I would like to continue with sankirtan, but not every day, maybe twice a week and it seems possible. I can't understand what is the real problem: I didn't surrender enough or it is that not everyone can do every service because we are not all the same?

The latter is correct. Krsna doesn't do rasa lila with Arjuna, nor does He drive a war chariot for Radharani. We all need to surrender more, but we can surrender in different ways in different services.

I also don't like England. The only things I like about it are the devotees, the Deities, and the tremendous preaching opportunities. I've sent you there for education and purification. Go on serving in whatever capacity you feel happy in. Krsna does not want us to be unhappy. If you can go out on sankirtan two days a week, that is nice.

It seems to me that I failed on the first test in my spiritual life.

It's not exactly a failure. More like a setback—Krsna's way of letting us know that we may not be so advanced or talented as we thought. Failure is the pillar of success.

Devotees were singing in temple room: Radhe Krsna Radhe Krsna … instead of the maha-mantra. I was surprised. Is it proper?

It is not improper as they are the holy names. Nevertheless Lord Caitanya and Srila Prabhupada have not taught us to sing like that. They always emphasized the maha mantra. So better stick to that.

3 December 1999

Deity worship according to the directives of sastra, following all the rules and regulations, can be properly performed only when one is initiated. This is because in Deity worship (a) one has to take permission from one's guru to worship; (b) the Deities have to be installed by the acarya or on his order; (c) mantras given on initiation are used in Deity worship; and (d) before the daily worship (puja) of the Lord is performed, worship of the guru is essential.

I have given directions for worship by uninitiated devotees of the picture form of the Lord in my "Beginner's Guide to KC." I suggest you worship like that for now, keep your stone Deities in a box for now, pray to the Lord for a guru, and prepare yourself to be eligible for initiation. You should keep a picture of Srila Prabhupada and pray to him for the same mercy also.

8 December 1999

Traditionally, prospective marriage partners would not meet each other before marriage. However, marriage arrangements were made based on astrological compatibility.

Even today in India, parents do not proceed with a match unless there is astrological compatibility. Association of partners before astrological matching is still not allowed, because attachment is sure to develop. But if there is poor compatibility, that attachment will be a cause of future suffering.

Here's a quote I just read: "Sometimes apparent resemblances of character will bring two people together and for a certain time unite them. But their mistake gradually becomes evident, and they are astonished to find themselves not only far apart, but even repelled, in some sort, at all their points of contact."

Your resolution to go ahead with this partnership is based upon a little association, and is against astrologer's advice. It certainly doesn't seem to be a good basis to make such an important decision. Please don't misunderstand me. I have nothing against *** Prabhu. I don't know him.

Probably you are thinking that if you don't go through with this arrangement, you will be unlikely to get another devotee of his caliber. But even if both of you are very sincere devotees (which I'm sure you are) it doesn't mean that you are suited for each other.

Please try to think about this in a detached way, if that is possible for you at this point.

16 December 1999

Especially in times of difficulties, it is most important to connect with Krsna and get His mercy by chanting properly.

"Somehow or other, however, we have fallen into this material ocean, and as the waves toss, we suffer. Actually we have nothing to do with the tossing waves of material miseries. We must simply pray, "Krsna, please pick me up." As soon as we forget Krsna, the ocean of illusion is there, and it at once captures us. The chanting of Hare Krsna is most important in order to escape from this ocean." (Raja Vidya, chapter 2: Knowledge Beyond Samsara)

You are feeling the distress of material life, which is a good sign. Even karmis are frustrated in their endeavors to earn money, so it is expected that devotees should be more frustrated. You have to try to balance your life as best you can. It would be better if you got a job that doesn't take up so much time and energy.

Another avenue altogether is to consider Srila Prabhupada's advice to get out of the bestial society and go to the land. Srila Prabhupada was fully aware that modern life destroys spiritual instincts, and therefore recommended devotees to get out of the system and go back to nature.

If you did consider such a move, almost certainly most people you know, including devotees, would disapprove of it. However, you have to think about what you really want and need to do with your life. Now you have the responsibility to deliver a son from birth and death. Will you be able to do it by bringing him up in modern civilization?

"Civilization is drugs, alcohol, engines of war, prostitution, machines and machine slaves, low wages, bad food, bad taste, prisons, reformatories, lunatic asylums, divorce, perversion, brutal sports, suicides, infanticide, cinema, quackery, demagogy, strikes, lockouts, revolutions, putsches, colonization, electric chairs, guillotines, sabotage, floods, famine, disease, gangsters, money barons, horse racing, fashion shows, poodle dogs, chow dogs, Siamese cats, condoms, pessaries, syphilis, gonorrhea, insanity, neuroses, etc., etc." Henry Miller (1891–1980), U.S. author.

Good intentions may not be enough. Even the children of *** Prabhu, an ardent protagonist of Indian culture, are growing up as karmis, with little interest in spiritual life. Why? Because they are brought up in the city, and he has little time for them. So, realistically speaking, if you want the best for your kid(s), you are going to have to do some serious thinking about how to lead your life. You can't save them unless you first save yourself.

17 December 1999

You certainly are in a difficult situation there, and I doubt if it will go away soon. You are certainly surrounded by persons of not very favorable disposition. If they ask, "Do you really know what ISKCON leaders are doing?" You can put the same question back to them. How do they know except what they hear from others?

There definitely are problems in ISKCON, as there have been and probably always will be. However, at present time, Kali seems to be testing particularly severely. These difficulties, however, are not eternal. What is eternal is Sri Krsna, His divine pastimes, His holy names, and His loving devotees. Let us try to focus on this, the true reality, while living in this tempestuous material atmosphere.

19 December 1999

This is the first letter I've written to you, and I'm going to give some advice that may not be very palatable to you. Please don't mind for that. It is my duty as a sannyasi to instruct, especially if one of my disciples is involved.

*** wrote me:

On Dec 24 we are going to Nrsimha ksetra until the New Year.

There is no time to inquire exactly what "we" here means but presumably it refers to she and you. However, according to the Vedic culture we are supposed to be adopting, pre-marital assocation of spouses is restricted or nil. There is no concept of courting or of boyfriends and girlfriends.

There are several reasons for this, one of them being the danger of falling into illicit sex. I presume you are both sincere devotees, but you are not great self-controlled rishis. Even if you were, you would still be in danger of falldown by intimate contact.

In the West, it is presumed that spouses must get to know each other before marriage. Considering the lack of marital support from parents and others in the West, it may be of some merit for the proposed spouses to get at least some indication of what each other are like, so that they don't marry someone they dislike from the beginning.

However, it takes much time and intimate contact to properly know another person. It is especially not possible to do so by courting, which, by the grace of maya, tends to foster illusory, unrealistic perceptions between partners. Often people presume they "love" each other, only later to be disappointed. They never actually knew the person they thought they loved.

Compatibility is a major consideration in Vedic marriage, but it is deduced before the partners start to associate. Because once they come together, attraction will certainly develop, whether or not they are actually suitable for each other. Therefore compatibility is assessed by astrology, and by comparison of age, social background, height etc.

I request you either to get married as soon as possible, or to maintain much stricter decorum until you are ready to do so. If you are to marry, please make sure that it is with astrologer's advice. At least that much should be there. Otherwise you are simply asking for trouble. Look around you. There are literally millions of couples who thought their union would be the source of all bliss, but who are now simply miserable with each other. Please consider carefully and do the needful.

25 December 1999

I am happy to know that you are happier now, as I could understand that you were feeling unhappy for sometime. I was feeling that you were not reciprocating the concern I have for you and I am glad that you are opening up now. It is especially good to know that you are feeling increasing love for Krsna, for this is the ultimate goal of life and all else besides that is meaningless.

Now that your love for Krsna is increasing, the best thing is to try to share it with others. That means by preaching Krsna consciousness, or at least assisting those who are preaching. After all, love is not simply a vague emotion, but is expressed through service.

We should be careful about how we apply love for others. As Srila Prabhupada explained, a saintly person sees all living beings equally, but he does not embrace a tiger. Loving means giving, but those who indiscriminately open themselves to others can easily be exploited. Even Krsna, the fountainhead of all love, judges others' motives and reciprocates accordingly. (cf. Gita 4.11) History is littered with the bitter annals of those who loved naively. Be careful!

I am certainly wary of New Age psychology. Certainly there may be good to be had of it, as you are experiencing with your new-found positive approach to life. However, we have to be careful of dabbling in such theories. After all, those who do not know Krsna are bewildered about the meaning of life. The love that New Agers profess, without clearly focusing on Krsna cannot be factual or complete, and tends towards impersonalism. At best it can be said that although New Age can help improve one's attitude towards life, it cannot teach the goal of life; and therefore ultimately cannot take one out of the confusion that is material life. I therefore suggest that having got into New Age this far, you now leave it and wholly and solely focus on the goal of life, which is service to Krsna.

Similarly, the teachings of Lord Jesus Christ have been sentimentalized, trivialized, and distorted. That they have still been such a powerful positive influence on the world speaks to the greatness of Jesus. Lord Jesus, as a genuine acarya, came to preach love of God, yet he was scathing in his condemnation of hypocrisy in the name of religion. His repeated and strident criticism of fake religionists upset them so much that eventually they had him crucified. Jesus certainly wasn't a sentimentalist!

You have written about discarding fear, yet some fear is healthy. A devotee should be afraid of Maya in the form of bad association, sinful activities, or anything else that disconnects us from Krsna.

Which again brings me to the point of your service. You have wished me well in my endeavor, for which I thank you, but what about yours? If you don't have a job and if you are adamant about not getting married, then how about doing something practical to serve the mission of the Lord? Both service and association are vital for advancement, but at present you have neither.

K wrote me that she is willing to sponsor a Croatian devotee to go to Ireland, as they are short staffed there. Croatians don't need visas for Ireland. Specifically a deity cook is required.

Or are you planning to come to India soon?

Have you read Srila Bhaktivinoda Thakur's books? I think you would appreciate them. Especially Harinama Chintamani would be nice for you, as it gives much encouragement and guidance in the chanting of the holy names. If you want I could send it to you.

Where are you staying now and with whom? How are you surviving financially? How are your parents? Is your mother still chanting?

Don't mind the strong tone of this letter. When you accepted me as your guru, you did so in knowledge of my straightforward approach to Krsna consciousness. As you have affirmed, I am your well-wisher, and have no intention of ceasing to be so by becoming a flatterer.

Please go on chanting, following the regulative principles, and studying Srila Prabhupada's books. Some time ago I wrote to you:

"As you were asking about which books to read I thought to advise you to read the whole 6 volume Srila Prabhupada Lilamrita (if you haven't read it yet), then the whole of Hari Sauri Prabhu's Transcendental Diary, followed by my Jaya Srila Prabhupada! This would help you more fully focus on the mood and mission of our glorious founder acarya and your own diksa guru's relationship with Srila Prabhupada."

If you didn't yet do this, please do so now.

I'll be happy to hear from you again soon.

25 December 1999

It is very good news that you have taken up Krsna bhakti so seriously so quickly and that Krsna is blessing you to preach also. Many strong young devotees are needed to spread this message very widely, especially to save the poor misguided youth from total downfall into pitiful hedonism.

So it is good that you have taken up this so seriously and I will be very happy to give you shelter as an aspiring disciple. For this, there are some formalities to be observed such as taking test etc. so please contact M Prabhu about that.

2000

12 January 2000

Wherever you may wander within the three worlds, please keep in touch with me. The best way to keep in touch is to chant your 16 rounds. Please do not neglect this. I recommend that you wander in Bangladesh and learn more Vaisnava songs and music. That will be better than going to America.

1 February 2000

It is not necessary that everybody be a full-fledged outgoing preacher. Actually, for women, shyness is considered most important. So you can try to set a good example by assisting the preaching in ways such as cooking prasada offerings, maybe talking sometimes to sincere individuals, and so on. Serve Krsna as best you can, without feeling uncomfortable. Feeling the need to be alone sometimes is not necessarily bad, but use the time to, for instance, study Srila Prabhupada books. The best thing always is to chant Hare Krsna and be happy, so please continue doing that.

26 February 2000

Thank you very much for your spiritual guidance.

Krsna consciousness is not meant to be like an eclectic coffee bar, where everyone fishes around for what he likes and simultaneously disgorges his own speculations and snippets of

197

trivia picked up here and there. The process is to follow guru, sadhu, and sastra. Anything outside of that has nothing to do with Krsna consciousness, even if it is propagated by so-called senior or advanced devotees.

11 April 2000

To Sri R. Ranganathan

All glories to Sri Ramanuja Iyengar and all glories to his glorious passing. Both his life and his apparent death assure him a place in the proximity of the Lord. Thus his departure is not an occasion for lamentation, but for exultation, that even in this dark era, devotees are practising bhakti to the extent that they qualify for entrance to the param padam.[7]

6 May 2000

Very good news that you are happy and progressing in Krsna consciousness.

… last two years: I moved from my parents, I have independent kitchen, I have morning program every day at the same time. I can feel big changes in my life, as if the whole world has changed. I can feel so much taste for chanting and reading and preparing food. But some devotees say that spiritual life starts only with initiation. Some other initiated devotes said that for them nothing changed in their life after initiation. Can you tell me, please, what really happens during initiation, and what the disciple is supposed to feel?

Spiritual life begins when the devotee seriously reaches out to guru and Krsna. For those who, even before initiation, seriously commit themselves to spiritual life, the initiation ceremony is in one sense a formality in that it recognizes the commitment that is already made. For others, the event of being initiated can

---

7. Sri Ramanuja Iyengar was the father of Sri R. Ranganathan. Param padam means "the spiritual world."

be like a wake up and a coming to terms with the reality of the commitment they have made.

18 May 2000

Don't feel bad about my not going to your home. I could have chosen to enter and preach to your mother, but felt loathe to enter and decided that not to enter was in itself giving a strong message. Of course, many people do sinful activities without properly knowing that they are wrong. They are more ignorant and misled than wicked. I am sure your mother is basically a good soul. If not, she would not be supporting your spiritual activities. Please be patient and slowly try to convince her, and after some time she will surely follow the right path.

I would be very happy to see you dedicate your life fully in preaching. There are many doctors in this world but very few preachers of Krsna-bhakti, which is needed even more than medication for the body. Especially needed are some capable devotees to present the proper siddhantas in Hindi. The Hindi-speaking field is vast and with great scope, yet little attended to by ISKCON preachers. It is also a great challenge, as the Hindi-speaking population is steeped in various misconceptions. It is a great challenge and I would be happy to see you concentrate on it as your life's mission.

Anyway there is time yet to decide exactly what you will do. Your attitude of chanting prayerfully will certainly attract Krsna's mercy on you.

18 May 2000

Krsna is blessing you. Please go on preaching sincerely. As much as possible, please do not be overly disturbed by the "unhealthy competition," as you have termed it. It is better not to be resentful towards others and not to concentrate towards others' faults or weaknesses, but rather to always and everywhere endeavor to glorify the names, forms, qualities, prowess, and pastimes of the unlimited Supreme Lord. If there is competition, let people decide for themselves which group they prefer to associate with. If by exhibiting true Vaisnava qualities, people decide that they would prefer to be with your group, that will be your success.

It will probably be the best, if asked about the "competition," to say that they are also devotees, but that they have some serious misconceptions, as deduced from guru, sadhu, and sastra. Directly calling them bad names could lead others to doubt you. Best is to speak on philosophy, and again, let others decide for themselves. We cannot legislate peoples' hearts.

These are just some thoughts of mine. I don't think that war with the ritvik-ites is going to work. Better to be as sweet as possible (it's difficult, that is for sure) and let them, if possible, gradually see the fault in their ways. What do you think?

19 May 2000

I have been chanting your pranama-mantra for 2 years. I'm afraid to commit Vaisnava-aparadha, but I don't feel the exclusive personal attachment, which—to my knowledge—is a prerequisite for accepting a guru.

Please, allow me to chant Srila Prabhupada's pranama mantra as before. Please, forgive my bothering you so much.

Accepting a spiritual master is the most important decision anyone can make in many, many lifetimes. So if you do not feel comfortable about accepting me, or anyone else, as a guru, you certainly shouldn't. However, it is best that you not delay making this commitment for too long. At some point one has to "make a leap of faith."

Thankyou for all the nice services you have done for me in the past and I wish you all the best for the future.

27 May 2000

Regarding the situation in ***: they are fighting over properties and money but they do not realize that it is Krsna who gives and that Krsna can take away also. Whatever assets a person may acquire, he cannot be happy unless Krsna is pleased with him. It would be better if they sold the building and used all the money to print books. Then those who want a building could work hard to raise funds by selling the books, and those who want money could be given it in books. But they should be warned of the reactions of taking that which is meant for Krsna's service and using it for sense gratification.

You wrote that "that in the new center, devotees would not be under such financial pressure, and they could preach and live more brahminically." But unless there is some pressure, they will simply eat, sleep, and fight among themselves.

The plan to make a Vedic cultural center in four years sounds like a phantasmagoria. So many things will change in four years. And when the original estimate increases, where will the extra laxmi come from? Better just to have a small house with a few dedicated devotees who are serious to preach. Let everything expand again naturally. Anyway, somehow or other it is best to close this situation and get on with the real business, which is preaching and book distribution.

These are some ideas that you are welcome to circulate. The point is that unless there is a strong sense of Krsna consciousness, any attempt will simply end in grief.

You must go on with the sankirtan mission, but don't go alone. You must have association.

20 June 2000

I know that you are very learned.

"Where there are no trees, a castor plant is taken as a tree." I live in India and I know people who are really learned. I may appear learned to those who know less than I do, but my learning is very little compared to many others. Still, I study Srila Prabhupada's books, and have faith in them, and the confidence that if I unduplicitously try to represent the knowledge Srila Prabhupada has given, then he will bless me to help impart it to others.

Why and if it is important to wear tilaka and dress in Vaisnava clothes?

Please see the attached file. It is a draft of part of my upcoming book on Vaisnava behavior.

As soon as we don't follow the Vaisnava etiquette in our dealings with others, we will follow our material conditioning.

Very good point.

Why and if female devotees are not allowed to pay obeisances to male devotees and vice versa. I have heard different opinions on that also.

Different opinions will come because of the dichotomy between acting according to the body and acting according to the soul. Vedic social dealings stress great care in maintaining separation between the sexes. Considering the "fire and butter" principle and the many falldowns we have seen, I personally prefer to stress conservatism in these matters. It is better that men deal with women (and vice versa) according to the Vedic model, as much as possible. It may not seem to be very possible in modern G, but we have to make a start somewhere or else we will permanently remain mlecchas.

I recommend that male and female devotees offer obeisances in a group (e.g. as is often done after tulasi arati in ISKCON temples), rather than walking up to each other and offering obeisances.

Apart from that, in Vedic culture women offer obeisances to sannyasis and to their husbands, and men and women offer obeisances to their parents and parents-in-law, so there are some cases even in traditional life of one sex offering obeisances to the other (although in these cases those offered obeisances would not return them).

21 June 2000

This book Nityananda-caritamrta has been around in Bengali for a long time ...

There is no evidence that it has been around a long time. Even if it were, that does not mean it is authorized or accepted by our acaryas.

... and it is definitely (as I mentioned before), not a product of Nityananda Parivara.

This is only your assertation, not a proven fact.

It is quite unfortunate that due to sectarianism, Vaisnavas would often discard an authentic scripture. There are several branches of Caitanya Mahaprabhu and Nityananda Prabhu's tree. Each of those branches surely have its own heritages of scriptural guidance.

They surely do, but our acarya, Srila Bhaktisiddhanta Sarasvati Thakura, came to cut away the rupanuga-viruddha-apasiddhantas that flourish in what he called unauthorized lines.

There may be some disagreement that Lord Nityananda did not have seminal lineage as Virabhadra Prabhu did not marry. But it is a fact there is a Nityananda Vat in Vrindavan, whose sevakas are purportedly the descendants of Lord Nityananda. Has there been anybody to disprove this fact?

Please see Cc. Adi 11.8 purport. Srila Bhaktisiddhanta Sarasvati Thakura clarifies that Nityananda Prabhu has no seminal descendants after Virabhadra Gosai, but that three disciples of the latter are accepted as his sons. Nityananda-vamsis, however, claim direct seminal descent from Nitai. However, the heart of the contention with the jata-gosais is not over whether or not

Nitai had sons, but that certain jata-gosais claim themselves as gurus by birthright.

kali yuge aneka vaisnava hoibe tattave na jani naraka ku yibe, "In Kali yuga many people may become Vaisnava but without knowing the tattva, they will go to hell."[8]

Exactly.

Nowadays, Vaisnavas are unwilling to digest information that may be somewhat different from what they might have heard from their immediate authorities.

That's good. Why accept an authority if you don't accept his statements as authoritative? Of course, no-one can be an authority without following the previous authorities. That is the parampara system. And that is why our acaryas have warned us about infiltrations from non-bona fide paramparas who do not follow the standard authorities of guru, sadhu, and sastra, but concoct for their own sense gratification.

Even people who heard from the same guru have difference of opinions as to what the conclusions of the sastras are. All the disciples of Srila Bhaktissidhanta definitely have different opinions as to what are his teachings and instructions. If not why do we see different branches of Gaudiya Matha today?

In my experience, their disagreements are mostly personal, and not on points of siddhanta.

Similarly all disciples of Srila Prabhupada do not have the same opinion about understanding Srila Prabhupada's teachings and instructions.

Are you inferring that any opinion is as good as another? That everyone should have their own opinion and do as they like? This is not the teaching of sastra. Please see Bg. 16.23.

Otherwise ISKCON would be a united organization today. Just because you don't believe that Lord Nityananda had a descendant, and I believe

8. This appears to be an attempted rendition of a Bengali or Oriya statement.

so, does that make me an offender? We should use mature intelligence in deliberating on these points.

Mature intelligence is insufficient. Everything must be based on guru, sadhu, and sastra. Particularly, we have to follow the words of our acarya. And they are very clear on the point that Nityananda-vamsa are bogus inasmuch as they claim to be seminal descendants of Nityananda Prabhu, and that their claims to be gurus on that basis are also bogus.

The facts remain that (a) although ascribed to Vrindavan das, the authorship is dubious; and (b) the last 3 chapters are in particular questionable.[9]

In this case you have to prove beyond reasonable doubt that the authorship is not Srila Vrindavan dasa Thakura.

Rather, you should explain why Srila Bhaktisiddhanta Sarasvati Thakura never mentioned this book, although it was his policy to list the works of major followers of Lord Caitanya.

Apart from the line cited in the verse of the 11th chapter, you have to prove line by line what is questionable in those last three chapters. You are saying that someone impersonated Vrindavan Dasa Thakura, to enhance the glories of Nityananda-vamsa, this I completely disagree with you.

Maybe you should learn more about the history of our parampara and not be so naive. The jata-gosais attacked Srila Bhaktisiddhanta Sarasvati Thakura and his followers during Navadvip Dham parikrama, and wanted to murder Srila Bhaktisiddhanta Sarasvati Thakura. These are historical facts. The whole ruse of the corrupt jata-gosais is to appear saintly so as to cheat people. Srila Bhaktisiddhanta Sarasvati Thakura exposed that and brought out the true colors of those rogues. Not necessarily that all jata-gosais are so bad, but the point is that people can do many things to maintain personal interests.

---

9. This sentence is from a previous letter by Bhakti Vikāsa Swami.

Printing a fabricated book in the name of a great acarya is certainly not beyond the doings of certain unscrupulous people. Indeed, it appears that in the late 19th and early 20th centuries, several such phony books were published with the deliberate intention of lending false credulity to various apasampradayas operating for pecuniary and self-aggrandizary motives. Their trick is to present something apparently devotional, and shrewdly insert their apasiddhanta along with it. Such books may be apparently devotional, but are actually as fraudulent as Putana.

Considering the history, we should not accept any book simply because it appears devotional, or is ascribed to a great acarya. To do so risks falling into the trap set by charlatans. Therefore, before publishing any book, we should first ascertain if it is accepted as bona fide by our acaryas. (Even many books that are adored by our acaryas are not approved by them for indiscriminate distribution. This especially refers to esoteric works of intimate pastimes. But that is another discussion.)

We have to be careful. Something may look good but not be. Even the Nitai Gaur Radhe Shyam group have done many good things (such as restoring and maintaining holy places) and much of what is in their books is not incorrect. But what is wrong about them is so wrong that Srila Bhaktisiddhanta Sarasvati Thakura thoroughly denounced them.

I am publishing works left behind by previous mahajanas especially the followers of Lord Caitanya Mahaprabhu. These works were not created for materialistic intentions.

That is my whole contention. It is not clear that "Nityananda Caritamrta" is written by Srila Vrindavan dasa Thakura. Several scholars suspect it may have been created with materialistic intentions. There are certainly grounds for doubt.

So how could you say these words were ascribed by materialistic people?

I am not saying that, just expressing a valid doubt that you have not answered. Our acaryas have taken such matters very seriously and we should also.

We should study an issue much more thoroughly before making our own judgements.

Again, I have not made a judgement, just expressed a doubt. Certainly we should investigate very thoroughly and only when we are certain that a book is authorized by our acaryas should we publish it.

As of this writing, I have not heard from any ISKCON scholars expressing their objections to this book. Instead I have been getting lots of praise and encouragement for publishing this book. When I initially asked *** Swami about whether I should publish the book or not due to this very issue, he at once gave me the encouragement to publish it. In making the decision of the publication, I had to use Franklin's method of making decisions. The decision to publish it far outweighed the decision not to publish it, therefore I went ahead with the publication, and it has been quite appreciated by the majority of devotees.

That many people may like it is not the criterion. The criterion is, is it authorized by our acaryas? There may be many scholars and great devotees but not all may be so expert as to discern the subtleties of deviation. In this regard, please see Cc. Antya ch. 15 for a description of how most of Lord Caitanya's internal associates did not recognize the Mayavada of a poet from Bengal. Only Svarupa Damodara could find the fault. From this pastime, enacted under the yogamaya potency of the Lord, we learn that maya may deviously present herself as bhakti, and that only certain devotees are empowered to deeply understand and present the siddhantas and refute apa-siddhantas. Being thus warned, we should be careful to follow the path of our acaryas and not be swayed by the dangerous enemy of populism.

28 June 2000

I'm not interested in *** going to USA and working 90 hours a week until he gets ulcers and a heart attack. I want him to be a fully dedicated devotee of Krsna who will be well-versed in sastra, preach the message of Lord Caitanya widely, and deliver many from birth and death.

There are millions of families all over the world with financial problems and every other kind of problem too. But there is hardly anyone prepared to dedicate body, mind, and soul, to the service of Krsna. If ***'s family think that he can solve their problems by earning money, they are wrong. He may temporarily seem to be able to help them, but they will continue to suffer many kinds of problems and be reborn again and again to do so until they surrender to Krsna. It is very fortunate for them that *** is ready to fully dedicate himself to solving their problems once and for all by delivering them from birth and death, and very unfortunate that they cannot understand this.

Whatever the problems in ISKCON may be does not in the slightest alter the fact that every spirit soul is eternally the servant of Krsna and has to surrender to him. ISKCON may have problems or not have problems, but it is up to every individual who has come into contact with Srila Prabhupada's teachings to take full advantage of them and go back to Godhead.

B, ***'s elder brother told me, "I am giving him to you." How can he think to take him back? This is not a good idea and should not be encouraged.

Please see the quotes below.

Once the mother and father of a young devotee complained to Srila Prabhupada that their son was a full-time student in the Krsna consciousness movement. They said they wanted him to become a doctor. Prabhupada replied that they should let the young man decide for himself, and that in any case, there were many doctors in the world but few serious devotees. Prabhupada said that the work of the devotee was more important than the work of a physician. A doctor can repair the health of a few hundred people, but even that is temporary. Medical cures do not free the patient from his karma, which forces him to take rebirth and suffer again in another material body. But a devotee who successfully distributes Krsna consciousness can help people achieve liberation from birth and death. So his work is the most important in the world. (Narada-bhakti-sutra, sutra 62, purport). See also SB 7.9.18 and purport.

2 July 2000

Thankyou for your letter. Very nice to hear from you.

First of all I would like to clarify that I am not calling him to support my financial burden. If that would have been the case, I would have never allowed him to join the movement in the first instance itself.

OK, that is good. Please forgive me if I have misunderstood you.

Now with reports coming in all news papers and all bizarre incidents happening in ISKCON *** and hearing the experiences of certain full time devotees here, my mother and my sister are very much opposing to the idea of +++ remaining full time in ISKCON. I also acknowledge their feelings.

This does not seem to be a very considered reaction. First of all, why consider that the press reports are all true? Undoubtedly in a large organization there will be some serious problems. But the aim and object of ISKCON is pure devotional service. It is not that devotees are disguised criminals or that most of them are seriously misbehaved.

Whatever has or may have happened in ISKCON, it remains an organisation meant for cultivating and propagating love of God. It gives an opportunity for young men like +++ to get out of the rat race and dedicate their lives in the service of Krsna. Whatever bad dealings you may have seen in ISKCON X, +++ has personally experienced a blissful loving atmosphere in ISKCON Y. I do not intend to keep +++ in X but in a place where he will be well looked after and cared for.

My sister in the US is more depressed than anybody and she is getting panic attacks after hearing that +++ is leaving home to join the movement full time.

Why is she panicking? If she was told that he was going to USA and working 80 hours a week under tremendous pressure, would she panic? So many Ayers go to the West, start eating meat and so many bad things, but their family members don't panic.[10] Rather, they are pleased. There seem to be some imbalanced priorities here.

I think the Vaishnava literature says that no living entity should be harassed knowingly or unknowingly.

This should not be misunderstood or taken out of context.

Srila Prabhupada gave the example of a man flying a kite at a cliff's edge. Totally absorbed, his eyes fixed in the sky, he does not perceive the danger of imminent death. Seeing his precarious situation, any commonsensical observer would call out to warn him. Only a madman would think, "He is enjoying flying the kite. Why should I disturb him?" A sane man must call out, "Watch out!" If the kite-flyer is a fool and a rascal, he will not heed the warning. Rather, keeping his eyes determinedly fixed in the air, he will rebuke his well-wisher, "Why are you disturbing me? Can't you see I'm flying my kite? Do you think I don't know what I'm doing?" Or, in arrogance, the foolish kite-flyer may simply ignore his well-wisher. Just to shock the rascal to come to his senses and save him from certain doom, the observer may urgently berate him, "You fool! You rascal!" The kite-flyer may not like such insulting words, although meant for his benefit.

---

10. Ayer—a Tamil-brahmin surname.

Harrassment is always there in material life. You know that very well from your office. You may want to save +++ from problems in ISKCON, but can you save him from being harrassed in his office? If he were to marry and his wife was not agreeable, could you save him from being harrassed by his wife? Even in your own family, where the members are all more or less cooperative (it seems), you are experiencing so many tensions and harrasments. If you want zero harrasment, then why are you harrassing me? Your thinking seems to be overly influenced by emotions.

I know for sure that Krsna consciousness is the highest thing. But the ground reality is different.

Your illusion is exposed. Krsna consciousness is reality, but you are thinking otherwise. Only due to maya you are thinking that pacifying the emotions of your supposed family members is more important than letting your supposed brother fully surrender to Krsna.

I myself am so much fried that I have no life both spiritually as well as materially. I am under extreme mental pressure.

Then why do you want to pull +++ back into such a situation?

I would also like to tell you that I will in no way spoil his spiritual life if he comes back.

According to your own description, your spiritual life is nowhere. How then, can you propose that his spiritual life would not be affected by going back? You are in no position to help him spiritually.

In fact I feel I should not have over reacted by taking the decision of sending him full time single handedly. Now everybody in my family feels that I have taken a wrong decision without getting proper consent from all his siblings who are very near and dear to him.

On top of this my mother tells me that I have forced her to agree with you in the temple to send +++ full time. She feels that she was not given time to think about the whole issue and was made to tell a big yes to you. She questions about my authority to have taken an independent decision and as a mother was not given the right to think about her son. She now shouts at me saying that "He is only your brother and not your son."

I did not canvass for +++ to make this move. I merely suggested that he think about it after finishing his course in two years. It was fully your decision and one that came as a surprise to me. Whatever you feel like now, the fact is that you are all fully grown responsible people and you all knew what was happening. You personally said to me, "I am giving him to you to engage in Krsna's service." Once having offered anything to Krsna, it is not right to take it back. I have offered +++ in the service of Srila Prabhupada and Krsna. It would be a great offense for me to take him back and I cannot consent to it.

In these circumstances I beg you to save me by sending my brother back home as per his mother's wish.

I will do everything I can to save you from the offense of trying to pull him away from full time service to Krsna, when you yourself have thus offered him.

Please don't misunderstand me. I feel no anger or animosity towards you and I hope that you feel none towards me. However, just as you feel that you have to act for +++ Prabhu's benefit, so I also feel the same way. The difference is that your thinking is overly influenced by the present, temporary circumstances you are in. It is my duty to see and act from the eternal platform, which is the only one that can actually benefit anyone in any way.

7 July 2000

In the absence of your father you are the head of the family and are supposed to act as a guru to the other family members. A householder should hear from his guru and instruct his family members accordingly. Sastra warns not to be dominated by women who are considered less intelligent as they are ruled by their emotions.

That we are seeing here. There is no reason that +++ should return home as your mother has one son there to comfort her, namely yourself. Being overcome by the tears of women you have descended to their level and have also become an emotional wreck not capable of thinking clearly for the highest benefit of all concerned. Instead of acting irresponsibly and putting everyone into anxiety by threatening suicide (which is a highly sinful act), you should be preaching to your family members how glorious it is that +++ has sacrificed his life in the service of Krsna.

Your family members are not suffering because of the absence of +++ but because they are in the maya of thinking him their bodily relation. Whether or not he goes home, they will continue to suffer as long as they are in maya and identify with their bodies. It is your duty to preach to them to come to the platform of transcendental knowledge and thus be happy.

It is not too late. You can still start preaching from the transcendental platform. It is, after all, only due to material attachment that you are reneging on your resolution to offer +++ in the service of Krsna. If you are really interested in the benefit of all concerned, you should not insist on such a disastrous step. You are offering me various quotes from sastra, but only to support the proposition of having your so-called brother go back to your so-called home, the doing of which is of no ultimate benefit to anyone but is only for the temporary sense gratification of your so-called family members.

***, you have read Srila Prabhupada's books. You are not supposed to act or think like an ordinary materialistic person. That some people superficially connected with ISKCON may do so is no reason for you to degrade yourself.

This is a test from Krsna to see if you are more attached to serving Him or to living a superficially pious life with no real commitment to Krsna. Somehow Krsna inspired you to offer +++ for full time devotional service and now Krsna wants to see if you are really serious. This is a great test and if you pass it you will certainly get Krsna's blessings to make rapid advancement in Krsna consciousness. However, if you now go back on your word, insisting on putting your supposed self-interest before that of pleasing Krsna, it would be a great step backwards in your devotional life. Krsna is being very kind to you to give you such a test and I pray that you have the good intelligence to see it as such and act accordingly.

"O son of Prtha, do not yield to this degrading impotence. It does not become you. Give up such petty weakness of heart and arise, O chastiser of the enemy."

8 July 2000

Please be clear that I have not asked you to go home and am not telling anyone that I have told you that. I have suggested it as a possibility, seeing that your family members are acting in such a disturbing manner. But I am not going to pressure or force you to go. Ultimately the decision has to fall on you, because it would not be good if I were to pressure you against your will, either to go or stay.

I do not approve of your family's behavior. They appear to be acting unreasonably, duplicitously, and selfishly. However, if they continue to make such a disturbance, you might consider making some compromise just to cool them down. On the other hand, if you don't compromise, they will probably just cool off after some time anyway. How long can they go on in this hysterical state?

5 August 2000

Some group of devotees say that we should not pay different fines for wrong parking and bus ticket and similar things (if we can easily escape) because the government are cheaters and rascals and if we take something from the robber it is not sin—we must use this laxmi in service to Krisna. Another group of devotees say that we must pay all these things because it is not good to develop a cheating mentality—if we don't pay we are cheating the material energy and because of that, material energy will bewilder us more and more, and we will in the future lose three times more money than we 'saved' in the case of not paying something. Please, tell me what is right and what is wrong.

A devotee should always act in such a way that is pleasing to Krsna. That may not be exactly the same in all circumstances. It is certainly good to save money for use in Krsna's service. In principle, if money can be saved for Krsna's service, it should be. But there is no surety of not getting caught, and the consequences of dodging paying are worse than the few pennies that might be saved. It certainly doesn't look good if devotees are exposed as cheapos who dodge paying bus fares.

It is also true that without being fully pure, such actions can develop a cheating mentality and spoil the character. Those that do not want to give to a government of cheaters and rascals should not themselves be cheaters and rascals. Not a few devotees who learned to "cheat for Krsna" now do so to maintain their families, e.g., by selling cheap paintings at exorbitant prices. This is against the principle mentioned in sastra, that grhasthas should earn a living by honest means.

In some countries where corruption is rife (e.g. India), it is almost impossible to live without giving a bribe at some point. But in general, illegal and corrupt activities should not be indulged in by devotees. Let us preach and have faith that Krsna will send whatever we require. Krsna is not a poor man and can at least cover our bus fares.

26 September 2000

How do we brahmacaris understand these actions?

Brahmacaris should take such incidents very soberly and assess
if they have what it takes to remain brahmacari. That many
sannyasis have fallen does not mean that no-one can make it, but
we should know that bravado alone is insufficient.

Are these actions by a sannyasi to get married as per guru, sadhu and
sastra?

There is almost certainly no sastra-vidhi for sannyasis to marry,
yet we cannot deny that Srila Prabhupada allowed it. Not that
he encouraged it; yet he has given some allowance so that fallen
sannyasis can continue in devotional service. Certainly Srila
Prabhupada didn't want sannyasis to marry, but the alternatives
that N Prabhu suggested (suicide or blooping) were less
acceptable to Srila Prabhupada. Unpalatable as it may be, as
followers of Srila Prabhupada we have to accept that he made
such an allowance.

In ISKCON in the past, many men took sannyasa against their
will or without proper consideration. Now we should be careful
in screening new candidates, and should extend support to those
who are presently in the sannyasa ashram but struggling. I'm not
at all happy with N's decision. I will be writing to him about this,
although I hardly know him. Better if those who know him well,
especially R Maharaja, try to discourage him from marrying.
But if he cannot take any other alternative, we have to allow
dedicated devotees like him scope to continue their service.

Aren't they demoralizing for other renunciants in the movement?

Probably. It may also help those who are more intelligent and
determined, so that they can learn from the errors of others.

What lessons do we learn from this?

We should be very careful in awarding sannyasa. Good sadhana, sastric knowledge, practical detachment—all these should be seen. Maybe some astrological screening should be done.

We should also tighten up the sannyasa ashram (be more strict on philosophical deviations, poor sadhana etc.), and respond early to danger signals from present sannyasis. Apparently a sannyasi who recently fell used to regularly go out from the temple for hours in karmi clothes. Maybe TPs should be enjoined to respond to such irregular behavior.

Don't these set a very dangerous trend for the sannyas ashram in our Society?

Yes. We are reaping the fruits of past imprudence. I feel that we, the sannyasis as a body, need to seriously discuss the continuing trend of falldown and see what to do about it. Probably the role of sannyasa minister should be more active.

*** Prabhu has justified his change of asrama from sannyas to grhastha by quotes from Prabhupada in the sixth canto and in 1977. Are you satisfied with that?

Srila Prabhupada was far from satisfied that his sannyasis fell, but the reality is that it is still happening. How to deal with it? Srila Prabhupada preferred that they get married and continue serving as an alternative to suicide or blooping.

I personally would prefer suicide in the Ganga at Mayapur than this fifth ashram business.

Such a mood should be the determination of a sannyasi.

I've added +++ Prabhu as a receiver here as I believe he once sent a posting on this subject. Although it is undoubtedly a painful topic for him, I request him to re-post that text for the benefit of us all.

I also request the blessings of all the Vaisnavas on this fallen soul, unqualified as I am even to ask for the mercy of the devotees.

"My path is very difficult. I am blind, and my feet are slipping again and again. Therefore, may the saints help me by granting me the stick of their mercy as my support."

31 October 2000

I got your letter in Mayapur, but as the devotee who brought it had already left by the time I arrived, and as I did not know your address nor could find another devotee returning to S, I was not able to reply to you.

I read that letter and your latest one with a mixture of happiness and sadness. Happiness that you still care for me and Srila Prabhupada and Krsna, and sadness at your present state of practice of Krsna consciousness.

Yet I am more happy than sad. After all, you do not have to write to me. You could just forget me. But you do not want to. For whatever reasons that you do not now strictly follow the practices of Krsna consciousness, you are still attached to Krsna. That attachment will certainly help you in the long run, for Krsna never forgets those who remain attached to Him. And what to speak of those who, like yourself, are engaged in the most important service of translating Srila Prabhupada's books into the various languages of the world. Surely Krsna will bless you.

Personally, as a tiny soul inadequately taking on the stupendous responsibility of trying to represent Krsna to others, I have always had affection for you and often think of you and your struggles in this nasty material world. It is of course my duty to always request you to improve your practices of sadhana.

Please keep in touch from time to time. By Krsna's grace, my life is ever getting busier, but I'll always be happy to hear from you.

1 November 2000

We hardly know each other, yet what few exchanges we have had have been brotherly and cordial. I have long respected your simplicity and straightforwardness. Now I'm taking the liberty of writing you about a difficult topic, so please don't mind for that.

When in ***, I was praising your qualities and encouraging the devotees to invite you there more often, but was told that you had been discussing with some disciples about the pros and cons of your getting married. Of course, I do not know for sure if this is true. But having heard it from a leader of the yatra, and having previously heard that you were similarly contemplating in the past, has led me to surmise that it probably is true. If not, please forgive me.

But if so, I strongly request you to reconsider your inclination towards marriage and to at least defer your decision for some time. Even if you consider that it was a wrong decision for you to take sannyasa, having done it and gone along with it for so many years, to renege on your vows now would be a far worse decision. Even if you feel a personal need to marry, it is not proper, for your role as a sannyasi is a public one with heavy responsibility. To marry now will lower the sannyasa asrama further in the eyes of devotees and discourage them. It will be especially discouraging for brahmacaris who are seriously striving to maintain their vrata to see yet another sannyasi get married.

Maharaja, you don't have long to live. At age 50 or so, you cannot be happy as a grhastha. At least for the sake of others, it is better to continue as a struggling sannyasi. And it need not be such a great struggle. If you were to go on Padayatra India, for instance, provocations for sexual attraction would be minimal. I'm sure Padayatra India would be more than happy to facilitate in this regard. There are many preaching opportunites including book distribution, constant chanting, and frequent visits to holy dhamas. And all this in the association of Gaura-Nitai and Prabhupada. The natural padayatra austerities are purifying and conducive for spiritual life. It is a paradise for brahmacaris and sannyasis.

I strongly urge and beg you to try joining Padayatra India and to put off your decision until after doing that for some time. If you were to come back from the brink, it would be a great inspiration for all devotees at a time when we need it most. Although Srila Prabhupada and his followers will certainly not reject you if you marry, they would surely be happier if you battle on, taking the help of the devotees.

"My path is very difficult. I am blind, and my feet are slipping again and again. Therefore, may the saints help me by granting me the stick of their mercy as my support."

What do you think?

3 November 2000

I'll be glad to write to you from time to time.

Thankyou very much. Please do so.

Even if you feel your advancement to be at snail pace, please never give up on Krsna or His service or His devotees.

11 November 2000

Please forgive me for this.

At present, I am working as a Software Engineer at a Software concern in B. When I accepted to translate Shri Ramayana written by Your Highness, I thought I would find some time to do that. But, the present job doesn't give me ample time for the translation.

Actually, I have translated just 6 pages in the past 3 months. I am very sorry for this. Since I am required to work on weekends also, I was unable to do this esteemed work. Even if I start translating on the available Sundays or other holidays, it takes me a lot of time to do this. Your Highness has written the book too beautiful, with good usage of power words in English and condensing a lot of information in small lines, coupled with 'rare-to-find' literary expertise. It takes me a large amount of time to reflect them exactly in Tamil. At this speed, I will surely make waste of this project.

I am extremely sorry for telling you this after wasting such a long time. Since I had a great interest for this, I thought I would dig out the required time somehow, to complete this work. But it is dawning on me now, that, at present I would be unable to do this, even though I like it very much.

So please relieve me from this most distinguished work and please assign this "kainkaryam" to some other Bhagavata. Let me not hinder this project any more.

My little mind was wavering back and forth for the last 4 days what I am going to do regarding this, till today. When I got the mail from Shri M dasa (I am forwarding that mail), I decided I should make a final decision.

So this mail. I am very very sorry Swamy. Please forgive this pleading soul for doing such a "papam." I have no other option.

I am not surprised at your inability to perform this service, and was even expecting it, for when one becomes the daasa of a computer company, he must dedicate mind, body, and words in its service with ananya-bhaava, day and night with no respite.

In this regard a Vaishnava acharya has written:

biphale sevinu krpana durajana
capala sukha-labha lagi' re

"Simply for the sake of a drop of flickering happiness, I am uselessly serving miserly rascals."

May Lord Rama be glorified.

19 November 2000

I know that you are a very sincere devotee of Lord Ranganathan and feel that He has sent you to this world for His service, but that somehow due to the effect of Kaliyuga you have become diverted. I would be very happy to arrange for various grhastha devotees to each contribute a small sum each month so that you could remain in Srirangam and lead a simple life dedicated only to the service of the Lord. It is perfectly honorable for a person fully engaged in devotional activities to accept donations for minimal personal requisites, so you need have no qualms about doing so. Please consider this and let me know what you think.

31 December 2000

Your wife has informed me that you wish to return to C to "enjoy your senses." I humbly beg you that if you have any regard for me to kindly reconsider your decision. Krsna has been very kind to you and given you an opportunity to serve Him and simultaneously fulfill your family needs. After waiting so long for such an opportunity, to give it up now would not be wise.

Furthermore, you have a very nice wife and child and to abandon them would be sinful. So please do not give up your responsibilities or succumb to the senses. To do so will only cause great suffering to yourself and others.

2001

7 February 2001

Thankyou for your letter and concern about the earthquake.[11] By Krsna's grace, no ISKCON devotees or properties were damaged. Devotees are now distributing thousands of plates of prasada daily in the affected area.

I never sent a letter of rejection to AV Prabhu. However, there have been serious accusations and your local GBC representative, H.H. B Maharaja, is responding by sending H.G. K Prabhu (a senior devotee) to investigate. Please cooperate with this investigation. I understand that you feel upset but it is the investigator's duty to impartially try to find out the actual facts. If there is no fault on the part of AV Prabhu then there is nothing to fear. So please remain cool-headed and cooperate, and remember that Krsna is the supreme controller and He has His plan for everything and everybody. Krsna tests His devotees in various ways, but those who stay faithful to His lotus feet can go on advancing in Krsna consciousness.

I pray to Krsna that this matter may be settled soon in a manner most conducive to the eternal benefit of all concerned.

13 February 2001

Thankyou very much for your letter. It is a little difficult to follow but I think I understood its essence.

---

11. This refers to a severe earthquake that had occurred in Gujarat shortly prior.

You misunderstood if you thought I advised you to marry. Rather, the opposite. I have never recommended a once married woman to again marry and do not intend to do so in future.

But it is true that women's power is very strong and that therefore not only among Muslims but in Vedic culture also there are strong restrictions to control this potentially damaging force. A major cause of the hellish condition in modern society is unrestricted mixing between men and women. Sastra speaks strongly against this; so did Srila Prabhupada; so do I.

Notwithstanding, you have children to support and no husband, so I wish you all the best in your business endeavors, as also your preaching activities, which I suggest you mostly conduct among women. The time for you to live a fully renounced life will come later.

I am sorry to hear of further injuries to your right arm. It must be a residual karmic reaction that Krsna wants you to go through. Tolerate it and learn from it.

14 February 2001

Thankyou for your letter and your nice (if not somewhat late) Vyasa-puja offering. Please thank *** also for hers.

Your letter expresses a mixture of sorrow and joy. Actually, Krsna consciousness is meant to be all joy. But as we are living in the material world, we are beset with the anarthas of ourselves and others. Therefore it is unrealistic to expect utopia. It is better to be grateful with the gifts that Krsna has given us in the form of association with devotees, worship of the Lord and tulasi, chanting the holy names, and so on. If we become overly disappointed with the inadequacies of others, we may develop apathy or offensiveness towards devotees and thus put ourselves into danger.

It is true that the condition of our movement in +++ and elsewhere is not what it used to be, and a manifestation of that is less deep exchanges between devotees. However, it is up to every one of us to behave positively towards others and thus make steps towards improving relationships. If everyone is waiting for everyone else to come forward, and in the meantime complaining about everyone else, then certainly relationships will be cold and impersonal. The solution lies with every one of us. Without making a genuine effort to open up to others and try to understand their problems, we ourselves will be perpetrating the selfishness and impersonalism that we ascribe to others.

However, I'm surprised that your experience of L was of devotees only looking after their own interests without caring for other peoples' feelings. My own impression, and that of other attending devotees who I spoke to, was of a warm family spirit. The mood was set by the hosts, A and B, who worked hard to make arrangements and financed everything from their own earnings. At least they cannot be accused of selfishness.

I hope that you did not feel I was neglecting you. It's a fact that I am perpetually busy with writing and traveling and preaching, and that as the number of my disciples increases I get less time to spend for each of them. I'm trying to compensate for that by writing books so as to give some valuable instructions, and to visit at least once a year the areas where my disciples live. Last time in L you unexpectedly left early so I didn't get much chance to see you.

But I also think of my disciples often and pray for their well being, and hope that they do the same for me. I will always remember the nice services you have done for me. I especially appreciate the enthusiasm you have for distributing my books.

I have sent a suggestion to several of my unmarried lady disciples who are not living in temples that they regularly correspond with a senior mataji disciple of mine, a very wonderful and sympathetic devotee (G dasi).

This was R's response to this suggestion:

Thank you very very much for this wonderful idea. I am accepting it this very moment and I will write to G mataji as soon as posible to introduce myself and my activities to her. I think that a senior mataji is absolutely necessary for me because she can understand me better and I feel more free and open to talk to her about so many things and rules and regulations in spiritual life.

I suggest that you also write to G regularly, and from time to time send me a report of your progress in Krsna consciousness. I think this would help you to broaden your vision in Krsna consciousness and develop relationships with devotees beyond the small circle you are in now. Even though they are no doubt wonderful devotees, it is better that you learn to associate with and appreciate other devotees also.

25 February 2001

You are wondering about accepting a siksa guru. You see some ex-disciples of *** who have not accepted siksa gurus. But without a spiritual authority they are prone to be misguided at any time, and many of them indeed are quite deviated. Judging from your distressed and confused tone, I suggest that it is imperative that you immediately accept guidance from properly placed spiritual authorities.

It is also important to become steady in your practices of Krsna consciousness, including mangal arati and at least 16 rounds. That depends upon developing determination and faith in the Holy Name. That may be achieved by chanting feelingly and developing a prayerful mood. The songs of Srila Bhaktivinoda Thakura are wonderful for helping us conditioned souls to start to feel for Krsna, and I recommend that you regularly read them.

I also suggest that you immediately start reading Sri Caitanya Caritamrta for at least one hour daily, and intensely pray for the mercy of Lord Caitanya and Lord Nityananda.

Apart from having a spiritual authority, you also need spiritual friends, especially as you are going through such a difficult period. May I put you in touch with a senior mataji disciple of mine? She is a very wonderful and sympathetic devotee (G dasi).

23 April 2001

Thankyou for your letter. It is not clear which point you want me to address in my reply, and anyway it is impossible for me at such a distance to ascertain exactly what is going on. But I will make some general observations appropriate to the situation.

Spiritual leadership in the Vaisnava tradition is based on adherence to guru, sadhu, and sastra. Only a committed follower of guru, sadhu, and sastra is competent to be a bona fide leader. A committed follower does not invent anything new or mix the process of Krsna consciousness with other processes, but simply presents what he has heard from his guru.

One of the claims about AV Prabhu is that he teaches some breathing technique along with chanting. I was aware of this as he had mentioned it to me. Although breathing techniques are not very important, sometimes in preaching such things are used to help bring people to Krsna consciousness. So I do not see anything intrinsically harmful in this, as long as it is not promoted as the main sadhana and it is gradually made clear that the essence is chanting Hare Krsna, and not breathing techniques.

However, if, as it is claimed, these breathing techniques are mixed with chanting Hare Krsna for the purpose of experiencing some extrasensory perception, then this would constitute a serious deviation from the knowledge we have received in parampara from Srila Prabhupada. Development of extrasensory perception has nothing to do with the process of Krsna consciousness, nor is it even considered desirable for those practising bhakti. Indeed, attempts to develop extrasensory perception are a deviation from the true goal of developing pure Krsna consciousness.

Also of concern is the accusation that, unknown to me, AV Prabhu has another guru than myself. If so, that would be a breach of the guru-disciple relationship on his part.

Other points were also mentioned by the investigative team, to which the same principle applies: anything not taught by Srila Prabhupada cannot be accepted as bona fide practice of Krsna consciousness, at least within ISKCON.

Hopefully you are all mature people who make important decisions affecting your lives only after carefully considering all points. You have to use your intelligence, based upon scrutinizing study of Srila Prabhupada's books, to ascertain whether or not the path and the leader you have chosen will truly benefit you or not.

But it seems that you have already made your decision to follow AV Prabhu. That is entirely up to you. But kindly consider that although AV Prabhu undoubtedly has charisma and leadership qualities, and is using that to attract people towards chanting Hare Krsna, still, he is a relatively inexperienced devotee, and therefore it would not be wise to place one's whole faith in him. After all, to be accepted as a bona fide guru in the Gaudiya Vaisnava paramapara requires not only unquestionable high character, but also a degree of scriptural understanding and maturity that is usually developed over many years of dedicated service to one's own guru and to the preaching mission; which AV Prabhu simply does not have.

As far as ISKCON authorities are concerned, it is their duty to make it clear that the path taught by AV Prabhu is not exactly according to the parampara system and therefore should not be considered to be representative of ISKCON. You should not have too much difficulty with this as anyway you consider yourselves to be separate.

I hope this makes my position in this matter clearer. I have nothing against anyone involved, and wish the best for all.

However, it is my duty as a follower of Srila Prabhupada to uphold the parampara principles and to cooperate with others who also do so.

2 May 2001

P.S. Maharaja please, please and please I beg you to pray for my spiritual strength.

Are you feeling difficulty? Of course I can and must pray for you, but you should also fully follow the process to gain spiritual strength, beginning with rising early and chanting rounds attentively. These are listed in the Nectar of Devotion. Please read this again and follow carefully. That will help you immensely.

6 June 2001

Thankyou very much for approaching this in a responsible manner and for keeping me informed.

However, I was not aware that Srila Prabhupada was in favor of premarital association, although I'm ready to be convinced otherwise if evidence can be provided.

I'm not very much in favor of extended premarital association of possible spouses, as I'm not sure that it serves much purpose, and could be harmful. The idea is to see how the possible spouses get on together, but that can never be properly understood unless they are fully committed to each other and have to face difficulties together. So I don't think that the answer lies so much in attempting to find the perfect match, which is hardly to be found anywhere, as in the sense of commitment that makes the best of a match which may not be perfect.

The traditional formula for the success of Indian marriages was based on character matching backed by firm commitment to marriage vows and the responsibilities that go with them.

In modern times this is considered outdated and irrelevant, but the unhappiness and instability in modern families suggest that the traditional system worked better.

I know that XXX herself is quite cautious, having seen the example of her own parents' divorce. However, I would prefer that you either marry without much delay or drop the whole thing now. If not, if you feel that you must go on with the experiment, then please do so with a clear understanding between you and her that you intend to marry and will only not do so if you find out in the meantime that you are wholly incompatible. In other words, that you are for all intents and purposes engaged.

Otherwise, this "maybe, maybe not" mentality may continue even after marriage, leading to separation due to caprice.

26 July 2001

It's difficult for me to give specific advice about a situation the intricacies of which I am not aware, but I suggest that if you feel shy to approach the relevant persons, that you ask D Prabhu to do so, or at least take D Prabhu's advice after explaining the whole situation to him. He is a wise and considerate devotee and presumably knows the persons involved and is therefore fit to guide you how to specifically behave in this instance.

7 August 2001

I heard that you are now not happy in Krsna consciousness and are aloof from devotional association. But I always knew you as a blissful and enthusiastic devotee. What happened? If there's any encouragement I can give you, please let me know, for having attained the gift of devotional service, we should always go forward positively towards perfection, whatever tests the external energy may present.

8 September 2001

Please excuse the delayed reply. I've been traveling extensively and have had little time and limited internet access.

And thank you for receiving me so nicely in your home and for giving us Nrsimha-prasada. As I quoted on that visit, by the prasada of Nrsimhadeva, a devotee can understand everything.

aham vedmi suko vetti
vyasa vetti na vetti va
sridhara sakalam vetti
sri-nrsimha-prasadatah

"I (Lord Siva) know and Sukadeva knows. Vyasa may or may not know. But Sridhara (Swami) knows everything, by the mercy of (his worshiped Deity) Nrsimhadeva."

I wish you had voiced your doubts to me when I was in *** so that we could have discussed them in some depth, as in writing it would take practically a whole book to cover the details of them all.

Basically, these doubts arise due to the perception that the essential principle in parampara is the giving of mantras from guru to disciple, whereas in our line we stress that the essence lies in giving siksa. In SB 10.80.32 Lord Krsna directly states that the spiritual master who gives siksa is more important than he who gives diksa:

"My dear friend, he who gives a person his physical birth is his first spiritual master, and he who initiates him as a twice-born *brāhmaṇa* and engages him in religious duties is indeed more directly his spiritual master. But the person who bestows transcendental knowledge upon the members of all the spiritual orders of society is one's ultimate spiritual master. Indeed, he is as good as My own self."

Regarding "missing" names in the parampara list, Srila Prabhupada wrote:

"Regarding your question about the disciplic succession coming down from Arjuna, it is just like I have got my disciples, so in the future these many disciples may have many branches of disciplic succession. So in one line of disciples we may not see another name coming from a different line. But this does not mean that person whose name does not appear was not in the disciplic succession. Narada was the Spiritual Master of Vyasadeva, and Arjuna was Vyasadeva's disciple, not as initiated disciple but there was some blood relation between them. So there is connection in this way, and it is not possible to list all such relationships in the short description given in Bhagavad-gita As It Is. Another point is that disciplic succession does not mean one has to be directly a disciple of a particular person. The conclusions which we have tried to explain in our Bhagavad-gita As It Is are the same as those conclusions of Arjuna. Arjuna accepted Krsna as the Supreme Personality of Godhead, and we also accept the same truth under the disciplic succession of Caitanya Mahaprabhu. Things equal to the same thing are equal to one another. This is an axiomatic truth. So there is no difference of opinion of understanding Krsna between ourselves and Arjuna. Another example is that a tree has many branches, and you will find one leaf here and another leaf there. But if you take this leaf and the other leaf and you press them both, you will see that the taste is the same. The taste is the conclusion, and from the taste you can understand that both leaves are from the same tree."

There are literally thousands of gurus in parampara, but in the list given in Bhagavad-gita as It Is, only the names of the most influential acaryas have been given. Srila Prabhupada and other great scholarly acaryas before him were certainly aware that Narottam das Thakur was initiated by Lokanath Goswami and not Krsnadasa Kaviraja, yet deliberately chose to present the paramapara in this way to stress that the essence of parampara lies where the essence has been communicated, which is apparent where there is the life of Krsna consciousness.

In this regard, please consider that Srila Prabhupada most certainly did give Krsna consciousness to the world in a manner that is only possible for a divinely inspired person, and that he was therefore certainly connected to Krsna. To deny this is to deny tangible reality. Therefore it would be wise to accept that Srila Prabhupada is in parampara, even if the technicalities of his being so are difficult to understand. To give an analogy, it would be foolish to deny the existence of milk due to the apparent improbability that it is produced from grass within the body of a cow. Even without understanding the technicalities of how this is so, an intelligent person does not refuse to drink milk, and is thus able to benefit from it. It would be unwise to distrust milk and refuse to accept it on the grounds of not being convinced of its source.

If you distrust Srila Prabhupada and his parampara, then why trust those that are doubting him? They profess to accept Caitanya Mahaprabhu, but Caitanya Mahaprabhu said that His name would be preached in every town and village of the world, and it is therefore clear that Srila Prabhupada has been blessed by Caitanya Mahaprabhu to fulfill His mission. Those who criticize Srila Prabhupada have not been able to serve Caitanya Mahaprabhu in even a billionth of the way that Srila Prabhupada has.

But if we are to doubt, then why accept even Caitanya Mahaprabhu? Many proponents of sastra deny that Lord Caitanya is Bhagavan. Or why accept Krsna? Or why accept sastra? Or that God exists? Or that anything exists?

Doubt is a function of intelligence, but unless doubt is intelligently applied, it becomes skepticism, or doubt of everything, which is foolishness born of the mode of ignorance. For although everything everyone does can be questioned, unless a person accepts some axioms, he cannot start to progress in spiritual life or even function as a sane human being. In other words, we have to put our faith somewhere.

It is not unreasonable to accept as axiomatic that there is God and that Srila Prabhupada was a highly empowered representative of God who was neither deluded himself, nor deluded (i.e., cheated) others. He knew what he was doing and was fully aware of all sastric conclusions and principles.

[Here were extensive citations from my at that time unpublished book on Śrīla Bhaktisiddhanta Sarasvati, and from *Sri Tattva-Sutra* by Srila Bhaktivinoda Thakura; these have been deleted.]

Please consider that although parampara is conventionally understood to mean a diksa line, there is not to my knowledge any sastric injunction that it must be so. Parampara simply means succession, and the true succession is that in which Krsna consciousness is alive and apparent. The term "bhagavata-parampara" was coined to distinguish real, living parampara from the kind of parampara that can, as Krsna indicates in Gita (4.2) become spoiled if even one member in the chain alters it. Although "bhagavata-parampara" may apparently be a relatively new term, bhagavata-parampara is the only true parampara that eternally exists, for it is the descent of the Absolute Truth through the succession of pure devotees.

Indeed the Srimad Bhagavatam which is the most essential scripture for all Gaudiya Vaishnavas, only comes to us via a siksa or bhagavata-parampara. Krsna spoke the essence of the Bhagavata to Brahma. Brahma spoke it to Narada, and Narada in turn taught it to Vyasa. Sukadeva, who was known not to have undergone any diksha samskara, learned its essence from Vyasa. Sukadeva spoke it to Emperor Pariksit. At that time Suta heard it as well, and he in turn spoke it to Saunaka. This is the Bhagavata-guru-parampara, a siksa-parampara. Without the bhagavata-parampara (as mentioned above) there is no Srimad Bhagavatam!

The importance of bhagavatas over conventional gurus is also apparent in that without realized devotees to explain sastra, the very existence of Radha as the essence of Srimad Bhagavatam would remain unknown, for Her name is not mentioned therein.

Much more could be written about this, but please carefully consider this much first. It will also help, if you have not yet done so, to read the English translation of "Brahmana O Vaisnava" by Srila Bhaktisiddhanta Sarasvati Thakur. Try to get a copy there and if you can't get one I'll send a copy from India.

30 September 2001

Not every endeavor in Krsna consciousness works out succesfully. Srila Prabhupada himself started and stopped several projects before founding ISKCON, most notably his League of Devotees in Jhansi, in which, as in your endeavor, persons who had promised to help later reneged. On seeing that circumstances had changed, Srila Prabhupada also changed to serve Krsna in a manner more likely to be fruitful. So I don't think that in this case it will be wrong for you to also face the fact that every endeavor in this world, even those done for Lord Krsna, cannot be successful, and thus go on to serve Him in another way.

22 October 2001

Congratulations on your success in your studies. It's also heartwarming to know of your spiritual rejuvenation. But it's really a pity, almost a curse, that your husband doubts Srila Prabhupada, especially considering that practically all sampradayas in India (even non-Vaisnavas) accept him as an extraordinarily empowered pure devotee, and that only a tiny handful of not very prominent people have anything bad to say against Srila Prabhupada or his movement. If your husband is to accept shelter in another sampradaya then probably most auspicious, considering that he is apparently unable to directly accept Srila Prabhupada yet has strong attachment to Lord Nrsimhadeva, would be for him to enter the Sri sampradaya, whose members (at least all those I've met), although adherents of a somewhat different siddhanta, are nevertheless highly appreciative of Srila Prabhupada.

Hoping this meets you well and ever improving in Krsna consciousness.

3 December 2001

In many places in his books Srila Prabhupada stated that there is no love in the material world but only a reflection of it in the form of lust. As well as all other kinds of relations too. So the meaning is that love is only possible and real in relations with God and for His pleasure, otherwise it'll be some or other form of lust. Right?

But also in many other places he used the word love to describe relations between husband and wife—not only between a devotee and God. Like Devahuti served Kardama in intimacy and with love. One can find many references in the Vedabase.

We can see that actually love is possible between living beings as well.

Many places in the Vedas describe the family life and relations in it etc. Other philosophies also talk about yin-yang etc.—the need to have a balance of these energies. Also lots of cases in ISKCON history provide the examples of the need for love or whatever it's called.

So what is that if not love? And then what is love? Is it not possible between living entities? How is it supposed to be if it is possible (what I believe)? How to make it successful and not interfering with our love of God?

I feel that the need for finding the "life-partner" or what is it called properly is always there even may be for some realised souls. And the desire to find such and fullfil these loving relations is essential and may be also important in our growth to love of God. I don't know how to express or explain it properly—I'm sure you had thought, discussed, and studied all that with more experienced persons and know and understand it much better. So I hope to get your explanations.

I don't want to bother you much, yet I wish I could have your sufficient attention and kind help for full clarification of all this matter for me. Otherwise I'm not sure even how to continue with my life and my spiritual practice.

Love is ultimately meant for Krsna but is also shared between jivas who cooperate to serve Krsna and to mutually enhance their love for Krsna. Any other form of love in this material world may appear to be very meaningful but ultimately isn't as it simply entangles the living beings in illusion and resultant repeated birth and death.

Nevertheless, for stability in society the cultivation of love within marriage is recommended for persons at a certain level. Such affection can help save one from bestial irresponsibility, yet it is also entangling and is therefore ultimately to be transcended. However, if family responsibility is renounced prematurely, there is a high risk of falldown. The Vedic directions for family life may thus sometimes appear to contradict those for sannyasis. Neither are incorrect, but are meant for persons on different levels. Most people are not ready for renunciation, although without coming to the stage of material non-attachment, no-one can achieve the perfection of life, namely full Krsna consciousness.

There is no harm in having a life partner, but it should be understood that there is nothing inherently spiritual in such a relationship, although it can be spiritualized if service to Krsna is made the center of the relationship.

It is certainly important that devotees develop meaningful relationships between themselves. Krsna consciousness is not meant to be impersonal but to bring out the best in each person and to share that with others. However, relationships in Krsna consciousness are not established on a sentimental basis, but with a true understanding of what it means to love all living beings by seeing them as parts and parcels of Krsna.

It is better not to be enamored by such materialistic philosophies as those expounding yin and yang. They may have useful insights for living in the material world, but cannot lead us beyond it. The perfection of life is not to balance yin and yang but to develop pure love of Krsna.

(The following is from Srila Prabhupada-lilamrta, Ch. 24)

"Swamiji," he began, "may I ask a question?"

"Yes," Srila Prabhupada replied, stopping his pacing.

"If a boy is separate from a girl, then how can he learn to love her?" Prabhupada began to walk back and forth again, chanting on his beads. After a moment he turned and said softly, "Love? Love is for Krsna." And he walked toward the window and looked down at the street below. "You want a girl? Pick one." He pointed toward some women passing on the street. "There is no love in this material world," he said. "Love is for Krsna."

For you it is advisable to fully consider the meaning of responsibility in family life and on that basis to prepare yourself to enter into a stable religious marital partnership.

13 December 2001

It is with a mixture of sadness and happiness that I heard of K's passing. Sadness in sharing your sadness, and happiness that Krsna has released him from his state of suffering and brought him to a better destination. Throughout his life he performed no sin and was always in the association of devotees, taking prasada, hearing and chanting Hare Krsna, and seeing the Deities. It seems that K was an exalted soul who just had a little more purification to make and that now it is done Krsna has taken him to Him. As a loving mother and sister you have done your duty and more to him, thus giving you the chance to serve a Vaishnava. Naturally you will feel the pain of losing your son and brother, but you need not lament, knowing that he is safe in the shelter of Krsna.

20 December 2001

"Women in general are unable to speculate like philosophers, but they are blessed by the Lord because they believe at once in the superiority and almightiness of the Lord, and thus they offer obeisances without reservation." (SB 1.8.20 purport)

Perhaps it would have been more appropriate to have said "women in general are less likely to speculate like philosophers" ... women in Krsna consciousness do enjoy philosophising and discussing—I believe it would be fairer to say that whilst women are able to speculate like philosophers, they are blessed by the Lord in that they accept more readily the tenets and precepts of a philosophy and religion without the NECESSITY to philosophise ...

Although it is nowadays a fashion to challenge what Srila Prabhupada says and present one's own opinion as superior, it should be remembered that as miniscule beings our intelligence is insignificant before that of realized acaryas, and that therefore the basic principle of understanding Vaisnava philosophy is faith in the words of such acaryas. *Guru mukha padma vakya cittete kariya aikya, ara na kariha mane asa.* If what an acarya says seems difficult to accept or apparently defies observed reality, a submissive disciple may present his doubt to get it cleared, as Arjuna did (see Bg 4.4). A man or woman who with intrinsic faith (which Srila Prabhupada mentions above is more common in women) thus applies their intelligence to understand the acaryas' teachings is blessed by them with realization.

2002

8 January 2002

Praying that there is a little space somewhere by your lotus feet for me.

My duty is to hold onto Srila Prabhupada's lotus feet. That means to follow his instructions. So if you follow my instructions, which I am duty bound to give as nondifferent from Srila Prabhupada's instructions, then we can all happily go back to Godhead together.

1 February 2002

Thankyou so much for your kind letter. Yes, I remember you writing to me some time ago.

It is good to purify earned laxmi by giving donations.

"Lord Sri Caitanya Mahaprabhu is the father and inaugurator of the sankirtana movement. One who worships Him by sacrificing his life, money, intelligence and words for the sankirtana movement is recognized by the Lord and endowed with His blessings. All others may be said to be foolish, for of all sacrifices in which a man may apply his energy, a sacrifice made for the sankirtana movement is the most glorious." (from Srila Prabhupada's purport to CC Adi 3.77-78)

By Krsna's grace I am now receiving sufficient laxmi for my publishing work but every little helps and Srila Prabhupada has

240

written that a Vaisnava sannyasi never refuses a donation so if you would like to send some you are most welcome to, although please don't strain yourself in doing so.

It is certainly good to be near a temple. Despite whatever problems may be there in ISKCON temples they still give the opportunity for hearing and chanting about and serving Krsna and His devotees. Kalacandji is exceptionally beautiful.

Actually I didn't resign from the GBC as I was never on it. I respect the GBC members. They're all great souls individually but as a group they just don't seem to function properly.

I have no objection to having female followers as I consider it my duty to Srila Prabhupada to instruct devotees who approach me for guidance, regardless of the body they come in. In the traditional Vedic culture which we are supposed to try to revive, women were directed by their husbands, but your case, like many others, doesn't fit that mold.

I generally advise devotees to take shelter of a senior devotee who they can regularly associate with, i.e. those who preach in the areas they live in. Nevertheless I have a few disciples in USA.

14 February 2002

1. Which is better, atheism or Mayavada and why?

This is a little like asking, "Which is worse, yellow stool or brown stool?" Both are despicable. It is difficult to give a clear answer as there are many strains both of atheism and Mayavada. And actually Mayavada is simply another form of atheism. Caitanya Mahaprabhu considered Mayavada more dangerous than Buddhist agnosticism (See Cc. Madhya 6.168).

2. Some devotees say that we should not wear silk clothes. What is your opinion?

There is no restriction against devotees wearing silk.

3. Is it a must that devotees should take brahmin initiation? What are the qualifications for it?

It is not a must as harinama alone can give all perfection. Brahminical initiation is required only for doing Deity worship, especially formally in temples and even for home worship of Sri Sri Radha-Krsna. Brahminical initiation may also be awarded to devotees not engaged in Deity worship, but they must be strictly following the principles of sadhana-bhakti, by rising early, chanting attentively, studying sastra, eating only Krsna prasada, etc. They should also have a proper understanding of Vaisnava philosophy.

4 March 2002

I have a doubt related to the Kurukshetra battlefield. It is regarding the size of the battlefield and the number of men, horses, elephants, and chariots it could accommodate. Since you are amongst the highly read swamijis in ISKCON, I humbly forward this doubt for clarification.

The total number of warriors alone numbers to 65 crores, and probably another 10 crores, 5 crores, and 1 crores of horses, elephants, and chariots respectively.

How could the battlefield accommodate all these men, animals, and carriages? The warriors definitely needed their support staff for cooking and sanitation. Animals would require food and shelter. They would have picketed at least a week before the commencement of the battle.

I am comparing the above mentioned numbers with the current population of India at 100 crores, spread over the entire country and yet struggling for accommodation and daily food and infrastructure. How was it possible for the Kurukshetra Bhumi to accommodate such a vast number of men, animals, and equipment?

I can't "explain" this because it's not explainable in terms consistent with observable reality. But it makes sense to accept that there is more to reality than the observable. Some things are inconceivable (acintya).

The nature of Krsna's acintya-sakti is nicely illustrated by the following story of a visit by Lord Brahma to Krsna in Dvaraka. In the story, Krsna first responds to Brahma's request to see Him by having His secretary ask, "Which Brahma wishes to see Me?" Brahma later begins his conversation with Krsna by asking why Krsna made this inquiry:

"Why did you inquire which Brahma had come see You? What is the purpose of such an inquiry? Is there any other Brahma besides me within this universe?"

Upon hearing this, Sri Krsna smiled and immediately meditated. Unlimited Brahmas arrived instantly. These Brahmas had different numbers of heads. Some had ten heads, some twenty, some a hundred, some a thousand, some ten thousand, some a hundred thousand, some ten million, and others a hundred million. No one can count the number of faces they had.

There also arrived many Lord Sivas with various heads numbering one hundred thousand and ten million.

Many Indras also arrived, and they had hundreds of thousands of eyes all over their bodies.

When the four-headed Brahma of this universe saw all these opulences of Krsna, he became very bewildered and considered himself a rabbit among many elephants.

All the Brahmas who came to see Krsna offered their respects at His lotus feet, and when they did this, their helmets touched His lotus feet. No one can estimate the inconceivable potency of Krsna. All the Brahmas who were there were resting in the one body of Krsna. When all the helmets struck together at Krsna's lotus feet, there was a tumultuous sound. It appeared that the helmets themselves were offering prayers unto Krsna's lotus feet.

With folded hands, all the Brahmas and Sivas began to offer prayers unto Lord Krsna, saying, "O Lord, You have shown me a great favor. I have been able to see Your lotus feet."

Each of them then said, "It is my great fortune, Lord, that You have called me, thinking of me as Your servant. Now let me know what Your order is so that I may carry it on my heads."

Lord Krsna replied, "Since I wanted to see all of you together, I have called all of you here. All of you should be happy. Is there any fear of the demons?"

They replied, "By Your mercy, we are victorious everywhere. Whatever burden there was upon the earth You have taken away by descending on that planet."

This is the proof of Dvaraka's opulence: all the Brahmas thought, "Krsna is now staying in my jurisdiction." Thus the opulence of Dvaraka was perceived by each and every one of them. Although they were all assembled together, no one could see anyone but himself.

Lord Krsna then bade farewell to all the Brahmas there, and after offering their obeisances, they all returned to their respective homes [Cc. Madhya 21.65-80].

In this story it is significant that each of the Brahmas remained within his own universe. This means that Krsna was simultaneously manifesting His Dvaraka pastimes in all of those universes. Each Brahma except ours thought that he was alone with Krsna in Dvaraka within his own universe, but by Krsna's grace our Brahma could simultaneously see all the others. This illustrates that Krsna has access to all locations at once, and it also shows that, by Krsna's grace, different living beings can be given different degrees of spatial access, either permanently or temporarily.

"With your experimental logic you cannot understand. It is inconceivable. Just accept the sastra. True understanding only comes by the mercy of the spiritual master. You cannot adjust the description of the Bhagavatam within the limits of your knowledge. Our Narada Muni went to Vaikuntha. After coming back, he told a cobbler about an elephant passing through the eye of a needle. The cobbler said, 'Oh, Narayana is so great!' But a brahmana said, 'It is simply stories!' Narada then asked the cobbler, 'How can you believe that Narayana was passing an elephant through the head of a needle?' The cobbler explained, 'Why not? We are sitting under a banyan tree. There are so many fruits; and each fruit contains so many seeds, which each will grow into a huge banyan tree.' Everything is inconceivable, and these rascals want to bring it as conceivable. Don't be puffed up by your so-called education. It has no value." Srila Prabhupada gave us the spiritual solution to a mundane question. (From *TKG's Diary*)

Srila Jiva Gosvami says that unless we accept this principle that Krsna or God has got inconceivable power, acintya-sakti, we cannot understand. (Srila Prabhupada's lecture, London, August 27, 1973)

15 May 2002

Another approach is just not to take it too seriously. Laugh it off. When you have nice association and service to Srila Prabhupada, Sri Sri Gaura Nitai, Sri Sri Radha London Isvara, Sri Sri Sri Jagannath, Subhadra, Baladeva, and Giri Govardhana, then does it matter so much if *** Prabhu sometimes seems unreasonable? Better to rejoice for the good things than lament for the not-so-good.

I hope this little advice will be of some help.

21 May 2002

Is there any reference where Srila Prabhupada says that Chanakya Pandit is a mayavadi/impersonalist?

And is it true that Srila Prabhupada carefully used only those quotes of Chanakya Pandit for preaching purposes?

Could some of Chanakya's thinking be different from Srila Prabhupada?

It is well known from his writings that Canakya Pandita was not a devotee. Srila Prabhupada often referred to him as a great politician and moralist, but never as a devotee. And if he wasn't a devotee it could be implied that he was some kind of impersonalist, although I know of no incident of Srila Prabhupada explicitly referring to him as such.

Yet we can quote any statement if not contrary to our siddhanta, even if spoken by a person whose overall siddhanta is contrary to ours. Canakya hardly touched directly on spiritual matters so it is not known what his siddhanta was, if any. His maxims are mostly concerned with material wisdom, which is useful also for all classes of aspiring transcendentalists to know. We can accept as authoritative at least those statements of Canakya's that Srila Prabhupada would cite.

21 April 2002

I am very happy to have accepted you as my disciple and pray to Srila Prabhupada that I may properly discharge my duty to him by guiding you according to his divine wishes.

I was rather astonished when I saw the amount you gave as dakshina. Of course different people have different capacities to donate, and what really matters in a donation is the feeling that goes with it. Yet it is not everyone who even having the ability to do so makes large offerings, so I can understand that your intention in doing so is very pure, and I thank you for that.

A word of caution though—Srila Prabhupada once asked a householder devotee if he could really afford to give the amount he had proffered. So please be careful in managing your household finances. In this regard please see Cc. Madhya 15.93–96.

And please go on chanting Hare Krsna and being happy!

May 2002

(Regarding book distribution)

Maya always gives some excuse. In summer it's too hot, in winter too cold, in monsoon too wet. In the meantime people are going to hell. The men should go out both in the morning and also after 5.30 p.m. in the evening. When I did book distribution in Andhra Pradesh in the summer we would be out for at least 6-7 hours a day.

22 May 2002

Thankyou for the appreciation of my humble services to you. I've also appreciated the excellent service you have rendered to me in the last few months.

Regarding your problem: such things happen and have been happening and will happen. The attraction between male and female is the basic principle of material existence. Now that your mind has become attached to that lady it should just become unattached. Use a little intelligence and consider practically that anyway she is older than you and from a totally different background so even if you were to marry at some point it shouldn't be to her. At least I would never recommend it.

Unmarried women are always in anxiety about how to get a man, so they can't be blamed. But you'd better get a hold of your intelligence and let these thoughts subside.

If possible you might take up the service of dressing Srila Prabhupada. And certainly you must pray for his mercy.

And whatever the state of your mind may be, you have to continue your service.

26 May 2002

Yes, best if *** is going for family life, is to move now. +++ Prabhu
and yourself may please guide him in this regard. Your letter is
not inappropriate; it is most appropriate as it is with genuine
concern for a godbrother. I am not dissatisfied with this as I only
want the best for *** and if ashram life is not best for him then
let him be a Krsna conscious grhastha with my full blessings.
Much better that he goes to Dubai rather than Africa.

27 May 2002

Obviously you are in a very tight situation. Kaliyuga is so bad
that even if one wishes to serve the Lord, he is often constrained
by adverse circumstances. It is very common, not only in your
case. The apparent solution would be to drop everything and
join an ISKCON ashram, but nowadays it seems that young men
who wish to do so are mostly being advised to first finish their
exams. There are some good reasons for this. One is that often
young men wish to join more to be free from suffering than out
of desire to serve Krsna, and thus their resolve to really dedicate
themselves is not strong. Another reason, which in my mind is not
very valid, is that relatives become upset. Sometimes they cause
difficulties for devotees. Also it may be that the young man is
sincere to serve but not very mature in character, and therefore
a little struggle to be Krsna conscious in adverse circumstances
can be helpful to him.

Anyway as your exams are up ahead you might as well do them,
but don't neglect to chant your rounds also. After that I have
no objection if you join an ISKCON ashram as long as your
immediate family agrees. The reason for this is that you tried
joining an ashram once but then your family members brought
you back home, so there is no use in repeating such antics. ***
Prabhu previously told me that your parents would agree to you
joining ISKCON N, so that could be an option, to join there then
after some time shift to another ashram.

Although you are finding difficulties due to lack of association, you are in a much better situation than devotees living at home whose parents are against Krsna consciousness. So go on chanting, read Srila Prabhupada's books, and follow the basic principles of sadhana-bhakti as best you can. If we are sincere then Krsna will help us.

You may chant my pranama-mantra when you have steadily and regularly chanted 16 rounds daily without fail for at least six months.

I've added *** Prabhu as a receiver here in case he wishes to further comment.

30 May 2002

Thankyou for your letter. I'm very sorry that you are working so hard in conditions that are neither materially even slightly pleasant nor conducive to Krsna consciousness. Can't you get another job? Why go through such torture just for some money? Better to earn less money and lead a better life. I can offer you enough money to live and a lifelong engagement in book production. But somehow you feel obliged to destroy yourself in ugra-karma.

It is certainly proper to contribute some of your earnings for propagating Krsna consciousness. But you are right: more than money I want your soul.

25 May 2002

My best regards to you. Thankyou for sending the photo. Do I recognize M and S in it? It looks like Hari got baptized.

Fear of death is a prime symptom of material consciousness so it is not surprising if we are afflicted by it. But by advancement in Krsna consciousness we should transcend that fear by having full faith in Krsna's protection.

Can I say that I am free from fear of death? I could say so, but it remains to be seen when the time comes. I often remember that I have to die soon and there is so much to be done in Srila Prabhupada's service so I don't want to waste time. That is the best way to fear death. But we may be confident also that if we sincerely serve Krsna in this life, then even if we don't remember Him at the time of death, He will remember us, and will surely arrange that we again get an opportunity to serve Him, either in this world or in Goloka. So even if we feel fear of death, we can remember Krsna's promise (na me bhakta pranasyati) and not worry about it.

You wrote: "How can I develop the desire to return to Krsna? Lately, I can't stop thinking about it." That means the desire is there! Now it may be cultivated by very seriously hearing and chanting about Krsna. Actually Krsna is so wonderful and this material world so nasty that it is only due to total insanity that we do not immediately surrender to Krsna.

11 June 2002

I received a letter from a prisoner.

He's a prisoner who read a BTG article by me and has asked me to recommend an Indian girl to him for correspondence with view to eventual marriage. It's an unusual request but he seems to have good intentions—he wants a chaste devotee wife.

However I won't accede to his request because that's not the way things are done here. Still, traditional Indian families find spouses for their sons and daughters, and it would be frowned upon to enter into correspondence like that. Americans may or may not understand or appreciate this but that's the way it is and I—especially being a sannyasi—don't want to go against this.

Could you please kindly convey this to him in a manner that he wouldn't be offended? Presumably you are already in contact with him. If not, you got a new contact.

23 June 2002

Paper marriage seems to be the best solution in the present situation. But more problems will arise. Who will look after *** when you work? If you work then it will be difficult to maintain sadhana. If your health is poor then it may be difficult to work and then your health will decline more and how will the medical bills be paid?

Anyway I am sure you must have thought about these problems. Please remain strong by remembering Kuntidevi and other great women devotees of the past who had to suffer much but kept full faith in Krsna.

30 June 2002

Thankyou for your news and appreciation. Please continue to keep faith in Srila Prabhupada, Vaisnavas, and the process of Krsna consciousness. Whatever difficulties may be there in life, if we remain fixed in our determination to serve Krsna, then surely He will help us.

30 June 2002

It is not at all proper that you disobeyed my instruction by failing to go to S. You did not even inform anyone, putting at least me into anxiety—I didn't know if you were alive or dead. You should now grow up and stop behaving whimsically like a child. Under the circumstances, I don't approve of your going to Puri for Rathayatra. You should immediately proceed to S. Did you send the letter I gave to you to give to G Prabhu? If not, hand it to him on arrival.

1 August 2002

This is all nice news. Please try to gradually infiltrate Krsna consciousness amongst the people there. You must also study

Srila Prabhupada's books daily otherwise you will not know what it is that you are supposed to be spreading.

Please note that the effectiveness of a devotee's lecturing cannot be measured by how it "suits the audience" nor is it required to tell many stories. Our aim is not to entertain the public but to give them real spiritual knowledge. We shall not imitate the entertaining so-called sadhus but will speak the truth for the benefit of those who are serious to receive it, never mind if that is only one in a million.

To understand this important point more fully please read "On Speaking Strongly in Srila Prabhupada's Service" which is the third section of my book, "My Memories of Srila Prabhupada."[12]

3 August 2002

It is now common knowledge that [you are] practicing and propagating behavior much discordant with standard parampara Vaisnavism. ***, this is a request from a very junior and insignificant Godbrother that you not spoil your life and that of the many others who have placed their faith in you as a bona fide representative of Srila Prabhupada. You have received tremendous mercy from Srila Prabhupada so please do not risk jeopardising your link with His Divine Grace by failing to faithfully and strictly follow the infallible path he has shown us. Please do not try to exercise your apparently vast but actually very tiny intelligence in judging matters inconceivable. You are known as a lion so please do not again become a mouse as have several "greats" before you such as B and K.

8 August 2002

Thankyou very much for taking the time and trouble to answer my letter even though it is clearly displeasing to you. And thank

---

12. "On Speaking Strongly in Srila Prabhupada's Service" is now published as a separate book.

you also for correcting my curtness. I'll try to bear your good advice in mind despite being a prude with no innate tendency for pleasing speech.

Although my previous letter may hardly suggest so, I like many others in Srila Prabhupada's wonderful family have always had a special regard for your unique, bold, frank, and incisive preaching. In the last few years however I maybe due to being of conservative disposition have been dismayed at your markedly altered approach. I didn't express this to you earlier, and can understand why my now firing a salvo strikes you as insulting and inappropriate.

It is true that misunderstandings are liable to arise when a person judges another's actions without consulting him as to his motive or perspective, and that if in doubt about another it is therefore prudent to openmindedly and nonaccusatively present that misgiving to him for clarification. Yet judging from the widespread concern being expressed by many sober Godbrothers as also by several of your disciples, the present seems to be a critical hour for your spiritual life. So kindly, by your Vaisnava quality of seeing good in others, adjudge my impropriety as based on consternation rather than malintent, and further please carefully examine if there is any substance in my otherwise denigrating missives.

That you express becoming stronger and stronger in spiritual life rather confirms my fears, for although you are far from being as outlandish as K, in many ways your approach seems to resemble his when he started overtly diverting from practices given us by Srila Prabhupada. At that time K appeared, to himself and those around him, to be receiving extraordinary blessings. But he would not listen to the many Godbrothers warning him that actually he was deviating, and thus he had to become a mouse.

Several other erstwhile leaders previously embarked on new courses that initially to them seemed wonderful, but that soon proved disastrous to themselves and whoever they had taken along with them. Surely it would be better that those who have inherited the mantle of Srila Prabhupada first consult with and take the full considered blessings of his trusted representatives before attempting simply on the basis of their own inclinations to institute novel approaches to devotional service.

So I beseech you, our dear and revered ***, to deeply reflect on whether your present trajectory is indeed truly satisfying to our beloved Srila Prabhupada, or whether it may lead you to disaster and humiliation. Of course Srila Prabhupada is always there to give guidance through the instructions in his books and his presence in your heart; nevertheless realizations thus received need be confirmed by submitting them to his faithful disciples.

***, please tolerate this maybe foolish prattling of a Godbrother inferior to you in every respect, who longs to again admire our leader and hero ***, taking Srila Prabhupada's full blessings on his head, once more dynamically spearheading the preaching battle in a manner for which he is singularly empowered. ***, we tiny souls need your guidance and inspiration so please don't veer away from the straight and sure path Srila Prabhupada gave us.

Thankyou very much for your patience if you have kindly read this far.

24 August 2002

I can understand that you feel very much upset by B Prabhu's untimely demise, and that you wish to spend some time in Vrindavan. But who will now oversee the sankirtana party? BP and JN cannot continue by themselves. P and DK Prabhus also wanted to join the party soon. Now is the time for you to step forward and take up the leadership. If you don't then the party will collapse. Just because one soldier dies on the battlefield doesn't mean that others should leave. Surely B Prabhu would want you to accept this responsibility and carry on the fight. Please don't disappoint me this time.

2 October 2002

I hope you are now more peaceful at heart and better prepared to accept the challenges of life in this difficult world.

As a noble hearted devotee you naturally aspire for fairness and propriety, so you should strive for these qualities in your dealings. However please do not be disappointed if you do not always find them where you had most hoped them to be. Pragmatism in Krsna consciousness is an essential quality without acquiring which a devotee cannot properly serve Krsna. This Krsna taught to Arjuna in Bhagavad-gita, so please read Bhagavad-gita daily and that will help you immeasurably.

4 December 2002

I am very proud and happy that you are in an exemplary manner fulfilling your duty as a Krsna conscious wife and mother. There is no more important service that you could be doing at the present time and although it is difficult for you, simply by being a chaste wife and bringing up children in Krsna consciousness you will become glorious. You are lucky to have such a nice devotee husband so please go on serving him to your best ability. Be patient, for when children are young is the most demanding period for mothers, but sooner than you can now imagine they will be teenagers and then married with their own children.

2003

8 January 2003

Thankyou for your letter and explanations therein. I can understand that you are much concerned about the welfare of others, which is the quality of a true Vaisnava.

However it seems that your concern for the welfare of one jiva has brought you to such a materially attached and emotional state that it is unlikely that you are ready to take my advice in this matter. Indeed from the very beginning of this affair you never consulted me or anyone else but went ahead with your private plans for a marriage that no one but your two selves approves of.

Your praying to Lord Nityananda for guidance is meaningless if you avoid taking guidance from your guru.

Anyway, *yatecchasi tatha kuru*—it seems that you will do as you wish even if I instruct you otherwise, so it's probably best that I not attempt to do so. But if at all you are ready to heed my words then please do not rush into anything, and do not marry before at least two years and until you have a reliable means of income.

Thankyou for all the nice work you have done on my books. I asked *** Prabhu to take up the service of layout as your position now is unpredictable; any time you may run off, so it's better that such an eventuality not upset production of my books.

21 March 2003

Thankyou for your deeply felt and meaningful letter.

Yes I may certainly accept you to be under my direction in the service of Srila Prabhupada and the acaryas. You should of course also remain under the direction of local senior devotees and, especially after marriage, of your devotee husband. I think you understand this point.

Cooking standards in restaraunts need not be as strict as in temples. Cleanliness should be high in both, and ideally initiated brahmanas should cook in both. But if initiated brahmanas are not available, others who strictly follow the regulative principles may cook. If cooking is however performed by formally initiated persons who do not strictly follow, then their infected consciousness will enter the food which will be unacceptable to Krsna and cannot benefit others.

Thankyou for your kind appreciation of this fallen soul's attempt to further sprinkle some drops from the great inundation of mercy that Srila Prabhupada brought. Such encouragement helps keep me enthused on the often thorny path to be traversed in this nasty material world. Please pray that I ever remain fixed in Srila Prabhupada's divine service.

21 March 2003

That your endeavour did not work out is no cause for disappointment. The important point is that you tried, and Krsna will be pleased with that. Even our most esteemed and beloved Srila Prabhupada had to undergo many apparently unfruitful attempts before his mission prospered. So please remain faithful and go on with your creative plans in Krsna's service, and He will surely bless you.

21 March 2003

Actually I had given the name Krsnarama, but if it was heard as Krsnabalarama and you are happy with that name then you may keep it as such. The meaning is the same. Srila Prabhupada sometimes for various reasons adjusted or changed names after giving them.

Radhamamata devi dasi is a purely spiritual and perfect name, although it may sound odd to materially infected ears. Even some of the names that Srila Prabhupada gave may have sounded odd, but devotees accepted them with faith that their spiritual master knew what was best. Mamata is a name of Srimati Radharani. Maybe because it is a common name (usually rendered in Hindi as Mamta) people think that it is not spiritual, but I was thinking that you could explain the name Radhamamata to others and thus give the proper spiritual perspective: that Radha is the personification of mamata, which is actually meant for Krsna; or that the perfection of mamata is to assist Radha in Her service to Krsna. But the name Radhamamata may be changed also. Which name do you deem better?

22 March 2003

Lord Sri Krsna is most kind to keep you in a similar situation to that of Maharajas Khatvanga and Pariksit, who in expectation of their imminent demise engaged in bhagavad-bhakti with an intenseness that cannot ordinarily be achieved. You are even more fortunate to suffer further material difficulties so that you cannot but pray for the shelter of Krsna's lotus feet.

You have asked my opinion about your intended marriage, but I think I will defer that to Puri Maharaja, who is of course far senior to me and is a greater wish-fulfilling tree than I could ever be. It is best that you get his direction first rather than I say something and Maharaja says something else, which might be confusing for you. So please see what Maharaja says and then, if you so wish, elicit my further comments.

Please go on chanting at least sixteen rounds of the Hare Krsna maha-mantra daily, with faith and attention.

7 April 2003

For the farm project in SA to succeed it needs not only to be okayed by the local ISKCON authorities, but overseen by them with a high degree of enthusiasm, commitment, and Krsna conscious missionary spirit. Considering that such positive input is highly unlikely, it is better that you shift to where your Krsna consciousness can grow, without which simply growing food is meaningless.

Actually GS Prabhu sent me a copy of his reply to you, to which my comment was:

"Bhakta G's heart is in farming for Krsna. However in the present situation there don't seem to be any viable openings. Under the circumstances going to Leicester for a year and seeing how things work out would be a good idea, especially if in the meantime he could study bhakti sastri etc."

I suggest you shift to Leicester, possibly with the option of joining me for about two months later this year while I travel in Europe and USA—for which you'd need to get some laxmi together (maybe from book distribution).

7 April 2003

I suggest that you write a humble but frank letter to the *** leaders and send a copy to B Maharaja, expressing your concerns at the way things are going. At first they may get angry but later if they see them themselves becoming unpopular and the yatra and their spiritual lives going down, they may turn to you for help before things get irretrievably bad. Writing such a letter wouldn't make you popular but at least you would have had the satisfaction of having done your duty, as did Vidura before he was driven out of the palace.

Your humility leaves me wondering how to reply. Surely, by distributing so many books and enthusing others to do so, you have done and are doing far more than I in Srila Prabhupada's service.

Thankyou for the offer to visit Malaga. I've been there a few times before. Let's see if I can fit it in. The only problem is that the more places I go the more I get spread out and the less time I have for writing.

15 April 2003

Different people come to Krsna consciousness at different levels and naturally some are more advanced due to previous practice. We should not be discouraged if we are less advanced than others. Rather we should be most grateful that despite our disqualifications guru and Gauranga are giving us a chance to be purified. We should take that opportunity and seriously apply ourselves to the process. Unless we follow strict sadhana then how can we hope to be free from bad thoughts? It is useless to consult a doctor unless we are ready to accept his advice.

You certainly have serious problems that may be difficult to overcome. But if you have faith in the process then Lord Caitanya, the savior of the fallen, will help you. Chant Hare Krsna loudly and dance madly in kirtan.

Please continue Deity worship. But if you cannot control wicked thoughts then better worship Deities by loud sankirtan.

Namaparadha can never give suddha nama so strive to at least come to the namabhasa stage.

More later when we meet.

16 April 2003

Naturally I'm extremely concerned because it is horrible to see anyone losing faith in Krsna consciousness and what to speak of you who are very very dear to me. Yet it is hardly surprising that exposure to the nasty academic system has worn you down.

I took the liberty of intimating your plight to my Godbrother *** Prabhu who is the best person for you to speak to for two reasons: one, because he spent many years in academics and is intimate with its pitfalls; and two, because in the galaxy of wonderful devotees in ISKCON, he is a very special soul which anyone who knows him will attest to. His association is so uplifting that I feel your present doubts may be Krsna's arrangement to make contact with such an advanced and humble devotee. He's agreed to talk to you so please without delay phone him and let me know how it goes.

You could also phone me but extended conversations would be costly, plus I'll be unable to get into long conversations for the next 5 days or so due to traveling and a full schedule.

I'm praying to Krsna for you even though I'm not qualified to, but surely Krsna will hear prayers for His devotee in trouble.

asraya laiya bhaje, krsna tare nahe tyaje[13]

21 April 2003

You are encountering some difficulties in your present service, in that your integrity has been called into question. You encountered similar difficulties previously. You wish to change your place of service, as you had changed previously. However it is likely that if you change to another place then problems will arise there also. I suggest that it is therefore better that you continue your

---

13. Whoever takes shelter of Krsna and worships Him will never be abandoned by Him. (From a song by Narottama Dasa Thakura)

service in the present place and by exhibiting excellent behavior and service attitude gradually convince those who doubt you that you are after all a sincere devotee.

25 April 2003

It is disappointing, and indeed ridiculous and insulting, that you think that I give unconditional support to anyone.

I have previously explained to you the rationale of my approach on this issue. Either you have forgotten or did not understand, in which case I could repeat the same. If however you insist on maintaining a different outlook then there is nothing I can do.

You have more than once complained about this yet restrained me from taking up the matter. Then again you complain that I don't take action. This is unreasonable.

Please send me the names of the many devotees who are unable to understand my "unconditional support."

Health permitting, it would be good if you go for some time on traveling sankirtana after finishing work on ***. Also, please read a chapter of Krsna book every day.

28 April 2003

It's best not to make major decisions, such as dropping your studies and going to Mayapur, on a purely emotional basis. Even if the emotion is powerful, as is despair, it is better to take things as calmly and cooly as possible.

Please therefore contact *** Prabhu first. I'm sure that if you talk with him regularly—it need not be about the present dilemma you face, better that you simply hear his wonderful Krsna katha—then that alone will help you immensely. I didn't mention that he also studied Sanskrit at the university and will be engaged as a BBT translator. So he should be able to both closely empathize with you and also help you with vision as to how you can utilize your studies in Krsna's service.

I'll of course be very happy to see you in Mayapur, and I'd really love to have you back working on my books. Yet I'm still inclined to advise that, as you have come so far in studies, you might as well finish them—as was Srila Prabhupada's policy. But the bottom line is, do whatever is best to progress (or at least stay in) Krsna consciousness—which may also entail fulfilling social obligations.

Is Krsna consciousness real? Yes, of course.

30 April 2003

But where to get detailed instructions about the details of ideal family life? (The one that's possible in Kali-yuga. I find Srimad Bhagavatam instructions too elevated.)

Do you mean you want to fight with your husband? Ideal means among other things not to fight. Be subtle, not gross. Please see the attached file, from a lecture by Radha Govinda Maharaja. Also please discuss this on the dharmapatni forum.

Congrats to your husband on his bold stance. Support him, encourage him. He is a good soul.

I have much appreciation of Sridhara Maharaja which has greatly increased seeing his strong desire to serve and preach despite death knocking at his door. I especially appreciate how he gives time to people and is very personal with them. We are very different persons but I don't have any major points of disagreement with him.

It's true that in the beginning Srila Prabhupada encouraged the rock opera but later he stopped it. If that lady's rock group distributes 900 Gitas then I'll also encourage it. Nevertheless the points that I made stand and have nothing to do with my being in India. Points such as that many people in the west appreciate kirtana as something different, because they hear rock all the time. Why would a cultured woman want to play in a rock band?

12 May 2003

I must admit I'm very happy to know that there is some serious endeavor for publishing my books in Croatian because up to now there really hasn't been much to show. I consider that writing books is at this stage my most important service to Srila Prabhupada so I take it very seriously and I would certainly be grateful to my disciples if they could help me produce them in different languages. These books are helping people to take up, remain steady in, and advance in Krsna consciousness. From the beginning you were eager to translate them and still you are maintaining that eagerness. So please go ahead and do what you can to get them translated and published. Please convey my thanks also to bhakta V for his enthusiasm in this regard.

Please convey my obeisances to P Maharaja. You are certainly fortunate to have the opportunity to hear from and serve such a great soul. P Maharaja is always very kind to me, usually by strongly chastising me, which I appreciate.

And please convey my regards also to your good husband. It seems that his health must have improved now.

Looking forward to seeing you at the summer camp.

22 May 2003

That just happened these days and we are having big tests. S ended up in hospital in Z today. The baby is still alive but he will not be capable to live on his own—he doesn't have kidneys. One option is that S waits in hospital for 2–3 months, then doctors perform an operation, take the baby out alive, which will die in a couple of days, and S will have to wait at least 1–2 years for again trying to be a mother. With every day of pregnancy the risk for S's life increases, but on the other side the option number 2 is not beautiful. This option 2, which I think is what the doctors could suggest, I wish to know what the sastras say about it (and what is your opinion about it, is it morally justified), so that we could know what to decide. I will be open. It's called medically justified abortion. The baby who can't live on his own, doctors kill and drag it out, because it jeopardizes the life of the mother, and by doing so they minimize the risk for the mother's death. I must confess that both options are horrible. Material world. In any case we need a lot of strength, Krsna's mercy and your prayers are in the first place.

This is certainly a very great test for you but you must know that whatever happens is Krsna's wish. It could be that the child has a particular bad karma, in which case you can help him by chanting so he can hear. Or it may be that he is destined to work off just a little more karma before going to Krsna, in which case you should also chant so he can hear. Whatever the case may be, it is your duty to help this child, and at the same time accept the fate ordained for him and for yourselves.

As doctors, even in your short careers you must have dealt with many distressful cases. How much more painful it must be when you are the subjects.

Since getting your letter I've made a few phone calls and discussed the matter with several devotees. Finally I got to speak to Dr. Sri K, who heads up the Ayurvedic unit at hospital in Mumbai. He said that there is no provision for or description of abortion in Ayurveda, and that having had a few such cases, they had been forced to make such decisions in the past. Their conclusion was that abortion could not be resorted to. In cases of death within the womb, if the mother's body does not automatically eject the foetus, then artificial labor has to be induced. Of course constant medical supervision will be required, and that too in an unfavorable environment as the karmi doctors will encourage abortion and call you crazy for not resorting to it. But then again abortion at this advanced stage is also very risky, is it not? So better let nature take its course.

If you need to phone me, I'll be available for the next few days at +91-6752-231440. Best for me would be from 12–3 p.m. by your time.

23 May 2003

As you know I don't write you letters very often. You have so many obligations and you are doing immense service and I do not wish to take away your precious time in the service of Srila Prabhupada. However, this time I have to write you and put a little burden on you. In this heavy test I am now going through, with the exception of prayers to Krsna, you are the person I have to confide my mind to. I will be sincere to you as I always were in my relationship to you.

My story began before our departure for India last year. M Prabhu and I have decided to visit the Holy Dhama once more, fix ourselves a bit more in service and ask the Deities for blessings to get children that we will raise in Krsna Consciousness. By the mercy of Krsna we went there and during the whole month of Kartik we prayed for beautiful Deities and for a child. If you remember that Govardhana Parikrama when the two of us got lost and came way after you in Radha-kunda, a very unusual thing happened there. Near the bench where we were waiting for you, one local mataji has worshiped a picture of Krsna with incense, flowers and fruits. In one moment she approached us but, already tired from all these beggars, we thought she will ask us for money or something like that. But instead, she approached and waving her hands she asked in Hindi if we have children. We said, no, and then, by touching me on my shoulder and my stomach, she clearly gave me her blessings to get a child who will be very beautiful, like that on her picture she worshiped. On the picture was little Damodara stealing butter. She smiled and, as quickly as she came, went away leaving us in confusion.

The first day upon returning from India my husband decided to have garbhadhana-samskara. I know that some things are not nice to tell to a sannyasi, and if everything went fine I would never write you about it, but now I will tell you all.

So, we read the instructions about performing samskara. I was very much afraid. That was supposed to be our first sexual relationship and I feared how it will be. However, we agreed that one has to perform his duties conscientiously and, completely in the mood of pilgrimage from which we returned just a day before, we easily chanted 50 rounds and had samskara.

I was completely shocked but I constantly prayed to Krsna to give me a child and somehow I went through it. Long time after that I was disturbed thinking of warnings in the shastras that a mother should be relaxed and in a good mood if she wants her baby to be healthy. I was not relaxed but soon I forgot about it looking forward to see my little baby.

After some time I entered in a special mood, some sort of tranquility, and I became fixed up in serving the Deities. I easily chanted my 25 rounds until I find out if I got pregnant or not. At our great surprise and happiness—it was true. Krsna has immediately sent us a jiva. As I once wrote, you and Srila Prabhupada have sent us immediately one of your servants. We were so happy. So many devotees are trying to have children, it takes so long for everything to come in the right place. But Krsna was immediately merciful to us.

In the beginning it was difficult, pregnancy nauseas, sickness, heavy weight loss, but spiritually it was wonderful. The first month I have chanted 25 rounds, and each following month I reduced my chanting for one round, planning to come to my usual 16 rounds by the time for delivery. The service for beautiful Sri Sri Nitai Gaurasundara became very nice and fulfilling. The following four months were filled with great endeavors, heavy work, building the guesthouse, maintaining our garden, working at the hospital … There were many different embarrassing situations, purifications, problems regarding the construction work, but we survived all this somehow. Being very enthusiastic about building nice rooms for receiving guests, I got over all that despite my pregnancy. There were times when we thought we are going crazy, but we made it.

We were very much pleased by your decision to spend so much time in L during your European Tour. We were a little worried how to organize all that during the last days of my pregnancy, but I had firmly decided and had written you a letter where I listed all my desires. That letter never made its way to you. I wrote that our mission of hosting devotees can not be hindered by anything and that we will teach this to our children, even while still in the womb. After carefully thinking over, I made my mind and chose the priority in my life: hosting devotees; I left you to make the final decision.

Suddenly maya has decided to put my decisions on a test. It all happened so sudden so I couldn't even write you. After two days we learned that our little baby has some kidney disease and also other problems that will probably cause her death, either in the womb or immediately after delivery. All the results of the tests I underwent in the hospital show no reason for encouragement. I am now lying in the hospital waiting; will I carry the baby to the end, give birth to a dead child, suffer a miscarriage? So many things fell on my shoulders in these three days. I had to leave the association of my dear Deities, my husband, other devotees and now I am fighting alone with my baby and with Krsna in my heart.

There is very little hope, almost none, but all the devotees are praying for me, encouraging me, bringing me prasadam, visiting me. It is very difficult for me going through all this what happened and is still happening, but I am aware that everything is under the control of the Supreme Lord. I keep reminding myself about it. Tests are coming and going. The greatest until now has come, difficult, almost insurmountable, but also very subtle. You often told me I have an emphasized parental instinct, so you can imagine how painfully this test stroke me. It hurts very much, but I know that does not mean I did not deserve it. Who knows what would I have to go through if Krsna mercifully didn't reduce my sinful activities, giving me minimal suffering. The very fact that I have got such a wonderful husband, wonderful Guru and a chance to serve Srila Prabhupada give evidence that Krsna has the best plan for me. I just have to patiently wait what will happen. So, after thinking it over, reading, and chanting, I have come to the conclusion that my Damodara has come to me to spiritually advance together with me. Every morning in the hospital we get up early, chant, have a morning program in my mind, worship the Deities, doing arati, offering fruit, reading loud, and I explain to him various points from Srimad-Bhagavatam. When we have time, we sew outfits for the Deities. In every moment Krsna is sending us answers to our doubts, and preaching to us through Prabhupada's purports. We are peacefully waiting for the outcome of present situation, happy to see how many nice devotees there are who are praying for us, visiting us, bringing prasadam …

We read a lot Srimad-Bhagavatam 7.8.22–33 and I explain to him how when Nrsimhadeva playfully let go Hiranyakasipu for a moment, he thought it was just by accident, or the Lord was maybe fearful of him. Even the demigods shared these thoughts. But in the next moment one can see that nothing is happening accidentally, but everything is in the hands of the Supreme. Our present situation is also a part of a plan, purification from our bad karma, expression of the Lord's special mercy … It is said that Hiranyakasipu was feeling helpless and afflicted when Krsna grabbed him and put him on His lap. We are always helpless when we are faced with some great purification. We struggle, fight, attack, accuse, but then comes distress and helplessness. The same happened to us. The first few days we fought with tears and with the burden; we couldn't believe it is happening, and will the Lord and His energy be so cruel. Then we relaxed in the Lord's hands, ready for everything He wants to do with us.

Nrsimhadeva was roaring and laughing fighting Hiranyakasipu and ripping him apart. The Lord always laughs and always protects His devotees. We have confidence in this. Today, when I was showing to little Damodara the picture of Lord Nrsimhadeva killing this demon, I explained to him that Krsna is like a bloodthirsty person and Hiranyakasipu like a victim. Naturally we would immediately feel compassion towards the victim, towards anyone in distress. But when we hear the complete story about the activities of this demon, about the fight, then it becomes clear that Hiranyakasipu deserved it and that he actually got the mercy that the Lord personally killed him. In this way I explained to little Damodara how everybody can now think it isn't fair that all this is happening to us, that Krsna is cruel to let this happen, but the two of us complied. We know we deserved much worse things and Krsna has come closer to us in a special way.

I beg you for your support and prayers for my Damodara and for me to keep the proper attitude in this difficult situation. Please pray also for my husband who is also suffering.

P.S. We just received your letter of support and I see my perspective exactly corresponds to yours.

Thankyou very much, dear S, for this very feelingful and very Krsna conscious response. I am proud to have such a wonderful disciple. Fortunate indeed is that soul sheltered in your womb. I pray to Krsna that if I have to take birth again I may be blessed with such a worthy mother.

3 June 2003

Thankyou for your letter which could form the basis of much discussion. But I'll try to keep the reply brief and to the point.

One side I am claiming that the Lord is taking care of everything so if I make efforts to study more to keep myself updated then is it foolishness and a waste of time?

We understand that ultimately everything is in Krsna's hands. Yet He nevertheless induced Arjuna not to renounce work. Everyone has to do something and Krsna consciousness is not meant to be an excuse for laziness.

Or should I try to create a balance between my profession and Bhakti by fixing up a time for studying devotional books and simultaneously finding time to do my professional studies?

This is the best suggestion. Certainly Krsna will be very satisfied at your sincere endeavors to rise early and perform sadhana despite having a demanding work life. This is indeed very surrendered. Surrender does not necessarily mean to attempt to renounce everything of this world, but rather to live in this world while dedicating everything to Krsna. Many responsible persons in the past, and even at present, have been fully Krsna conscious while performing their worldly duties.

3 June 2003

I am very proud of S and am remembering her again and again every day. Simply remembering her purity is giving me much inspiration and forcing me to be more serious in Krsna consciousness. I pray for the association of such devotees life after life. Please always keep association with M and S and help them in whatever way you can during this difficult test.

7 July 2003

I hadn't been attending to emails due to being fully engaged otherwise.

G Prabhu is neither replying his emails nor answering his phone (I tried) which suggests that he is presently not in Vrindavan (probably due to the overwhelming heat, if the monsoon hasn't yet begun there). It may be that now is not the time for you to be able to stay there. You may be tested much before being able to stay in Vrindavan. I recently heard of a Godbrother who took over 10 attempts before being able to stay in Govardhan. Even Lord Caitanya's first attempt to go to Vrindavan was stunted. Indeed Sanatana Goswami in advising Lord Caitanya not to go to Vrindavan with a large retinue indicated that even in fulfilling his heart's topmost desire, a devotee should not act out of sentiment alone but should be pragmatic also.

Maybe try again later.

11 July 2003

With best wishes as sincere as they come from My Lowliness, I beg to submit that your statement "for my own continued progress in Krsna consciousness it seems appropriate to do so" is coming from a deluded mind which is hardly fit to ascertain appropriateness or otherwise. You are dreaming of Cinderella—where in the world is the woman to fit your job description? Which woman is dreaming of marrying a divorced half dead pauper? And how would you maintain the one or two children that you would so religiously give her with your dying breaths?

Really it would be better to get yourself out of this dangerous situation. Why enter a well at the age prescribed for quitting wells? It's still not too late as you didn't remarry yet and Krsna consciousness always works. But you need a heavy dose of surrender. Crooning bhajanas on a harmonium won't help. How about getting out on a book distribution party? That is a really appropriate medicine for maya.

Of course I'm not going to hate you if you fall down another well although my straightforwardness about it might make you feel uncomfortable. I hope so. You're already uncomfortable due to the dictates of maya so better experience some discomfort that will benefit you.

My bottom line advice: get the hell out of whatever you are doing and get into intense devotional service. Don't listen to the advice of pragmatists who are pragmatically stuck in wells. Krsna has arranged for you to be free to serve Him so take this opportunity and do whatever is required to get yourself back to Godhead in this life. Don't pick up any baggage on the way. If you were to do so, you would surely regret it within a few days. But then it would be too late and you would be stuck.

Please consider carefully and do the needful.

15 July 2003

Regarding the old enemies of mind and senses that despite all efforts remain just like demons: please anyway continue with your spiritual practices. This is a test. Please have faith that in due course of time Krsna will respond to your sincere efforts to serve Him despite the influence of these demons, and will remove them. Daily recitation of Srila Bhaktivinoda Thakura's prayer "Gopinatha" will be very helpful.

16 July 2003

Thankyou for at last getting the papers posted. However it seems I was misunderstood as I wanted posted only the relatively short (two and a half page) paper herewith attached (a slightly revised version). I suggest that *** Prabhu allow this to be posted for a couple of weeks or so just so that people can get the idea that from now on as much as possible I wish to avoid initiating people who are not serious about Krsna consciousness. At present as the only "ISKCON guru" visiting B regularly I am expected to initiate whoever lives in the temple or otherwise hangs around for some time.

Your comment, "by collecting money for ISKCON, one can do or say whatever he wants and no steps will be taken against such a rascal" is a fairly accurate summary of much of what goes on in ISKCON India today, and it is not in my power to change such a paradigm wherever it exists. It is up to you whether or not you wish to participate in such an atmosphere. Whatever others may say or do, Krsna will accept the services of those who are sincere, and reciprocate with others accordingly. See Bg. 4.11 and SB 8.9.28 text and purports.

17 July 2003

I agree, we have to do the best we can in far from ideal circumstances in this miserable Kali-yuga, and work toward making things better, which will in most cases be a slow task that requires much sincerity and patience. In the meantime we should stick to our basic practices of Krsna consciousness and try to not be overly disturbed by others.

17 July 2003

I suspect that at this point direction from me to *** will subtly further undermine your influence. The temple president's standing is automatically reduced if he appeals to the gurus to keep disciples in line. You should not have to do so as obedience to the temple president is a basic condition for staying in any temple. You have every right as temple president to insist that he accepts your authority. I suggest that you have a talk with ***, point out the difficulties you are having in dealing with him, and gently but firmly give the bottom line that your authority has to be respected otherwise you cannot perform your service properly and others will also be spoiled, and that if he can't submit to this condition then despite his good qualities it would be better that he moves on. Let others see that non-cooperators are given a chance to reform, failing which they have to go and work on their anarthas elsewhere.

My experience as temple president of a few temples and traveling sankirtana party leader is that allowing devotees to scorn authority gradually engenders a horrible defiant situation which is simply hellish to try to manage.

What do you think?

21 July 2003

The principle of following authority is an important one. Please give your support to *** Prabhu and help him in this great attempt to revive Krsna consciousness in L. Hardly anyone nowadays is prepared to take such a risk for Krsna so he deserves all support. It's not easy to be a TP and it may be that he is not naturally cut out as a leader but he sincerely wants to do something for Srila Prabhupada and Krsna so please help him with the faith that if we are all sincere we will all progress and learn, although sometimes the learning process may be painful. Be patient and take the present adversity as an opportunity to become more mature in Krsna consciousness.

Another point is that you are probably more senior than most there so your example will be crucial. Please bear this in mind and help to maintain the fragile faith of newcomers.

2 August 2003

Happy adventures in the material world, if that is the way you decide to go. But please also consider that Krsna has given you certain abilities in writing and editing which should not be neglected; and that My Lowliness is very grateful for all services rendered by Your Grace and eager to avail of your talents to help me as much as possible in producing important books for the Krsna consciousness movement. So you might consider moving back to Bharat, marrying there if you so desire, and being supported in a simple manner as you work on my books. Please think about it.

8 August 2003

So now this episode is over. But it is not over. Just as you carried your child in your womb, now you will carry him in your heart, and together you will help to carry each other back to the lotus feet of our eternal object of love, Sri Krsna.

I am fortunate to have such a genuine devotee as yourself as my disciple. Thankyou very much.

Now you must rest. Please do not strain yourself.

11 August 2003

Thankyou dear devotees for receiving me so nicely and all glories to your dedicated service to Lord Nrsimhadeva and Srila Prabhupada.

*** Prabhu assured me that there really is very little chance of the farm being sold, despite what some devotees may say. So please continue with your service, knowing that it won't be easy but that even if no-one else cares, Lord Nrsimhadeva is certainly very satisfied with you. Please remember how Prahlada Maharaja pleased Lord Nrsimhadeva by his fortitude amidst difficulties, and how after undergoing many tests he thus received the full mercy of the Lord.

7 September 2003

I certainly have no objection to home Deity worship but just want that it be done properly. So please do so.

As the wife is supposed to follow the husband it is best if you follow what *** Maharaja says as he is your husband's guru and is seeing you regularly which I am not. There may be differences in details between what he and I say but such differences will not be very important as long as the essence is the same. If as in this case you feel you need further clarification from me then you are of course always welcome to contact me.

It is Krsna's mercy on you that you are now nicely situated in family life. However, adjustment to a new situation is always a test so please be patient.

8 September 2003

Cruel as it may seem, I think it best not to get involved in devotees' financial problems. There could be some exception, for instance if a grhastha devotee who has served faithfully for years suddenly dies and his family is left without any means of support. But once we start to give loans or take responsibility for paying others' debts, there will be no end to it and everyone will want, expect, and even demand such help: "You gave to him so why not to me?"

8 October 2003

I am writing you this email because something strange happened. I hope I am not doing the wrong thing. You see, I learned about you from a devotee, and I thought to myself 'maybe he is my spiritual master' and then I felt this blissful feeling which lasted until the next day, but I then brushed it off. I was afraid to approach you because of what my senior devotees would think about me. But since then I have had three dreams about you, after the second dream, I wanted to get in touch with you, and I said 'ok if I have one more dream then I'll write ...' and that same night I did really dream about you. So I feel it is my duty now as well as my wish to write to you. I have been speculating about this in fear all day, and worrying about what I would write, but it is my duty, because that was the deal, that I would write to you if I dreamed about you. So here is my email. Please could you write back to me? I am very nervous and I think a lot, so I don't know what to say. If you agree to write to me, then I will tell you whatever you ask me to, is this ok?

Although generally dreams are simply nonsense mixtures of thoughts, Srila Prabhupada said that dreams of the guru are to be taken as real.

I feel some encouragement from this, that despite my lack of qualifications, my miniscule attempts to serve Srila Prabhupada by accepting the role of guru seem to be appreciated by His Divine Grace.

However it is not simply by dream that a guru is to be accepted, but by hearing from, following the instructions, and serving.

If you wish to pursue this further, please let me know more about yourself, your material background, and your present standing in Krsna consciousness (i.e. how many rounds you are chanting etc.).

May Lord Krsna and Srila Prabhupada bless you always.

30 October 2003

R, you are making a big fuss over nothing. It is you who is mistaken, not Srila Prabhupada.

From "rascal's version, Sankara's version" it could be understood that the speaker is calling Sankara a rascal. But it could also be understood as "the version made by Sankara for rascals"—which is in accord with Srila Prabhupada's standard description of Mayavada.

Just like if it is said "sinner's place, Yama's place" it is understood that "Yama's place" means "the place for sinners that is governed by Yama"—not that Yama is being accused of being a sinner.

To surmise that Srila Prabhupada was calling Sankara a rascal is inconsistent with everything else Srila Prabhupada said about Sankaracarya.

To take some stray words out of an informal conversation among Srila Prabhupada and disciples (who were familiar with his stance on Mayavada), and to interpret them out of context to come up with a conclusion different to that intended by the speaker, is called word jugglery, which is a popular resort of Mayavadis. And we all know what Srila Prabhupada called Mayavadis. Something beginning with "r."

10 November 2003

A young brahmacari can best grow in Krsna consciousness if he serves the sankirtan mission under competent guidance without making his own plans, which as you are seeing cause unnecessary complexities. If you could understand the importance of preaching and distributing Srila Prabhupada's books then you wouldn't have so many different plans. Actually Krsna consciousness really begins when we stop thinking what I want to do and start thinking what Krsna and His representatives want me to do.

Anyway it's nice that you have put aside some of your valuable time to do book distribution. And under the present circumstances if the devotees there agree then I have no objection if you now revert to personal fund collection. But on the whole it would be better if you seriously considered how best to utilize your valuable human life in the service of the sankirtan mission. Simply touring around doing what you like, when you like, how you like, even if superficially within the scope of Krsna consciousness, will not help you very much, nor can you ever do any solid service that way.

10 November 2003

Please take the opportunity to have darshan of your wonderful Guru Maharaja whenever possible. Just to see and hear him will be uplifting even if you can't honestly tell him "I surrender."

Probably after a year doing community service with AA your future direction will become clearer.[14] Whatever happens just keep on chanting. I feel Krsna has a wonderful future arranged for you, whatever or wherever it may be.

As for my advice: ashram life is uncertain, but then so is any mode of life in this world. Ashram life affords better opportunities for being Krsna conscious and thus getting out of the otherwise certain repeated struggles of material life.

---

14. AA—Alcoholics Anonymous, an association of alcoholics who try, especially by mutual assistance and faith in God, to overcome alcoholism.

12 November 2003

I understand that you have had to do a lot of unnecessary work and that it is a heavy workload for you. Much of this has been due to misunderstanding caused by faulty communication, your suddenly having to leave M at the time I'd allotted to be with you, the newness of this arrangement, and the newness of yourself to this service.

My experience with book production over the last 26 years is that it's never easy, always beset with various snags and tangles.

Sreyamsi bahu vighnani: many obstacles arise in auspicious activities.

So please keep in good spirits. I think you can appreciate how important this service is to me in my service to Srila Prabhupada and that it will gradually have its effect and indeed already is.

13 November 2003

My sincere best wishes to you.

Please don't misunderstand me. I'm not against the method you are following as I don't know enough about it to make much comment. Obviously if it helps attentive chanting then it's worth considering seriously. I personally regularly stress to devotees the importance of attentive chanting.

However my fear is that too much importance is put on technique so that it becomes more like a yogic process. A problem with "new techniques" is that there are so many of them. We can take up one then jump to another, and another ... Hence I prefer to stick closely to guru, sadhu, and sastra.

It is not necessary to read all of Srila Prabhupada's books before striving for attentive chanting or good Vaisnava relationships. Rather, from the beginning of our Krsna consciousness we should strive for these. But certainly we should not neglect to read all of Srila Prabhupada's books. So I suggest that in your preaching you also stress this important point.

Harinama Cintamani is certainly a wonderful book and although the general process we recommend is to first read all of Srila Prabhupada's books, if you find such great inspiration from Harinama Cintamani then I encourage you to keep on developing that.

20 November 2003

I am of course shocked and very sorry to hear of C Prabhu's untimely demise. Please extend my commiserations to your father and mother also.

Truly, birth, death, old age and disease surround us on all sides. However, we should know that no one can withhold the inexorable hand of fate, which is totally beyond our control. No one knows what is Krsna's wish. In life or death, a devotee is always protected by Krsna.

Certainly he led a pure life in Krsna consciousness and Krsna is looking after him.

27 December 2003

Recently we were insulted badly for not taking part in one of the dance programs for the ISKCON New Year program 2004. I'm not interested in these dances. I'm very upset about all this and a few other matters. Guru Maharaja, please tell me some way by which I can keep away from all these problems!

ISKCON is a big society trying to cater to the spiritual needs and aspirations of many aspiring devotees—which means that there will be different outlooks. ISKCON leaders also have different approaches.

Personally I cannot at all recommend that young girls like yourself be asked to dance in public, even if the program is said to be for the sake of Krsna consciousness. I am often criticized for this "conservative" stance but nevertheless prefer to be careful in my practices even if it means not satisfying the demands of others. Others who similarly try to practice strictly are also liable to be censured. It is a burden one has to accept.

2004

9 January 2004

Thankyou for your offering and letter. You have raised an important question. Is it enough simply to go on with service and neglect our inner feelings and problems?

The answer could be both yes and no.

If we are happy in our service then why be concerned about our minds? Better just forget it and concentrate on serving Krsna.

On the other hand, serious anarthas, if not dealt with, can in course of time strangle our devotional advancement.

So on the whole I recommend that you go on with your service of book distribution, but also be introspective and work on identifying and overcoming anarthas. This does not mean becoming "mental" but, rather, thoughtful.

12 January 2004

Medical science advises that if malignant tumor is in advanced stage, it should be excised as soon as possible, otherwise it causes the patient's death. I am seriously thinking of divorce.

The analogy here is inappropriate as divorce is not sanctioned by sastra.

You yourself told me just a few days ago that she was improving. Your sudden and extreme change of position suggests that your own perspective is not very stable.

Please be patient and don't do anything adharmic.

7 February 2004

Thankyou for your letter and the welcome news of your continued positive engagement in Krsna conscious activities.

You asked what to do about your habit of reading non-Krsna conscious books. My answer is: stop it. If you know that it is impeding your advancement then why do so? Better that you set yourself a goal to read all of Srila Prabhupada's books by a certain date. Then you won't have time for other books.

Generally samskaras are performed by grhasthas but in today's unusual world we see brahmacaris and sannyasis doing so also. Considering the lack of devotees in L knowledgeable about samskaras, it will be a good service if you can do so. You may perform any samskaras, as long as you don't feel disturbed in doing so.

7 February 2004

Thankyou for writing to me—at last. It was certainly unusual that you left India without consulting or even informing me, and I took this as an indication that you were not in clear consciousness.

I am glad that you are still chanting 16 rounds and wish to continue in spiritual life. And I can understand that you wish to marry. That is almost inevitable, as you have never been steady as a brahmacari, never staying long anywhere, always moving here and there. So for you to take the responsibility of family life might help you to become steady.

However I cannot at all approve of your marrying this particular lady. To do so would be a very bad move on your part. Please consider that I am preaching a high standard of moral responsibility and that if you as my disciple indulge in such whimsical affairs then it will make me an object of scorn and much undermine my attempts to lift devotees up to a better standard.

Furthermore your proposed alliance is unlikely to last long. You are proposing to protect her but you cannot even protect yourself. You cannot provide for her at the standard she is used to. You are entering into a hellish situation.

But being blinded by infatuation you are unlikely to accept my guidance. Then I will become your "pet dog" guru. You will consider that you know better than me but will keep my picture as a sign of affection for the unfortunate soul who you call your guru.

But if you actually wish to live by the principle of *jive daya,* then please begin by being merciful to this jiva, myself. If you are my disciple then you should obey my instruction, which is: get out of that situation immediately and never speak to that woman again. Get married, but do so to a never-married woman and in a gentlemanly manner, not like this.

12 March 2004

Thankyou for the news about the soul who is trying to avoid being G dasa.

Better read Srila Prabhupada's books than get caught up with smelly fish in the net.

Chant Hare Krsna loudly and associate with devotees who will help you to remain pure.

26 March 2004

My best regards to you and Thankyou for your letter. Let's hope you can go to the bhakta program before too long.

It's true that in ISKCON as probably in any religious institution there are various discrepancies toward which many of us might turn a blind eye in the hope that things will improve by God's grace. Of course if things get too much out of hand it might be incumbent on us to speak out. However in your present stage of Krsna consciousness it's probably by far best that you concentrate on the essentials of hearing and chanting about Krsna, avoiding controversy, which could damage your faith in the very essence of bhakti.

I have a question, where is the border between if somebody recommended something and I'm not able to do it, and offense that I don't do it.

This is too general a query to give a specific reply to. On the whole it is understood that offense occurs when there is malintent, so if that is not present, you are probably not making an offense.

Considering your age and situation I would not advise you to re-marry.

8 April 2004

Naturally I'm very concerned with your difficulties. As *** Prabhu is helping in your spiritual progress, I'd like to get his feedback on what advice to give you; he and I shouldn't give conflicting advice. So I'll get back to you after conferring with him.

Certainly this ritvikism isn't good. Please go to Sri Krsna Matt and pray daily to Lord Krsna there. Also if you get the opportunity you may have the saintly darshan of Sri +++ Swami.

Another thing you should do is to serve R and P Prabhus in whatever way you may. It was wrong that you criticized them and your spiritual difficulties are no doubt aggravated by that. So try to rectify that fault by serving them.

Jump and dance in kirtana! That will help you immensely. Also be sure to read Srila Prabhupada's books daily. This will help to keep everything in clear perspective.

13 April 2004

Thankyou for contacting me in your difficulty. This, despite your profession of lack of faith in me, indicates that you think I could help you and that you sincerely want help.

This is not the ISKCON I wanted to join. I am not losing faith in Prabhupada or his books, but it is very, very difficult for me to continue now with the present-day ISKCON.

I could have written the same myself! But I certainly can't seriously contemplate going back to karmi life. Whatever ISKCON's present difficulties may be, we have to take advantage of the great gifts Srila Prabhupada gave us and try to propagate his mission as best we can, hoping for better days. By no means is all lost.

Please consider that there are many sober intelligent devotees who are as or more aware of ISKCON's problems yet who nevertheless go on serving the mission. If they can, why not you? What is your service to Srila Prabhupada's mission?

Quite likely your problems are at least as much mental or emotional rather than on principle or philosophy. You probably need to make some real friends in Krsna consciousness— philosophy is not in itself enough.

You could and should have a (or a few) heart to heart talks with a devotee there who you respect and trust. Maybe S, C, N, or Y.

I can try to administer to you by email, but as your problems are deep-rooted, an email exchange is unlikely to help much. Maybe you could come and see me—I'm in Puri now. Why not take a break, and bring your family here for a few days?

You suggest that I'm neglecting you but please consider I have almost 400 disciples plus writing service and that you have had considerably more direct attention from me than most of my disciples, and far more than most devotees in ISKCON get from their gurus.

Here's something interesting about faith, which although not directly applicable to you could be partially so:

> Strange as may seem that anomaly called Liberal Catholicism, its reason is not far to seek. It takes its root in a false conception of the nature of the act of faith. The Liberal Catholic assumes as the formal motive of the act of faith, not the infallible authority of God revealing supernatural truth, but his own reason deigning to accept as true what appears rational to him according to the appreciation and measure of his own individual judgment. He subjects God's authority to the scrutiny of his reason, and not his reason to God's authority. He accepts Revelation, not on account of the infallible Revealer, but because of the "infallible" receiver. With him the individual judgment is the rule of faith. He believes in the independence of reason. (From a website)

How is your sadhana? If your sadhana is weak then your Krsna consciousness cannot be strong.

18 April 2004

Thankyou to both of you for kindly helping with the production, storage, and distribution of my books. It is a very great help for me and leaves me freer for other services. It has to be a labour of love as there is nothing very attractive or interesting in this service. So from this I can understand your love for me, by assisting me in this, my major service in Srila Prabhupada's mission.

24 May 2004

Thankyou for communicating your decision to me. And thankyou for the services you performed as a brahmacari in the ashram. I trust that you learned many things that will be useful in your onward march back to Godhead.

Do not think that you have failed. Take it that your brahmacari life was a training period. Please continue to associate with the devotees in D, and go on chanting your prescribed rounds and studying Srila Prabhupada's books. If possible please visit me at Lord Jagannatha's Rathayatra in Baroda on June 19.

What did you do with the books I had given you for safe-keeping?

Please convey my regards to the devotees there.

2 June 2004

Don't worry too much as mistakes made in ignorance are not very blameful.

I am much disturbed at the manner in which Deities are bought, sold, given away, worshiped, ceased to be worshiped, and so on, that is common nowadays, as if They were toy dolls or something like a bar of soap to be passed around.

But you should have considered that any important decision affecting your spiritual life should be first submitted to your guru. A guru is not meant just to be kept in a photo for waving incense at.

Better that you return the Deities to those who gave Them and tell those persons that you made a mistake in accepting Them so readily. Deity worship can only be accepted under certain conditions, such as being brahmana initiated and in a position to undertake such worship uninterruptedly throughout life.

The main worship of Gaura Nitai is by chanting. Continue with that.

15 June 2004

Dandavat. All glories to Srila Prabhupada, without whose profound humility, infinite compassion and patience, authoritative teachings, personal qualities, unbelievably arduous sacrifices, and simply pure love, this world would have been lost long ago.

As a grhastha devotee in Denmark (G) once told me that H had told him regarding family problems, "there are no easy solutions to such difficult problems." But as you mention, you have many times talked it out with your wife and it seems like it's time for a long talk. I suggest that you center the talk on what you can both do best for your child.

Definitely the hormonal change can make women very irrational—I've heard quite a few tales about that.

Another suggestion: sit together daily as a family, have a little kirtana, and read from Krsna book or a child's version of it.

I'm more and more seeing how traditional cultures, in which women were both strictly controlled and highly respected, were best. In the absence of such an ethos women have freedom to indulge their minds, which simply causes chaos and misery for themselves and others.

Please keep in touch with me about this. I'm ready to help in whatever way I can to help avert disaster. But as you know, once someone's mind goes completely out of control then they become like a ghost and cannot listen even to those they love and respect.

Bhn. *** wrote to me from your wife's email address that she wants to work for your wife (I suppose to help with housework and child care) and thus earn some laxmi to clear debts. I gave my approval, but I wonder if it will affect the situation, especially if bhn. *** goes to you for advice and guidance. What do you think?

One point is that simply moving close to a temple may have a wonderful effect for you all, so it might be worth waiting to see if that happens.

7 July 2004

Had I been in a man's body I would have served you everywhere, but my biggest disappointment in life is that I am situated in a woman's body which brings along so many shortcomings in my spiritual life, but I know they are my karmas.

Although a woman's body necessitates different duties and facilities than those of men, it is not an impediment in Krsna consciousness. Particularly at the present time it is much required that women in Krsna consciousness set an ideal example of combining traditional stri-dharma with the transcendental practices of devotional service. If you can do so it will be most conducive for your own spiritual advancement and will be first class preaching by practical example.

9 July 2004

I thought some more about your proposal to divorce. I feel that whatever the reason for doing so, it will not look good and will add to the ongoing culture of family instability that plagues ISKCON. The more devotees that divorce, the more others will think it normal and acceptable to do so—especially if leaders divorce and remain in their positions. I hence feel that if you do so it would be better if you resign all official positions in ISKCON. By doing so you would make it clear that you yourself understand that divorce is not very honorable, and not suitable for spiritual leaders of society.

It would be another matter if the divorce went through after your wife had instigated proceedings against you, and you had fought against it on the grounds that it is against sastra.

This is my seemingly harsh outlook, based on the principle that unless and until ISKCON members and especially leaders set ideal examples, there will be no hope of progressing toward Srila Prabhupada's dream of ISKCON showing the right path to the misdirected civilization.

10 July 2004

If you, a well-known spokesman for dharma, institute divorce proceedings, it will be a major setback for those attempting to establish dharma within ISKCON. Others will criticise that we don't live according to our ideals, that even those who preach such high standards can't stick to them and that hence we should just be realistic and not attempt to follow a culture that we're not fit for … etc.

19 July 2004

It is certainly a laudable desire to have a son who possesses all good qualities like Srila Prabhupada in serving Krsna and Srimati Radharani with great determination throughout his whole life. Yet considering the rarity of such exalted devotees, it is unlikely that such a great personality would appear in your family unless you elevate yourself to a similarly high standard of consciousness.

Srila Prabhupada said, "If you want to know me, read my books." This is a more important sadhana for you than performing austerities and feeding cows. If you want to have a pure devotee in your home then you must be prepared to train him in bhagavat philosophy. To date you have not made an intensive study of Srila Prabhupada's books. You have neglected to take advantage of the teachings of the great Vaisnava acaryas and thus your understanding of Krsna consciousness is almost certainly both lacking in depth and mixed with misconceptions. As such it is unlikely that an acarya-purusa will agree to appear as your son.

You have asked me to chant an extra round of japa daily during Purusottama-masa to help fulfill your desire. As it happens I was not able to attend to your letter until after the start of this month. And anyway I try to chant all my rounds in a mood of service to Srila Prabhupada and Krsna, which service includes my endeavors to act for the benefit of those I have accepted as disciples in their service. So whatever is required for my disciples' benefit is already included in my regular chanting.

Please study Srila Prabhupada's books regularly and deeply. That will be beneficial for you and for all other jivas who come in contact with you.

2 August 2004

What you have described is horrible violence against the jiva who you had caused to take shelter in the womb of your then girlfriend and now wife. In the present social ethos of India this act is considered a commendable method of population control, but according to sastra it is highly sinful.

Of course genuine devotional service removes all sins but to have knowingly done this after coming to Krsna consciousness compounds the offense.

However it is good that you have informed me of this, for in Krsna consciousness there is always hope for a better future, however bad the past might have been. A devotee who has sinned need not perform prayascitta (atonement) for devotional service itself removes all sins. However after sinning, one's service must be fully sincere, otherwise the effect of sinful activities will remain.

I suggest that both yourself and your wife immediately take up chanting minimum sixteen rounds of the mahamantra daily and petition Krsna to give a better opportunity to the jiva that you so cruelly sent away. You should utilize a significant portion of your income—at least Rs. 1000 per month—for promoting Krsna consciousness. Best is that you donate to the shastra daan program.

After doing thus for two years please ask me again about shelter. In the meantime you are welcome to come and see me, attend lectures and other programs at the temple, etc.

2 August 2004

Thankyou for meeting me at the ISKCON *** festival. It certainly was a wonderful event, with so many Vaisnavas chanting and dancing together.

I appreciate that you are a very sincere devotee and may be frustrated by certain attitudes of some others. Nevertheless I request you to continue your activities in Krsna consciousness without too much concern about the deficiencies of others. Especially in the beginning stages of our devotional lives, it is best to concentrate on our own improvement than to become critical of others.

Your proposed life's activities in bhakti-yoga, based on the Holy Name, peaceful atmosphere, plain living, high thinking, brahmanas, cows, and care for women, are all certainly commendable, and I wish you all the best in your chosen way of life.

6 August 2004

Thankyou for your letter and the well intentioned advice proffered therein.

I had at one point declined to speak to X, but that was put behind. My last exchange with him was a morning congenially spent together visiting temples. But unpredictable as ever, he has again flared up. Similarly, you faithfully accept X's version that I insulted his mother, and thus advise me to apologize to her. It seems unfair that you listened to him for hours but didn't care to get my version before advising me based on his word only.

You may be suprised to know that I'm not fanatically against marriage: [quoting from a letter to a disciple] "Certainly my best wishes are there for your happy and ideal grhastha life in Krsna consciousness."

S Prabhu is pressing me to order Y to marry. However I never pressurize disciples into accepting any ashram against their will. I might advise someone to marry if I consider it is for their ultimate benefit. But in the case of Y and X, I suspect that X wants Y married because he wants to control Y and his income— and that Y's aversion to marriage is largely because he realizes this. He wants to escape X's control (wouldn't you?), X wants to impose it, and thus even if Y were pressured into marriage, it's likely that X would continue to pressurize devotees into making Y fully surrender to him, which is never likely to happen. In short, I doubt that apart from a temporary respite, the X syndrome would be solved by pressurizing Y into marriage. And that thus another approach should be sought to tackle this issue.

I could write more about this but I don't wish to tax you further as you are suffering from stress. Also I am pressed for time, and anyway you have withdrawn from this affair. Please carefully look after your health, and please continue to consider me favorably. But also please don't judge me based solely on others' assessments.

Thankyou for your time and trouble.

6 August 2004

Certainly my best wishes are there for your happy and ideal grhastha life in Krsna consciousness. I suggest that you ask ***

Prabhu or any other sober senior grhastha devotee to give you detailed guidelines on grhastha life and to act as your ongoing mentor to help you advance in Krsna consciousness within that ashram.

6 August 2004

Congratulations on your appointment as the temple president of ISKCON ***. Your immediate engagement is to build a glorious temple for Sri Sri Gaura Nitai, Sri Sri Radha Krsna, and Sri Sri Sri Jagannath, Subhadra, Baladeva. May Krsna and Srila Prabhupada give you the necessary strength, intelligence, and resources to do so.

Please also remember that even more important—and difficult—than building temples is to build people in Krsna consciousness, and that your real success will be measured not in bricks and mortar but in souls offered at the feet of the Lord.

25 August 2004

I suggest that you analyze not only ancient Lithuanian culture as deduced from fairy tales, but also more recent culture, for even a few years ago family values etc. were much stronger and closer to the Vedic ideal.

Reading mundane academic books is certainly potentially contaminating. I hence am very concerned that you get solid training in Vaisnava siddhanta before going more deeply into the mundane academic ethos. So many devotees have compromised their Krsna consciousness and even become offensive to guru-sadhu-sastra due to taking these learned fools too seriously. Please bear in mind that more important than pursuing university education is becoming strong in Krsna consciousness and that the whole attempt to present Krsna consciousness through the secular academic system will become undone if the aspiring preacher is not himself solidly fixed in Krsna consciousness. One who goes into the lions' den has to be powerful enough to defeat the lions, otherwise he will become their victim.

You should at least theoretically have faith that whatever guru-sadhu-sastra teach must be correct, even if you cannot understand it, and that you may be able to understand it by submissively inquiring from and serving sadhus.

As stated in "The Real Nature of Sree Krsna," Introductory Chapter 2 of Sree Krsna Chaitanya, vol. 1 (written under the supervision of Srila Bhaktisiddhanta Sarasvati Thakura, by one of his leading disciples):

> The empiric historian, with his geographical and chronological apparatus of observation, can have really no proper idea of the grotesque anomaly that he unconsciously perpetrates by his pedantic effort to gauze (sic) the absolute by the standard supplied to her victim by His deluding energy in the form of the mundane categories that can only limit and define them, whereas the function to be performed is to get rid of the necessity to do either. The empiric consciousness is not in the absolute consciousness at all. It can only bungle and commit a deliberate blunder by attempting to limit and define the immeasurable under the pleas of a necessity that need not be supposed to exist at all. By the empiric attitude one is led to launch out on the quest of the Absolute Truth with the resources of admittedly utter ignorance. This foolhardiness must be made to cease. The method of submissive inquiry enjoined by the scriptures should be substituted after being properly learnt by those who have themselves attained to the right knowledge of the same by the right method of submission.

30 September 2004

There have been not a few devotees who have desired to become well known musicians and thus promote Krsna consciousness, but I'm not aware of any who have succeeded. It's not so easy to succeed in the music world. It is another matter for already famous musicians who subsequently take to Krsna consciousness and use their popularity for preaching. Anyway I wish you all the best on your meandering path to Krsna and have added you as a receiver to two interesting texts I recently received about music.

26 October 2004

After considering your situation I wish to tell you that Srila Prabhupada also faced a similar situation in his life. He was married and had many responsibilites. His family also did not co-operate with Him in devotional activities. Nevertheless He did not leave His responsibilities. He continued supporting His family with all difficulties. So it is not good of a follower of Srila Prabhupada to leave his family like this and take sannyasa. This would go against the example set by Srila Prabhupada. If your family is unwilling to come to India and settle down, it would be in your best interest to go back to them and continue your devotional service from there.

As far as taking sannyasa is concerned, at present you are not fit for taking it. Taking sannyasa is not so easy as you are thinking. First try and become a responsible householder then you can become a responsible sannyasi.

11 November 2004

I'm sorry to hear of your injury and am glad to know that it is not serious; and that all your other news is favorable.

Several devotees have told me of having visions and other esoteric experiences. Interestingly, all such devotees are women. I wonder if it is connected with sentiment rather than pure realization. Anyway visions or no visions everyone has to follow the process of Krsna consciousness as given by our acaryas. Hearing about Krsna from bona fide sources is more reliable than visions. It is nice if you have visions but then so many sahajiyas do also.

So the real test is if we continue unflinchingly with our service, and give up all material desires. Visions are not the substance of spiritual life; service is. So whatever visions come, just continue with service.

Whether or not such visions are substantial is also to be considered from the standpoint of sastra. As there is no authorized description of Lord Jesus in Vraja-lila, such visions are unlikely to be from the platform of substantive reality and are thus probably from an illusory source.

Govardhan Sila may be worshiped on Govardhan Puja day by the standard procedures. These should be known to senior devotees and there is nothing extra for me to instruct in this regard.

19 November 2004

I understand that *** Prabhu is heavy, but that heaviness is for the benefit of others, for instance to pressurize devotees weak in surrender to do so. He is considerably more advanced than yourself and can help you advance in Krsna consciousness, if you agree to be helped. I suggest that you say no to your mind, resolve to wholeheartedly try to cooperate with *** Prabhu, and strive to develop an enthusiastic service attitude.

You have to consider what you want. If you really want to become a pure devotee, then you need to be under strong guidance and you have to surrender. *** Prabhu can help you. And he needs help also. Please try to help him in the difficult services he has taken on.

Soon the Bhakti sastri course will begin. That will be very valuable for you. Please remain patient, stay where you are, and take advantage of that course. In the meantime please be sure to read Srila Prabhupada's books carefully for at least an hour each day.

Please be well. Please be happy. Please always try to dip daily, afresh, into the ocean of transcendental chanting of the Holy Name of the Lord and the beautiful worship and other sadhana Srila Prabhupada has left us.

29 November 2004

Guru Maharaj, here in D we have a Bhagavatam speaker from Vrindavan. His name is ***. From what I have learned from others, he hails from the Nimbarka Sampradaya. He is conducting a Bhagavat Saptah at the Srinathji Mandir. 80% of our ISKCON regular satsangis are attending his lectures and everybody is saying that he speaks very nicely and sings very nicely too. He is very famous around the world and lectures on many tv channels also. Guru Maharaj, I want to know your opinion on this, should we go and listen to such Bhagavatam speakers of other Sampradayas or should we stick to Srila Prabhupada and listen to his lectures? Won't we be called as fanatic if we do so? Please enlighten me.

That he is praised for speaking and singing "nicely" suggests that the hearers want to be entertained rather than enlightened; which again suggests that they never actually heard Bhagavat-katha in their lives—certainly not in the manner that Pariksit heard Sukadeva. Does this "nice" speaker explain Bhagavatam in a manner to uproot misconceptions and anarthas? Does he discuss Bhagavatam topics relevant to the hearers such as *grhesu grha-medhinam* and *nayam deho deha-bhajam*? Does he maintain a family by donations received from so-called Bhagavat-katha? Is he himself free from anarthas such as drinking tea and viewing TV, and if not how can anyone be freed from such anarthas by hearing him?

If these questions have not been considered before going to hear him, or if initiated devotees have not consulted their gurus before doing so, then it is to be understood that they are materialistic devotees interested in sense gratification in the name of Krsna consciousness, that they consider Krsna as an object of their enjoyment rather than as the object of their surrender.

Please bless me that I never become a popular speaker or that my speaking or singing be considered nice. Please protect me from the association of persons who wish to hijack for their own sense gratification my feeble attempts to serve Krsna. May I ever be considered a fanatic and scorned by such persons.

3 December 2004

It is inappropriate that you recommend others to me for diksha when you yourself lack faith in me.

I appreciate your desire to see things improved, but not your unwillingness to do more than complain. There are two types of complainers: one that simply grouses, and the other who is prepared to do something. How were slavery, apartheid, and child labor abolished? Not simply by complaining, but by people who felt they had to do something, and remained determined despite gross mistreatment by those whose malpractices they sought to reform.

ISKCON Law provides a systematic process for resolving internal complaints. If the complainant is dissatisfied with the outcome at a lower level he may take it higher. I have requested that the procedures be sent to me, after which I will forward them to you. If you are prepared to "walk the walk" and not just "talk the talk" then I will support your right to complain—even though, if you are to make the complaint fair and complete, I should also be one of those complained against.

5 December 2004

You will have to decide yourself whether it is appropriate that you continue in the diksha recommendation committee. I am not banning you.

I understand your frustration and hence previously suggested that you move to ***. Somehow that didn't happen and maybe it's Krsna's will, as you are contributing to Krsna consciousness in +++.

I have not got much involved in trying to resolve issues in +++ as it would take much of my energy which is better channelled into various national and international issues of ISKCON, which I have been addressing in various forums for several years—for which I am sometimes considered a maverick. I can't do everything, but would be willing to support you if you are serious to make a difference in +++.

Even among nondevotees it is considered that one who is not willing to pursue his complaints is not very serious about them. Simply by saying that you won't complain will not remove your discontent. Indeed you have previously told me that you will just mind your own business and not complain, but now again are complaining, being unable to restrain yourself.

I am not against your complaining per se but find it vexing that you are so willing to declare your lack of faith in me (three times now) but so unwilling to do anything to attempt to rectify the subject of your complaints. Big talk, no action.

Anyway considering the reality of your situation, maybe it is Krsna's arrangement that you are aloof from temple activities and can concentrate on study and preaching of Krsna katha. *Smarantah smaarayantas ca*. (SB 11.3.31)

23 December 2004

Thankyou for your frank and feelingful letter. According to ISKCON Law there are certain procedures to be fulfilled before approaching gurus to chant their pranama-mantras. However I think that in your case an exception may be made, to help to give you strength to come up in Krsna consciousness after all these years. Please consult *** Prabhu about this and if he agrees you may chant the pranama mantra offered to my very poor self. However you should be very serious about overcoming anarthas. And of course actual initiation would depend upon coming up to the required standard.

Please chant a lot, read Srila Prabhupada's books a lot, and associate with and serve devotees a lot. This will help you advance in Krsna consciousness. I am at your service.

24 December 2004

Even more important than working for a political solution to the mess in *** is to yourself always set an ideal example of hearing and chanting about Krsna by reading Srila Prabhupada's books and preaching Srila Prabhupada's message. That way you will get the mercy of Srila Prabhupada and always remain inspired, and in due course those who are sincere will be able to understand who is who.

24 December 2004

I know that your wife is a very good girl as I have seen her coming for so many years and sincerely engaging in Krsna conscious activities. So now I am very, very sorry to learn that she is manifesting materialistic tendencies.

Certainly the young grhastha devotees there need lots of help and attention. Probably very soon it will not be forthcoming on a permanent basis, but please try to invite some senior and responsible grhastha devotees for regular meetings with the young grhasthas. You could ask S Prabhu to take some interest although he is very busy with ISKCON V. R Prabhu in X could also be invited.

Also it would be good if the young wives could be engaged in classes for children and in preaching in the women's hostels. If they have taste in Krsna consciousness they will not have taste for anything else.

31 December 2004

Thankyou for accepting such great austerities to bring the message of Krsna to the suffering people of this world. There is no doubt that Srila Prabhupada is extremely pleased with your sacrifices on book distribution.

You are very fortunate to have the association of such an exemplary devotee as A Prabhu. Leaving his association might in some ways be easier for you, but it is unlikely that anywhere else you will get the opportunity to be so closely guided by such an advanced devotee. Considering this I feel it better that you adjust yourself to the austerities and continue serving under A Prabhu, at least up until Gaura Purnima. You should also frankly discuss with him the difficulties you are having.

If after Gaura Purnima you still feel you need a change, then let's consider it then.

2005

11 January 2005

We live in an era of doubt.

Open questioning of Srila Prabhupada and outright offenses against him go unreplied by the GBC despite pressure on them to do so.

Guru falldown is common.

In such an ethos it is not surprising that disciples will question their gurus' actions and very motives. It happens to me and I admit it's not pleasant. But if disciples are seriously practising Krsna consciousness then it is best to take their questioning seriously and try to reply.

Regarding reinitiation, please see SB 8.20.1 purport, especially "a useless guru, a family priest acting as guru, should be given up, and that the proper, bona-fide guru should be accepted."

Also,

avaisnavopadistena
mantrena nirayam vrajet
punas ca vidhina samyag
grahayed vaisnavad guroh

"One who is initiated into a mantra by a non-Vaisnava must go to hell. Therefore he should again be initiated properly, according

305

to the prescribed method, by a Vaisnava guru." (From SB 11.3.48, purport)

Faith, dedication, and affection cannot be forced or legislated. I understand your position and know that you are extremely sincere and that you have a good guide in your husband. Therefore if you wish to relate to me in a less than absolute way that is probably the best in your situation at present. There is no use to try to force faith that isn't there. As far as guilt feelings, well, you were a victim of certain circumstances. Be sure that if you are sincere, Srila Prabhupada and Krsna will reveal everything and take you back to Godhead. They will also reveal all that is necessary to go there. I can try to help you along the way. And you can also help me.

Email has its limitations so I'll keep this short. We could talk more in Mayapur if you could get out there, unless you feel inclined to discuss on the phone. But my feeling is that this may need not much discussion but that our future dealings depend on continued mutual respect between yourself, your husband, and myself.

22 January 2005

Thank you for your letter and request. I have been giving you siksa in an informal manner for some time. If you wish to formalize that relationship, it is fine with me. Formalization probably won't mean any great change in the manner of our dealings, but is more to do with the way we see each other. Put simply, this is an affair of the heart. Faith cannot be legislated, but faith that arouses out of genuine trust is the most valuable commodity as we reach out toward Krsna on a path we know little about.

Please go on serving your husband and looking after your children, knowing that performing stri-dharma and bhagavat-dharma side by side is a great service in this confused and unstable world.

23 January 2005

To Bhakti-tirtha Swami

Maharaja, I know that you've done a lot of service for Srila Prabhupada and I respect that. Mistakenly or otherwise, in a spirit of service to Srila Prabhupada I took up issues with you. Frankly, if you weren't in your present condition then I'd probably still be stoking those issues. But as it seems that you won't be present with us long I'd like to state again that I never intended anything personally against you and hereby apologize for any unnecessary disturbance I may have caused you. I wish you well in your onward journey.

3 February 2005

I suggest that in the meantime, along with your regular book distribution and other preaching activities, you take the opportunity for Krsna conscious self improvement, especially by deep study of Srila Prabhupada's books, plus learning to play mrdanga nicely, learning various bhajanas, going on harinama as much as possible, etc. Become advanced in Krsna consciousness.

14 April 2005

At the risk of threatened legal action I am writing to you in the hope of touching any spot in your heart that has not become wholly hardened. I beg that if somewhere in your heart you have even a glimmer of affection for me that you cool-headedly peruse this letter.

I address you as "my dear" for I have always regarded you as such. However you haven't been much in touch with me for the last few years although I have tried to contact you on many occasions. For instance the following letter to which I got no reply:

> I understand that you are in a state of great mental turbulence. I strongly request you to meet me in Juhu

on 21 Sep (when I am set to arrive from Japan) and to celebrate Radhastami with me there. It is my duty to try to help you when you are in difficulty but you have to come to me so I can help you. Please do.

In the meantime please go somewhere where you can get congenial association. I suggest going to Juhu and being with B for some time.

You were eager to go overseas but that didn't work out. You wanted to marry one lady in Punjab but that also came to nothing. Please consider if unfulfilled personal desires are a factor in the frustration by which you are now writing to me very aggressively. I have always appreciated you as a strong spirited, serious devotee of Krsna, but I find it unfair that now you are accusing me of torturing you, for I cannot recall even one occasion when I have acted in a manner calculated to harm you or anyone else.

I openly admit that I am far from perfect but can honestly say that I am not deliberately trying to manipulate people, as you claim. I have always given you full scope to indulge your free-spirited nature and as such you have served largely according to your own wish practically since you joined ISKCON.

Undoubtedly there are many discrepancies in ISKCON, and I am ready to cooperate with you in attempting to rectify them as far as possible. Indeed I am already active in this field as I deem it a major responsibility to Srila Prabhupada to try to preserve the spirit of his movement in these difficult times.

What else can I do to help you? Please let me know. It is not possible to understand exactly what difficulties you are undergoing from vague accusations in an email. Please come and be with me for some time as I have several times requested you, and let us work together to be better devotees and to serve Srila Prabhupada's mission in the best possible way.

Otherwise to suddenly reject me and ISKCON without even once trying to discuss your problems with me suggests that this is an excuse to renege on or much decrease your commitment to devotional life. Please also consider if it is actually conducive to your eternal welfare to compare to skunks persons trying to serve Srila Prabhupada.

22 June 2005

Your desire to improve chanting is laudable. However our acaryas have advised to cultivate *nama-ruci* simultaneously with *jive daya*. It can be difficult to balance the demands of preaching with sadhana, but somehow we have to do it, knowing that for our sadhana to bear fruit, we have to get the mercy of our acaryas, who become very pleased when they see a devotee is compassionate to help others. Specifically as you are maybe the only capable preacher in a large language area, and aspiring devotees are very much desirous of your spiritual input, I suggest that it is not proper for you to presently consider reducing your preaching, but rather to improve your sadhana side by side with preaching.

I am planning to later this year for the first time perform Kartik-vrata by staying in a holy place, with extra chanting etc., and feel this could be useful for preachers to get spiritually recharged. But really our first duty is as suggested by Sri Prahlada Maharaja (SB 7.9.44).

Devotees in D told me that you will organize Rathayatra there. If it is held a few days after Kartik, I would be able to attend.

13 July 2005

Don't worry about not knowing English. There is plenty of preaching to be done in Hindi also. English might impress some people but sincere people will be impressed by genuinely saintly qualities. So please try to develop all good qualities as a sincere devotee and ideal wife and that will please Srila Prabhupada and myself very much and your life will be successful.

The best way to learn English is to read Srila Prabhupada's books in English.

16 July 2005

I pray that you may be ever happy at the lotus feet of Sri Sri Gaur Nitai. Please continue serving Them with full sincerity, cooperating in all ways with A Prabhu, and the day will soon come when you will be fully situated in pure devotional service.

16 July 2005

You yourself note that it is best if women not work outside. Many problems arise because of this, which may not be immediately or overtly apparent. As a temporary measure it may sometimes be adopted due to various conditions in this strange age we live in, but it is best avoided and not at all advisable as a long-term policy.

I would be happy to discuss this further with your husband and yourself as and when possible. Now I am heading for Europe.

1 August 2005

Thankyou for consulting me on this. About two years ago a disciple of mine in Europe was in a similar situation. Like yourself, both he and his wife are doctors. In his wife's first pregnancy it was ascertained that her child had no kidneys and could not survive outside the womb. They were advised to abort, and asked my opinion. It took me a little time to consult various learned devotees and ayurvedic doctors but the opinion was unanimous: sastra does not under any circumstances allow abortion.

By the time I communicated this to that disciple, he and his wife had already decided that they could not terminate the pregnancy, that for some reason known to Krsna He had sent them a soul to be nourished and cared for as long as possible. She went through the whole pregnancy, singing and talking of Krsna to the baby in her womb, who died within two hours of delivery. Her conscience is clear and she is happy that she did the right thing.

I request you to take the same stance. If it is Krsna's wish or some karmic due that your child be physically or mentally retarded, accept that burden as Krsna's mercy and help the child as responsible parents should. Other persons will advise you that it is practical and proper to kill the foetus, but such a sinful action would bring upon you distress in the present and in future lives. Please consider this very carefully and inform me of your decision. I pray that you act in a manner pleasing to Krsna and worthy of His devotee.

2 August 2005

I am a member of the Indian community in G and some time ago I have joined the bhakta-program here. I have been attending S Maharaja's lectures and I am thinking of accepting him as my diksha-guru. However, Srila Prabhupada says that if we accept a wrong person as guru, our whole life is spoiled. So, before taking a final step, I would like to be sure about my decision. Some way or other I heard that you do not have a very good opinion about S Swami. I am sure you have better things to do than talking about other's lives, but if you can tell me anything that I should know before becoming his disciple, please do it. This is just for my personal information, as it is so important in my spiritual life, so I promise I will not comment about whatever you may say.

A weighty query indeed, especially coming from a person unknown to me. It is certainly wise to be careful in selecting who to approach to lead one to Krsna, especially in these turbulent days of ISKCON. You could read the section on Guru and Disciple in my book *A Beginner's Guide to Krsna consciousness*.

I have very little interaction with HH S Maharaja and as far as I remember have not publicly or hardly even privately expressed opinions about him. Several devotees have confided to me that Maharaja's style is more eclectic than they feel comfortable with, and almost certainly my approach to Krsna consciousness would be considered more conservative or traditional. However you have to make your own decision, intelligently based on guru, sadhu, and sastra, with particular reference to Srila Prabhupada's books.

12 September 2005

There are certainly plus points for this match, yet I am reluctant to endorse it, because sastra states that the wife should be younger than the husband, and because sastra forbids women with children remarrying. As Srila Prabhupada wrote to a lady disciple:

I wish that the mothers who have no husband at present should not remarry, but should dedicate their time to seeing that their children are brought up very nicely in Krsna Consciousness. (Srila Prabhupada's letter to Silavati—New Vrindaban, 14 June 1969)

Probably you are quite enthusiastic about entering into this union, but particularly as you are one of my senior disciples, your going ahead with it would make more difficult my preaching intended for establishing Vedic dharma. More or less anything goes in modern ISKCON, but I am trying to point the way toward a better cultural ethos based on traditional Vedic dharma, and I would greatly appreciate if my disciples would help me in this endeavor, even if in doing so they have to make some sacrifices, or even if they don't fully understand why they should follow the edicts of a social system that they have no experience of.

I am sitting next to *** Prabhu, the well known astrologer, who says that the methodology that +++ Maharaja (who he has very high regard for) uses for giving marital matching is simplistic and quickly executed and although may give a general indication, is not very reliable.

It is a good idea that you get married but please reconsider this particular match.

28 September 2005

Transcendental mystic experiences, such as actual appearance of acaryas in dreams or in waking visions, should be taken seriously, although sometimes lower spirits deliberately mislead by impersonating spiritually realized souls. If you want we could discuss this when we meet but after all, mundane mystical experiences, however real and meaningful they may appear, are just more material noise for us to forget as we become absorbed in Krsna consciousness.

18 November 2005

My father and his forefathers had been performing Kedareswari vrata every year the full moon day after Diwali (the wedding day of Srimati Tulasidevi and Lord Salagrama). Once we got married, my father had given the vrata to me and my wife which in turn I have to give to my son once he is married. We also had the toran to be tied to our hand given by him. Please have mercy on us and let us know what we should do now.

The following is relevant in this regard.

... unlike other great devotees such as Arjuna, who sometimes worshiped demigods in order to comply with social customs or to show respect for their positions in the scheme of planetary management, Uddhava never worshiped any demigods.

Therefore, Uddhava is *prapannaya*, or completely surrendered to Lord Krsna, having no other shelter. (SB 11.11.26–27)

You may worship demigods just to comply with social customs, but that will mean an obstruction in your surrender to Krsna. I suggested to *** Prabhu, who was in a similar situation, to observe his vrata by distributing many books of Srila Prabhupada as a better offering to Lord Siva. Better that you also do the same in the name of Kedareswari. That would disappoint your father, unless he becomes Krsna conscious. You could try to explain to him based on Gita 18.66 etc., that Kedareswari vrata and other such observances simply bind us to this material world birth after birth and that we can better serve ongoing generations by directing them toward Krsna.

20 November 2005

Thankyou for your letter and your concern. I am of course very sorry to learn of the unjustifiable behavior of your husband. It seems like a classic case of an aspiring spiritualist caught between high ideals and habitual gross desires.

However, your wish that he goes away and leaves you is also not very laudable. You are fortunate to have a husband with lofty spiritual aspirations. Even if he falls far short of them, that he is thus inclined is itself rare in this modern age of gross materialism and selfishness. Your duty as his wife is to try and help him in all respects, not merely separate from him in times of difficulty. Your son also needs his father at home. Children separated from their fathers are far more likely to have serious psychological problems and become social delinquents.

As fighting and arguing with him are likely to make the relationship even more strained, I suggest that you gradually, carefully try to improve your life and his. You claim to be a Buddhist, so you can probably understand that to lead a purer, more spiritual life, giving up eating meat and watching TV would be a good first step. Doing so would no doubt please your husband and help immensely in healing the rift between you. Please try to deal with him sweetly and tolerantly and in this way reach his heart.

What do you think?

22 November 2005

Guru Maharaja I'm P Devi Dasi. I'm the wife of N Das from D. Guru Maharaja now my English is ok, I had started to read Srila Prabhupada's books. Guru Maharaja, on 27th of October I fly to D, I will start my new life in full devotion. So I want your blessings, Guru Maharaja. I failed my T.Y. Bcom Exams in 2 Subject and 2 in S.Y. Bcom.

Please be blessed! Chant Hare Krsna, serve devotees, read Srila Prabhupada's books, be an ideal wife, and your life will be succesful in all respects.

23 November 2005

(In response to a letter to a devotee who had been advised to read about Mother Teresa to learn how to be more assertive, as Mother Teresa was)

Please do not worry about your inability to be aggressive and dominant. To enter the spiritual world it is required to be humble and submissive, not aggressive and dominant. Please read about Srila Prabhupada and books by him. You should know that whereas Srila Prabhupada is fully Krsna conscious, Mother Teresa was on the mundane platform of identifying the body as the self. Hence even one moment of Srila Prabhupada's pastimes, one word from him, is more valuable than anything Mother Teresa could give in millions of lifetimes.

26 November 2005

I know that you are a very sincere bhakta. That you have made a mistake is not surprising. We are all prone to do so, as we are all weak. It would be better if you go where you can get strong association. For this I recommend that you spend some time with *** Prabhu in X. Later if you want to work outside you may, but please get some good training and association while you can.

Please see +++ Prabhu, who I've added as a receiver here, to arrange your travel to X.

28 November 2005

Therefore we are asking Your Holinesses kind blessings for our endeavour so we could do something pleasing for Srila Prabhupada and His mission.

By whatever power Srila Prabhupada may have invested in me, please be blessed for fulfilment of this pure desire.

There is also one question regarding association with parents. We usually go visit our families during Christmas holidays. But my family they are all meat eaters etc. and my little brother is the managing director in a wholesale meat company. I haven't been preaching to them strongly against their nasty habits since my milder approaches haven't got any effect. Should I try to minimize my association with them or have a stronger stand with them regarding meat eating etc.? They are very supportive otherwise, brother letting us borrow his company's forklift for free and my mother just bought me winter equipment with almost 1000 Euros. But they have no idea about anything spiritual.

Maybe your mild approach has no overt effect, but that they are supportive and rendering service will not go in vain. They are already becoming imperceptibly purified and Krsna will arrange for their further purification if you remain patient with them. I suggest that you not risk disrupting the tangible service that they are doing, and continue to do your part by giving them lots of books and prasada. You could even give them prasada of the variety that Srila Prabhupada called "meat-eaters delight"—as described in Kurma Prabhu's description of Srila Prabhupada-lila in Australia. Contact him for the recipe.

18 November 2005

Sri Chaitanya Mahaprabhu's dictum, *bhala na khaibe ara bhala na paribe,* "Do not dress luxuriously and do not eat delicious foodstuffs," was specifically meant for vairagis. Nevertheless it is good for grhasthas also to remain simple. I suggest that you keep a few fancy clothes for special social occasions and otherwise dress simply but neatly. For makeup on special occasions, better remain traditional and use kajjal and mehendi. I suggest that you live simply, save money, and retire early so that you can serve Krsna full time as soon as possible.

23 November 2005

Please pray to Sri Sri Gaura Nitai to return to you. If They wish to, they will. If not, They won't.

30 November 2005

Please accept my best wishes, offered with great concern. All glories to our eternal master, His Divine Grace, ISKCON Founder Acharya, Srila A. C. Bhaktivedanta Swami Prabhupada.

Krsna will help you as long as you maintain a desire to be connected to Him. At the same time, as you know, acting against the principles of bhakti is not pleasing to Krsna. I suggest that if you are not already doing so, keep pictures of Srila Prabhupada, the Panca-tattva, and Sri Sri Radha Krsna in a place where you can regularly see them, and daily offer them at least incense. And, however disqualified you feel yourself, daily pick up your beads and chant at least one round on them. Get some beads if you don't have them. Also it would tremendously help you if you were to daily read a page of Bhagavad Gita As It Is. Please try. Krsna is ready to help you, and no one is too fallen to get His mercy.

12 December 2005

Please tell your wife that out of great concern for her I strongly request her to wholly put out of her mind any thought of divorce.

Please contact *** and/or +++ Prabhus or any other senior grhasthas who you trust and ask if they can help you through this difficult period.

It will probably be necessary for you to work and earn some regular income, without which most women, even devotees, feel insecure.

I suggest you not talk to her a lot of philosophy but more of how Krsna is kind, sweet etc. A devotee and his wife in USA who are married for about 30 years told me that they joke a lot; instead of quarreling they just make light of each others foibles and of themselves. Instead of getting angry they just laugh.

15 December 2005

I suggest that you daily read together out loud a chapter of Krsna book. Also you might suggest to her to develop some home-based business such as making sweetballs, jam, and cake prasada for selling.

31 December 2005

I understand that you wish to serve Krsna on a very high level, and that others may not understand your doing so. Still, within an institution some rules need be followed. You write that you decided to change your diet, but better than unilaterally deciding is to take permission and blessings from other devotees, without which nothing we do can please Krsna. Indeed shastra states that before performing a vrata one should take permission and blessings from one's guru, otherwise the vrata will be useless. Just imagine the chaos if everyone decided to perform devotional service in their own way.

Undoubtedly there are various difficulties connected with your service, but as I have several times told you, I will be happy if you continue it. And it seems that Sri Sri Gaura Nitai will not let you go. So please return and continue your service in a cool-headed way, and that will make me happy and you will be happy also. Do not become a servant of your imperfect mind.

Please try to understand these points. *** Prabhu may also explain them to you in more detail.

2006

4 January 2006

Two devotees I know in India have been following a partially naturopathic diet for the last many months. They take one meal a day with chapatis, dal, and raw vegetables, and once a day fully raw: sprouted chickpeas etc. And I think also milk once a day. It's not as purifying a diet as 100% raw food, but that way they get enough strength to do their service and also gradually the benefit of raw food.

I wish that you might do the same. Please don't be unreasonably attached to a diet that renders you so weak that you can't go to mangal arati and the devotees become anxious over your health.

27 January 2006

Although recognizing that there are and will be different approaches in Krsna consciousness, and that we can aspire to in a Krsna conscious manner emulate misapplied qualities of non-Krsna conscious persons, I still feel it better that we find role models in those great devotees whose qualities are purely Krsna conscious.

10 April 2006

Dearest brother, friend and Prabhu Maharaji

Thankyou dear ** Prabhu-Garu for your efforts to inject

personalism into this impersonalism-promoting media. My dandavat to you.[15]

However I have two difficulties in giving you advice. One is that I really don't feel qualified to do so as you are so much more capable and senior than me. And on this particular issue I don't have much to offer of practical help other than "Just pray to guru and Krsna and dive in."

Language skills seem to be largely a gift. +++ Maharaja struggled unsuccessfully for years to learn Hindi and Nepali. Whereas H Maharaja and the erstwhile B Maharaja (R Prabhu) are both so brilliant that they start to speak a new language after a few hours of exposure to it.

Your problem seems to be more like stagefright than language abilities. I find it helpful when faced by mental blocks to remind myself that I'm an insignificant fool and to pray to Srila Prabhupada and Krsna for the ability to represent them properly without worrying what others think about my imperfect attempts to do so. Being properly rested also makes a lot of difference to my presentation. When I'm tired my brain doesn't move beyond second gear.

It is of course essential to practice, practice, practice. Fluency means getting beyond the stage of thinking in one language and speaking in another. As you have noted, Indian people are very tolerant of and even grateful for imperfect attempts to speak their tongues, so you have a supportive audience.

I hope these few words may be of some help.

I'm looking forward to seeing your books whenever they manifest.

_____

15. Garu—a suffix denoting respect, similar to *Ji* in Hindi.

12 April 2006

Pride comes before a fall.

But there is hope.

"Thus there is every chance of failure on the yogic path; even a great sage like Visvamitra Muni can fall down due to material allurement. Although the muni fell for the time being, he again resolved to go on with the yoga process, and this should be our resolve. Krsna informs us that such failures should not be cause for despair. There is the famous proverb that "failure is the pillar of success." In the spiritual life especially, failure is not discouraging. Krsna very clearly states that even if there is failure, there is no loss either in this world or in the next. One who takes to this auspicious line of spiritual culture is never completely vanquished." (The Path of Yoga, Chapter 6: The Fate of the Unsuccessful Yogi)

You will always be dear to me. Please make all efforts to remain strong. Try to become a humble servant of the Vaisnavas.

13 April 2006

Srila Prabhupada gave you that name for a specific reason. He clearly expected great things of you. Please accept my obeisances.

Still I go brain dead when I reach words I cannot speak and have to then start thinking in English which is like trying to skip rope with the wrong rhythm.

In that circumstance, Indian people just speak the English word. Hinglish: "Ye machine ke parts mein cooch problem he." South Indians do it all the time. It's quite fashionable. How about Anglolugu?

One thing I do if I don't know the word is to ask the listeners: "unknown word" kya bolte he?

On the whole it's best not to get hung up. Jump in with the awareness that most listeners don't care too much what you are saying, being happily mesmerized by your speaking something resembling their language. That's OK for the beginning. By the time they're ready to hear your message, your language should have improved enough to convey it.

Both the languages I've picked up were a struggle in the beginning, but at some point suddenly, mystically, things clicked and speaking became natural.

Srila Prabhupada: When there is fire in a house, the inmates of the house go out to get help from the neighbors who may be foreigners, and yet without knowing the language the victims of the fire express themselves, and the neighbors understand the need, even though not expressed in the same language. The same spirit of cooperation is needed to broadcast this transcendental message of the Srimad-Bhagavatam throughout the polluted atmosphere of the world. After all, it is a technical science of spiritual values, and thus we are concerned with the techniques and not with the language. If the techniques of this great literature are understood by the people of the world, there will be success. (SB 1.5.11)

14 April 2006

It is not good to be whimsical especially in such an important matter. He gave his word that he would marry that girl and he should follow it through. Changing his mind like this will only cause disturbance to himself and others.

17 April 2006

It is sad news that *** has become so foolish. It is clear that she never carefully read Srila Prabhupada's books or heard my lectures; for if she had, she could not have been attracted to these shallow people. Her deviation underscores the importance of undertaking bhakti-sastra study.

Someone should try to explain to her why the path she has taken is wrong. But she has been duplicitous inasmuch as she did not consult me before adventuring on it, which indicates that she has very little regard for me. So I am not very hopeful for her.

Now she has to choose: she can either be my disciple or the disciple of that cheater. If she wants to be my disciple she must immediately give up all contact and sympathy with that cheater and his followers. Unless she gives up this nonsense, devotees should be advised that she is deviated and should not be associated with. And even if she does agree to give up that nonsense, then for at least a year she should not have any kind of leadership role, including conducting Nama Hatta programs.

21 April 2006

It is good that you are living as a brahmacari in ISKCON Vrndavan. Best that you continue doing so for at least two years more and for the time being not consider doing anything else. Submit yourself to any service you may be asked to perform and study Srila Prabhupada's books carefully. That will help you progress in Krsna consciousness.

6 July 2006

Is it wrong if I try to make my living from my Mahabharat narrations?

A better attitude is to desire simply to glorify Krsna and live on whatever He provides, even if that is very little.

I can sell this recordings in the form of mp3 and thus make a good business.

Thinking of making a good business from Krsna-katha renders one unfit to speak Krsna-katha.

In this way my mind will always be absorbed in Krsna katha also because I have to make nice recordings.

"Nice" in this context means what will appeal to the hearers, rather than what they need to hear. In this way you may join the ranks of professional speakers who Srila Prabhupada speaks against so strongly. I pray never to become a nice speaker but for the blessing to be a servant of the non-duplicitous parampara.

24 July 2006

You need the courage to face the fact that you are not fit for brahmacari life and should get married and practice Krsna consciousness as an honest grhastha.

22 August 2006

I have received your letters and deliberated over their contents. Of course, I don't know all the nuances of this situation, but on the whole it seems wise not to marry unless there is mutual respect, trust, and appreciation, which is clearly lacking in your case. Cancelling the marriage will bring difficulties but better to suffer them for a short time rather than suffering throughout life.

However if you can reconcile then you might reconsider. But such reconciliation would have to be more than surface deep. For instance it might be difficult for H to forswear his understandable resentment for another proposal having been mooted after the engagement had been made.

When I agreed to the proposal for your marriage I did so presuming that all factors had been carefully considered. The idea was to make an alliance between devotees, as marriage to a nondevotee can devastate efforts in bhakti. However it seems that we are sometimes naive in presuming that devotees can overcome their material conditioning and live peacefully with persons with whom they are basically incompatible. Astrological matching gives but an indication, and factors such as financial and social expectations and cultural background must also be considered. As there are not so many devotees and matching can be difficult, sometimes in good faith we overlook differences in devotees' temperaments and marry them anyway, but the result is not often happy.

Please do not blame anyone for this unfortunate situation. In today's disturbed world it is not easy to arrange solid marriages, and those who sincerely attempt to do so are often paid with scorn.

I wish that whatever you decide, you both remain convinced that the lotus feet of Lord Krsna are the ultimate refuge for all persons suffering in material existence, and that we should commit ourselves to His service under the guidance of Srila Prabhupada and his representatives.

17 October 2006

It is a good idea if you spend more time in India before marriage, although it might not be easy to find a devotee community that will accept you on a full time basis. Please do not get married or live with that young girl devotee for at least a year. You got engaged once then it broke, so better be slow, steady, and sure.

3 November 2006

Below is an extract from a letter from yet another devotee who performed much austerity for several years and whose health is now broken.

Finally the fever has come down. But I am so tired and it will take some time to get energy. But the past two years have proved that I have a serious setback in health and I collapsed so many times. It seems to me that I have to take some gap in my service to ISKCON and improve my health. Otherwise I am afraid that in long term my health will not allow me at all to serve ISKCON and yourself.

Please consider carefully and don't push your body too hard. It is not your property and should be properly maintained for serving Krsna.

3 November 2006

You will get many different answers as there are many different levels of understanding guru-tattva. Once Srila Prabhupada approved that a disciple of his be further initiated by a Gaudiya Math sannyasi and other times he was much against it.

It's interesting that you are interested to follow Vaisnava etiquette whereas your diksa-guru seems to consider it his duty to reinitiate disciples of gurus in ISKCON and other Gaudiya Maths with the reasoning that such gurus are fallen if they don't allow their disciples to be initiated by him.

I would not recommend that you again be initiated but you might consider yourself in need of guidance or at least someone you can look up to and wholeheartedly bow down to. That you don't think you could find a guru is your misfortune as you certainly need to become more respectful in dealings with your peers what to speak of seniors. Frankly I found your recent responses to *** Prabhu and +++ Prabhu quite distasteful. Of course my own attack on B Swami is well-known, but that took place after nearly two years of privately trying to point out to him that some of his statements needed rectification.

6 November 2006

Chanting at least sixteen rounds of the maha-mantra is the basis of the spiritual practices given to us by Srila Prabhupada, in pursuance of the teachings of Lord Caitanya and sastra, and it is not within my right to endorse a different standard for you.

There are thousands of devotees throughout the world in similar circumstances to yourself—almost all have to struggle one way or another in this difficult Kali-yuga—who nevertheless retain their commitment to chant sixteen rounds.

I understand that you lead an arduous life, but nevertheless again request you to maintain your initiation vows, and to not try to justify reneging on them.

Please carefully study Srila Prabhupada's books as well as distributing them, and you will understand better.

6 November 2006

I've given clear guidelines to S Das but he is ignoring them. I told him that as far as possible I don't want to get involved in disputes between disciples and that he should sort it out with "lower level" devotees. But he insists that I must instruct B—presumably meaning that I must order him according to S Das's direction. What if after hearing everything I were to instruct S Das to do something against his wishes? Would S Das follow? I doubt it because some years ago when S Das was campaigning against the local ISKCON management (including forging a complaint from A Prabhu), I instructed him to join padayatra in G. S Das did not follow that order but now he wants me to follow his order and give his orders to someone else. He has severe misconceptions regarding the roles of gurus and disciples.

7 November 2006

Please forgive my innumerable offenses at your lotus feet. I could not realize your exalted position.

As I am not fit to communicate with you, and as I do not wish to divert you from your many important services, and as I am also very busy, I request that you not send me any more mails.

7 November 2006

Sorry I do not want to hear any excuses or unnecessary topics to prolong this matter. Do not twist the matter again.

And sorry I don't want to hear any more such offensive statements from you again. You should apologize to B Prabhu. Go look up the word in the dictionary: "apologize."

I am not interested to be involved in this affair. You have demonstrated not an iota of humility (look up that word also) and just demand that I do as you say. I refuse. I am not your chela.[16] Do not write to me about this again.

11 November 2006

Thankyou so much for the trust and affection you have expressed for me. However according to tradition and plain common sense, I cannot instruct you without your husband's knowledge and involvement. Doing so would almost certainly lead to unpleasant misunderstandings.

Srila Prabhupada recalled:

"I am a sannyasi. I am forbidden to make any association with women. I cannot talk even with woman in a lonely place. That is forbidden. I cannot talk with a woman. I give you one practical example. When my Guru Maharaja, my spiritual master, was living … I am speaking about fifty years before. We were all young men at that time, and one of my Godbrothers, he was also young man, Dr. O. B. Kapoor, and his wife was also young. So his wife wanted to speak with my Guru Maharaja. My Guru Maharaja was at that time not less than sixty or more than that, and the girl, my friend's wife, she was not more than twenty-two years. But actually, she was just like his granddaughter. But she proposed, "Sir, I wanted to speak with you something confidentially." My Guru Maharaja said, "Oh, no, no. I cannot speak with you confidentially. You can speak whatever you like here." Just see. "I cannot speak." Now the so much age difference, so much, I mean to say, affection, still, he refused:

---

16. *Chela* (Hindi and Bengali)—disciple.

"No, no. I cannot talk with you confidentially because you are woman." (From a lecture on *Bhagavad-gita* 7.8–14, 2 October 1966)

Nevertheless I will be happy to reply to your queries when I go to Mayapur, which would probably be in February. And I can give you the best instruction, to always chant the holy names and study Srila Prabhupada's books very carefully, serve the Vaisnavas and especially your husband, and always be happy in Krsna consciousness. For intimate advice on a day to day basis it would be better to request one of the senior ladies living in Mayapur.

13 November 2006

Please accept my apologies for offenses to you by my disciples. It gives me much distress. Some seem to be incorrigible. Or maybe I'm so incompetent as a guru that I'm unable to reform them. Just see that fellow who I ordered to apologize for his blatant offense to you, and he replied "explaining" that he had a right to do so!

You could consider asking why the girls aren't coming much to the temple. It may be due to exam pressure, hostel restrictions, or whatever. And if you don't get a satisfactory reply, it might be better to heed Lord Krsna's advice: *na buddhi bhedam janayed* ...

As far as certain persons being trained to consider other centers on a lower level, all I can say is "pride comes before a fall." Can the bubble last forever without bursting? I suggest you mention what you were told to the superguru of that whole colossus, next time you see him.

Now I'd better get back to editing the disputes—and the triumphs—of the past.[17]

---

17. This refers to work on my book *Sri Bhaktisiddhanta Vaibhava*.

16 November 2006

How about calling all the gripers together regularly for kirtana? Otherwise the kali-kolahala will continue.[18]

harer namaiva kevalam

"This chanting should go on. Instead of meetings, resolutions, dissolutions, revolutions and then no solutions, there should be chanting."[19]

21 November 2006

I wasn't displeased by your leaving the temple. I'm very grateful for all the very valuable service that you performed, and filling the gap hasn't been easy, but I accepted it as inevitable that you needed to move on and wish you all the best for your future.

There is no doubt that we live in a very difficult age and inside or outside the temple things can be almost unimaginably rough. A philosophical outlook helps. Did you see the recent posting I sent on BVKS Sanga, re the Avanti brahmana's acceptance of his fate? And of course we need to organize farm communities as Srila Prabhupada envisioned. Doing so won't be easy nor is country life a guaranteed utopia, but at least there should be more opportunity to engage in the yuga dharma of chanting Hare Krsna, which is the only genuine elixir.

26 November 2006

For you to be accepted as a sannyasa candidate in ISKCON you would have to change your lifestyle in ways that you may not wish to, and then wait a few years, which you also may not wish to do. And to take sannyasa elsewhere would effectively place you outside of ISKCON, which you also may not desire.

---

18. *Kali-kolahala* (Sankrit, Bengali, Hindi)—an uproar or quarrel typical of the Age of Kali.

19. From *Srila Prabhupada-lilamrita*, by Satsvarupa Dasa Goswami.

In other words, in whatever way you might take sannyasa, it would mean significant changes in your life that you might not desire. So practically you have to consider what is most important to you.

27 November 2006

Get off the mental platform. Read, chant, and distribute Srila Prabhupada's books. Pray a lot. Krsna will help you. For any particular advice ask *** Prabhu.

3 December 2006

*** Prabhu's estrangement from many of his godbrothers is probably largely due to his sharp criticism of everything he perceives as wrong. Even though often accurate, his comments may not be always appropriate, and may be the cause of his present suffering.

If he wants to avail of the devotee association that is the only hope for his rectification then he has to admit that he is in no position to criticize others, and that to effect change where it is needed, first he has to change himself. Just as patience is needed to cure his sickness, so patience is required to rectify anomalies in ISKCON.

Here is a letter from Srila Prabhupada addressing a disciple sick in another way. Srila Prabhupada challenges the disciple to prove his sincerity.

> My Dear Lalitananda dasa,
>
> Please accept my blessings. I am in due receipt of your letter dated May 13rd, 1975 and have noted the contents. I am very sorry that you have taken to homosex. It will not help you advance in your attempt for spiritual life. In fact, it will only hamper your advancement. I do not know why you have taken to such abominable activities.

What can I say? Anyway, try to render whatever service you can to Krsna. Even though you are in a very degraded condition Krsna, being pleased with your service attitude, can pick you up from your fallen state. You should stop this homosex immediately. It is illicit sex, otherwise, your chances of advancing in spiritual life are nil. Show Krsna you are serious, if you are.

I hope this meets you in good health.

Your ever well-wisher,

A. C. Bhaktivedanta Swami

*** Prabhu needs strong determination, strong humility to admit he needs help, and strong, caring assistance. The first two are in his own hands. As for help, there is probably only you in a position, emotionally and logistically, to do so. Beyond your capacity? Maybe. But you are the only one who cares enough about him. You have to decide if you are ready to put in much sustained energy with apparently little chance of success, and the risk of arrest if caught with him when he has drugs.

Please also consider that mere unsubmissiveness does not qualify one as a ksatriya, who is characterized more by determination to perform heroic acts than by wanton unsubmissiveness, a trait typical of criminals rather than devotees. A real ksatriya is always submissive to brahmanas, who he recognizes as superior and competent and necessary to guide him. The "I'm right and all others are wrong" attitude suggests that of the demonic as detailed in Gita chapter sixteen. I'm not saying that *** Prabhu is demonic, but that his anarthas should be understood as such and not attributed to noble causes.

A harsh analysis? Possibly. Realistic? Probably.

Please consider and decide what to do.

3 December 2006

It is good that you wish to wholly dedicate your life in Krsna's service and I commend that decision. But you have to do so in a way that your parents will be satisfied and will not harrass the devotees. You also have to be fully convinced, not that later you have doubts and feel disturbed.

5 December 2006

I'm sorry to learn of your sickness. Just see how maya can strike any time even at the beginning of the marathon.

Do I chant missed gayatri and japa next day?

Best.

… likely ask me to take away kanthimala and upavita atleast during the operation so are there anything to overcome this lack of protection?

Wear tilak, pray and chant. Listen as much as possible, all day more or less, to lectures and kirtans. Be super nice to the staff and fellow patients because they will judge ISKCON and Srila Prabhupada based on you. Distribute prasad and never complain and they will be impressed.

Don't rush back to book distribution against doctor's advice. In fact don't do any physical effort that the doctors don't advise. My personal experience is that I wasted literally months of service due to rushing into service when I should have rested more after illness.

Please let me know how things turn out.

23 December 2006

Thankyou for preparing these books. I appreciate your sticking to this service and getting things done. However, now that there are others ready to help, it would be better if you were to work with them. For instance, devotees in Bosnia are ready to print more copies of each book, so by your printing just a few, more work is created by necessitating reprints.

In principle, the idea of the book on Srila Prabhupada is good. But as several of my VP offerings appear in My Memories of Srila Prabhupada, they should be published in that book only, not elsewhere. If you have English transcripts of the lectures you planned to publish, please send them to me.

I was and will always be acting correctly and sincerely toward you.

Thankyou.

If you really want to act correctly and sincerely toward me, then better than asking me to support you in what you are doing would be to first ask if what you are doing is what I want you to do. These are my books, not yours, so if you wish to serve me in producing them, please consult me about how to do so instead of trying to force me and all others concerned to be servants of your plans.

What you are doing is good, but if you would work more cooperatively with others it could be much better.

2007

10 January 2007

As you've asked for input I'll give some even if it's viewed as impractical.

I see your most important service now as keeping your marriage together. Even more important than being with the book distributors. Excuse me if that sounds like heresy.

Just two days ago I was speaking with a godbrother who provided well for his family yet saw several of his kids turn into drug abusers and womanizers. They told him that he had never provided a home for them. House yes, money yes, but not a home, because many times either one of the parents was away, and when they were together they mostly fought.

Exactly what you should do I can't suggest but I request that you bear this in mind.

Just an aside: a recently married devotee here in G committed suicide a few days before his scheduled initiation. He left behind a pregnant wife (the sister of one of my disciples) and a widowed mother. He was a bit mentally unstable it seems and had been dismissed from his job, and was mostly at home trying to balance his mother and wife, who didn't get along well.

10 January 2007

I'm sorry to hear that you are feeling hopeless about the situation in C. Time is often the best healer. The Pandavas had to wait 13 years for their wrongs to be addressed. And the Avanti brahmana (see SB Canto 11) just tolerated the dreadful insults piled on him, considering them his karmic dues.

I also feel on one side hopeless about many things in ISKCON but at the same time hopeful that *satyam eva jayate*—truth will prevail. I try to look on the bright side and see that there are many inspiring devotees I can associate with, who even though like me going through struggles with anarthas and sometimes having more downs than ups, are nevertheless sticking with faith and sincerity to Srila Prabhupada's lotus feet. They for me are the real ISKCON, never mind where the signboard is.

You are also fortunate to be in a community of devotees whose aim is clearly to serve Srila Prabhupada. Above all you have a husband whose dedication to and enthusiasm for Srila Prabhupada's most dear book distribution has not diminished since his legendary days as a brahmacari maharathi.

So please do not feel hopeless. Negative emotions are just as misleading as blind positiveness. By sentimental positiveness, we see everything wrong as right, but by a negative attitude we see everything right as wrong. Both are maya because they are not accurate assessments of reality. Reality, or truth, means to see things as Krsna sees them; maya means to see things as we think correct, without caring for guru-sadhu-sastra.

Please give careful attention to chanting attentively and reading daily Srila Prabhupada's books, and you will find that no external situation can impede your progress in Krsna consciousness.

11 January 2007

I have no objection on principle to your joining the army, if your wife agrees. But please consider that you will probably have to associate thickly with persons who use bad language and talk a lot about sex, and who may be more cruel than noble. You might also have a problem in taking only prasadam.

Please also consider that much of the hooha about Muslim terrorism is politicians' hype, for conditioning and manipulating people. I'm not saying that terrorism isn't a threat, but certain Muslims aren't the only terrorists. Those who torture and slaughter millions of animals and birds each year are guilty of similar crimes, by which they invite karmic retribution, for instance in the form of terrorist strikes.

17 January 2007

Conundrum. We need to perform devotional service and associate with devotees, and temples facilitate this. Yet at temples we tend to get caught up in gossip and seeing things that disturb our Krsna consciousness.

To maximize the benefits of visiting the temple and minimize the drawbacks, you might go just for arati, kirtan, and class, and leave right after that. Previously you were performing Deity service and it would be good if you could continue with that, or any other service for that matter. If someone starts to tell you their woes you could say, "I appreciate that there are problems, Prabhu, but please refer your matter to someone who can do something about it, for my guru has advised me to avoid getting involved in such matters."

You could also have regular satsangs with like-minded devotees, with strict rules against discussing topics outside of sastra. Even then the temple should not be neglected—you should go at least to offer obeisances to the Deities.

Even if we consider all devotees too neophyte and contaminated to associate with, if we cut ourselves off then we ourselves dry up. One should be intelligent enough to recognize and take good association whenever and however possible. *** Prabhu is there in M.

In researching for my book on Srila Bhaktisiddhanta Sarasvati, I came to appreciate that despite the Gaudiya Matha's problems being in many ways far worse than any ISKCON has yet faced, and although much of what exists now of the Gaudiya Matha is rather compromised, still its overall legacy is one of extraordinarily powerful bhakti. To find filth is not difficult when it's spread everywhere, but a more discerning person can detect if there is gold hidden in it, and if so extract it. And once you get gold, it doesn't really matter where it comes from.

Actually I don't get many devotees writing to me about their problems with the institution. Most devotees either find some way to fit in, or otherwise they slide out.

My long-term plan for addressing perennial discrepancies within ISKCON is to write a book called "The Mood and Mission of Srila Prabhupada." I have collected much material for it, and hope that after about two years I'll be ready to start organizing and refining it. Maybe you could put aside a few months at that time to help me—especially as you have always been much concerned with these issues.

Obviously a letter cannot fully answer your questions, nor can we understand everything of why Krsna has arranged things. Please read the "Putana" issue of Krsna Kathamrta as it is relevant to these topics.

17 January 2007

As far as I know (and I'm not an expert on this) samskaras are supposed to be in a series starting with vivaha and garbhadhana, so it might not be very meaningful to perform a first grains ceremony for a child born out of wedlock. You could ask Jaya Tirtha Charan Prabhu and Bhanu Maharaja who probably know more.

However another question is that of giving an air of legitimacy to illicit sex. By being asked to do this you are forced to take a position, either against illicit sex or in tacit approval of it. Agreeing to perform the ceremony would be easier but would compromise your position and leave you open to similar requests in future. Refusing to perform it would send a strong message. Someone has to stand up for principles or there won't be any for your children's generation to look up to.

18 January 2007

Definitely no abortion. That would be most sinful.

Brajahari Prabhu (President, ISKCON Juhu) related that his maternal uncle died young, leaving behind a widow aged sixteen, pregnant with their first child. She thereafter lived as a widow in her deceased husband's house, always keeping quiet, never talking intimately with anyone, nor attending social functions, or dressing nicely.

If *** can do similarly it is best. Remarriage may be allowed in certain situations (especially if the marriage has not been consummated) but generally is not a good idea. Best that she understand her fate as prarabdha karma and use the rest of her life to cultivate Krsna consciousness, just as your godsister J d.d. (who lives opposite ISKCON ***) is doing after her husband died young.

But living with her mother-in-law is not a good option. She should be under a man, although if your father is recommending abortion then that is horribly sinful. Last option is to stay with you.

Didn't you check with an astrologer before making the match?

See SB 9.18.23 purport.

26 March 2007

Your acceptance of inevitable fate, seeing it as the will of Krsna, is exemplary. You are even apologizing for giving bad news! But actually your courage in facing the inevitable is very good news.

My feeling is that if treatment can only briefly delay total destruction of the body, better just prepare for leaving it. Going to the dham is best, either Mayapur or Vrndavan, if there is someone who will care for you there. Otherwise maybe best to stay in Finland, where surely devotees will give you all material and spiritual support up to the last moment.

Now is a good time for you to preach through newspapers, TV etc. It's one thing to say "we're not the body" when the body is healthy, but to say it without fear when wasted by cancer will surely attract the attention of persons attached to their bodies.

What is T Prabhu's outlook on these points?

28 March 2007

It is not unusual that due to the mad mind a conditioned soul mentally offends spiritual superiors. Srila Bhaktisiddhanta Sarasvati Thakura wrote:

"What we hear from a true guru initially seems revolting. We feel a rising inclination to compensate what appears by our empirical means to be inadequacy of the guru's intelligence. But the current of thought prevalent in the material sphere cannot assail sri-gurudeva, who is too heavy for those who participate in that current. He has been able to keep them at a distance of innumerable crores of miles. He is guru, or the heaviest, because his position is not shifting. At the outset, we think that he sticks to his narrow conceptions due to his ignorance of external objects and thus we want to widen the scope of his conceptions and ideals by telling him all about the empiric world. Such a notion follows from dullness of comprehension gleaned from the school of empiricism. Our gurudeva is free from such an idea. He is the servant of the absolute truth, not partial truth."

Fortunately for us mad Kali-yuga-ites, in this age mental offenses are not punishable. So please chant Hare Krsna and be happy, and don't be too worried about any unintentional mental offense.

11 April 2007

Politics is always part of life in any institution especially when there is personal interest at stake as in the case of paid workers. And clearly A Prabhu's wife has no business getting involved in such matters and should be restrained from doing so.

But maybe you are being oversensitive, as comments such as "Don't blow it" and "Don't make a mess" can hardly be considered abusive. ISKCON *** is going through a somewhat strained period, and it's probably affecting everyone. However I request you to not prematurely think of resigning but to tolerate the words of immature people and continue your service to Sri Sri Radha Krsna, because leaving your service now would certainly make things considerably worse. Of course you need to discuss everything openly with A Prabhu, as soon as possible.

12 April 2007

Pls discuss everything clearly with him and surely by the grace of Srila Prabhupada and Sri Sri Radha Krsna matters will be cleared up and we can all go forward together in their divine service.

24 April 2007

I also feel the pain that *** feels, that pain being a major feature of my own unhappy youth. Luckily for me that pain brought me to the shelter of Srila Prabhupada's lotus feet. In this case it might destroy all the faith in bhakti that has been nurtured in *** since birth.

It is a time of great testing for you and and your faith in and commitment to Krsna consciousness. How you conduct yourself through this can be greatly beneficial for or greatly destructive of your own spiritual standing. For many devotees such apparently unfair batterings by the material energy has sapped their resolve to continue fighting against maya. Better to follow the example of Srila Prabhupada, who worked so hard to maintain a family that was practically useless that will distract you from your main service both materially and spiritually, and when he was told that his business had been looted, took it as a sign from Krsna that it was time for him to fully surrender. Of course Srila Prabhupada is nitya-siddha, but that is how he himself expressed the events of his life.

20 May 2007

Although I do not favor women working outside their home, especially nowadays social or financial pressure may practically necessitate it. Better if it can be avoided. One possible option is to work on a computer at home. Also not too bad are looking after children, or an occupation in which association is only with women. As long as you are under the control of your parents, it will be difficult not to do what they say.

11 June 2007

It is up to you to decide whether or not to use painkillers. Pain does not intrinsically promote advancement in Krsna consciousness although the experience can for a sober devotee enhance appreciation of the uselessness of clinging to hope of material enjoyment. On the other hand it may be easier to concentrate on hearing about Krsna if the body is not racked by pain.

21 June 2007

In the past few days I have received several queries from various disciples who are shocked and disappointed at reports circulating about yourself.

Those with the great good fortune to live in Vrindavan should know that the dhama is meant for living simply and purely and performing bhagavad-bhajana. Included among offenses to the dhama are to go there to engage in business and to consider any part of the dhama, which belongs to Srimati Radharani, as one's own property.

Unfortunately you have now created much enmity with devotees (yes, devotees, persons engaged in devotional service in ***-dhama, although you may have a different opinion about them). I understand that you consider the temple administration as corrupt, and indeed pertinent questions could be raised about various dealings of ISKCON leaders in *** and elsewhere. But it is not your duty to administer justice. Anyone misbehaving in *** will be dealt with by Krsna. That includes you.

Under the circumstances it is best that you extricate yourself from this complex tangle and go do business elsewhere, for instance in ***. You may suffer losses, but if Krsna wants He can very quickly turn a pauper into a billionaire. On the other hand you are now in danger of complete ruin, both materially and spiritually.

Previously you told me that [deleted]. It appears that you lied to me. What is the actual fact?

Please do not think that I am writing this at the instigation of others. No-one from the ISKCON hierarchy has contacted me about this matter. I am writing simply out of concern for your well-being, and hope that for once you can hear me.

22 June 2007

According to shastric understanding *** Prabhu is to be respected by you as a guru. So if there is a rift between you then the onus is on yourself to mend the relationship, even if according to your perception he is unreasonable. You may not wish to attend his programs, but you could phone him and try to re-establish mutual cordiality, despite disagreements and misunderstandings.

27 June 2007

I suggest that you write *** Prabhu and explain to him as politely as possible why your feelings are hurt. You could express again your gratitude to him and beg his forgiveness for this tension that has arisen. Whichever course of action you take, please keep up at least a semblance of cordiality—whatever may have happened, as a senior devotee he deserves at least that!

5 July 2007

Certainly the best decision you can make is to fully dedicate yourself in the sankirtan mission. But you are right, considering the present situation in many centers of ISKCON, one should consider carefully before joining. Please be assured that I wish to situate you with swan-like devotees, not wolves.

12 July 2007

It is not very practical that I advise you on personal difficulties without knowing all the factors involved. As general advice I may suggest that you seriously consider the standard direction given by Srila Prabhupada and sastra for young women, that they should be married and under the care of a competent husband to guide them in all such matters.

29 July 2007

Of course we must all serve as much as we can, but if there is too much strain then we have to adjust. If the services you have volunteered for are too much strain for you then you may withdraw.

29 July 2007

What you wrote was clearly a reply to my query, and if someone insists that you are speculating for doing so, then I would say that they are speculating. There will always be some unreasonable people and it's best not to be bothered by them.

3 August 2007

Unfortunately as you know you are by no means unique in being a devotee sincerely following Srila Prabhupada's instructions, with the faith that Krsna consciousness means to be happy, peaceful, and prosperous, yet finding their material situation disturbed, and hardly a model to show to others of happy, peaceful, and prosperous life.

As I understand it, Srila Prabhupada, although pleased in many ways with the efforts of his Western disciples, became disturbed and exasperated by the material and spiritual instability of most of us, and thus especially in the later part of his manifest presence began to emphasize the necessity of varnasrama. Varnasrama training is a huge area that we in ISKCON have hardly begun. In fact it seems that increasingly we are looking to non-Vedic disciplines, such as mundane psychology, for solutions to our individual and collective woes.

In the meantime we as pioneers are still suffering the distress of having to live with ourselves and others of uncontrolled mind and senses. Having little sense of commitment or responsibility, many of us who take vows or enter into relationships think nothing of reneging at whim.

The best I can suggest is that you keep faith in the ideal. Despite your sincere efforts, your own situation is far from ideal, so you can try to make the best of a bad bargain and encourage the younger generation to understand and adhere to traditional societal norms. Particularly the importance of and proper behavior within marriage needs to be inculcated.

My book *Glimpses of Traditional Indian Life* has been inspirational to some young married couples who after reading it decided to as far as possible pursue the ideals outlined therein. This book is a small but I pray useful contribution toward the massive task of respiritualizing human society.

I hope these thoughts are of some help in your difficult but nevertheless dedicated and glorious life.

12 August 2007

I hope that your wife and her relatives will forgive you. After all, you are honest enough to tell them your fault, whereas many others would have kept it secret. Now please be careful and make extra effort to be an ideal devotee and husband.

18 August 2007

In spiritual decline, the best thing to do is pick up your beads and prayerfully chant Hare Krsna, Hare Krsna, Krsna Krsna, Hare Hare/ Hare Rama, Hare Rama, Rama Rama, Hare Hare.

Try it; it works.

You wrote that you were "going to do operation on heart." Is that a physical operation, or is this statement figurative? Either way, chanting Hare Krsna will save you.

22 August 2007

If he said that then it is certainly very bad. But I cannot accept such a serious accusation merely on your word, as there are always two sides to a story.

And why is it that you are informing us now, after so many months?

And why do you speak reject without first thinking of reform? This was not Srila Prabhupada's policy, nor does it demonstrate the Vaisnava quality of compassion.

Srila Prabhupada wrote: "It is better to correct him to the standard point by friendly gestures. We can reject anyone, that is very easy, but to reform him that requires great skill and tact and if you can reform him by kind words and dealings, that is best. ... better to forget the past and try to reform him."

"Why you are complaining? You cannot reform him, your Godbrother?"

You are the witness, the prosecution, and the judge, and your verdict is that he is a devil and that I am to reject him. In your eagerness to tell of his offenses you could not offer respects when writing to your guru, but instead are giving me advice. Thus you are acting as if you are my guru, which is tantamount to rejecting me as your guru.

His spiritual standing is not good, but what about yours?

22 August 2007

Wherever you go, your mind will go with you. I advise that you stay in K and try to help the temple there develop. Keep a close relationship with R Prabhu and try to improve relationships with other devotees by always being humble and serving them.

24 August 2007

To a previous spate of complaints, I directed you to follow the prescribed procedure in ISKCON for making them, rather than directly bringing them to me. But you did not want to do that. So I will give you an alternative for your present and future gripes:

Please do not write to me directly. You may call a meeting of at least five initiated devotees to decide what, if anything, is to be done. If you collectively decide that it is necessary to send me a letter, then please compose it in sober language.

25 August 2007

Now that your father's ability to talk is almost finished, please encourage him to chant Hare Krsna at least mentally.

Distributing Srila Prabhupada's books is a wonderfully purifying service and I suggest that you stop lecturing and writing until you have personally sold at least five hundred of Srila Prabhupada's books door to door or at the train or bus station. You could give all the profit to the temple, or use it for some specific service at the temple such as buying gur[20] for the temple's cows.

31 August 2007

J Prabhu is a very good devotee and you should not disrespect him. Any problem you have should be told to him, not that you simply declare distrust. Do not be childish or offensive. Try to work matters out amicably between you and if necessary take help of any senior devotee who you trust.

1 September 2007

I thought you simply had mental disturbance as previously and was hence not eager to speak with you because these things come and go. If you were making plans to get married then you should certainly have told me.

I already stated that I don't approve of this marriage as the girl is older than you. Also it is not good that after leaving home against your parents' wishes, now within two years you

---

20 A type of raw sugar that is common in India.

want to get married. It is also not proper that in sadhu dress you independently approached a girl for marriage. I have no objection to your eventually getting married, but not soon, not by your own arrangement, and not to this particular young lady.

It is understandable that you are young and weak but still you should know the responsibility of brahmacari dress. Please leave Vrindavan immediately as you will not see Krsna there; simply your illusion will increase due to attachment to this female.

More when we meet.

2 September 2007

It seems that you have little idea of the heavy responsibility of marriage, and even after getting my objections expect me to bless this alliance. You may think that I am your enemy for not approving your plans, but actually I would be your enemy if I were to approve them.

3 September 2007

My position in this matter is clear and there is no need to repeatedly inquire about it. Please inform this lady (not directly, but via *** Prabhu) that I have absolutely nothing against her and that I wish her all the best in her ongoing advancement in Krsna consciousness, but that I object to this marriage due to the age disparity and due to the way it was attempted to be arranged.

If you are still in Vrindavan, please buy for me a lota and cover made of asta-dhatu, the same size as the copper lota I previously had.

On Janmastami you may chant and dance in the ecstacy of Krsna consciousness, and forget all these misadventures.

3 September 2007

Your mother has been released from a condition of suffering. Although she did not take very firmly to Krsna consciousness, she was undoubtedly benefited tremendously by the devotional activities she performed, such as chanting harinam and regularly taking prasada. And also by having two sons who are serious devotees, she will no doubt attain an auspicious destination.

Although you could not take her to Vrindavan, you have otherwise done the best you could for her. So do not be disturbed. As becomes clearly apparent on such occasions, we will all have to make the same journey some day.

5 September 2007

What news of ***? He is a capable boy, but tends to be unnecessarily critical. He needs a strong authority—maybe +++.

7 September 2007

I'm so happy to hear from you. Just yesterday I was thinking of you and all the nice service you performed for me. And now today I got your email.

So please come back to devotional service. You are welcome. It's an easy process and you know what to do: chant Hare Krsna, associate with devotees, take only prasada, etc. It's up to you to take advantage and not waste any more time in maya.

> *labdhva su-durlabham idam bahu-sambhavante*
> *manusyam artha-dam anityam apiha dhirah*
> *turnam yateta na pated anu-mrtyu yavan*
> *nihsreyasaya visayah khalu sarvatah syat*

After many, many births and deaths one achieves the rare human form of life, which, although temporary, affords one the opportunity to attain the highest perfection. Thus a sober human being should quickly endeavor for the ultimate perfection of life as long as his body, which is always subject to death, has not fallen down and died. After all, sense gratification is available even in the most abominable species of life, whereas Krsna consciousness is possible only for a human being. (SB 11.9.29)

I suggest that you use your fashion-designing skills in making gorgeous outfits for Sri Sri Gaura Nitai in ***.

You could also resubscribe to BVKS Sanga, for daily bytes of Krsna consciousness.

7 September 2007

I'm not at all convinced that modern psychological techniques are actually helpful. Being based on atheistic anthropology (evolutionary theory etc.), they might in some cases afford some temporary apparent improvement in disturbed persons' abilities to relate to others, but ultimately they simply deepen forgetfulness of Krsna. Particularly marriage counseling that attempts to bond relationships according to mundane concepts of compatibility is actually violence, for by failing to teach that the basis of marriage is the responsibility that goes with commitment to dharma, they indirectly promote imagined principles as being superior to dharma.

Psychological counseling is one of ISKCON's ongoing fads, but we would be better off with more kirtana and less counseling. Whatever counseling is required should be on the basis of sastric understanding, by advanced devotees fixed in knowledge of sastra and convinced of the worthlessness of mundane ideologies such as those spawned by Freud.

Elderly parents who have spent their lives raising children and know the ins and outs of family life are clearly best qualified to guide others in marriage, not a young woman like yourself who have not had children and who proposes to do so on the basis of some theoretical college degree.

8 September 2007

Especially for this time in ISKCON's history, I advocate that the best service lady devotees can perform is to set an example as ideal wives and mothers. Which means no outside career, because looking after young children should never be a part-time job. A woman's place is in the home—which doesn't mean she cannot perform some economic activities there.

11 September 2007

You have asked me for advice and counseling, but you are getting daily association with *** Maharaja. Take his help and go forward. No one is perfect but we have to try our best, and that will please Krsna.

20 September 2007

You wish to write to me weekly and to be 100% truthful about your going away from Krsna consciousness. But being 100% truthful is useless unless you make the effort to be Krsna conscious. Please write only if you are serious to take up Krsna consciousness. I am not interested in hearing of how you are in maya.

23 September 2007

I'd like to suggest that you sit down and ask *** "where do we go from here?" but it seems that you have tried that and not got any clear reply.

I still think that the path of tolerance that you are following is the best. Seems like she is trying to drive you to some extreme action. If you don't take it then she herself will eventually force the issue. Better that she does than you.

Of course I didn't hear from her side and there is always another side.

The whole thing is grim. With very few exceptions, marriages nowadays seem to be full of inordinate difficulties, and even those which are fairly OK divert much energy from the real goal of life.

26 September 2007

I don't see that anything is to be gained by legal moves. It will simply prolong and deepen the bitterness. If there is any punishing to do, let God do it.

28 September 2007

I did not say to X Prabhu that I was unhappy with you, but expressed concern that there are certain complaints about you. And that if they are true, it is bad, and if they are not true, it is also bad that devotees are spreading rumors.

At present there are signs of distrust and discontent at ISKCON ***. Let us pray to Srila Prabhupada and Krsna that this phase be got through quickly so that all may cooperate happily to serve Sri Sri Radha Krsna. The following quote from Srila Prabhupada is relevant in this regard and you may consult the letter from which it is taken for the whole context:

"There is some symptom of missing the point. The point is to be engaged in doing something for Krsna, never mind what is that job, but being so engaged in doing something very much satisfying to the devotee that he remains always enthusiastic." (Srila Prabhupada's letter to Karandhara—Bombay, 22 December 1972)

Now you have a great opportunity to study Srila Prabhupada's books while residing in Vrindavan Dham. So please become refreshed and enriched by doing so and prepare to return to service at ISKCON ***, always bearing in mind Lord Caitanya's spiritual success formula:

trnad api su-nicena
taror api sahisnuna
amanina manadena
kirtaniyah sada harih

"One can chant the holy name of the Lord in a humble state of mind, thinking himself lower than the straw in the street. One should be more tolerant than the tree, devoid of all sense of false prestige and ready to offer all respects to others. In such a state of mind one can chant the holy name of the Lord constantly."

2 October 2007

Direct deity worship is for initiated brahmanas. That is the standard Srila Prabhupada gave us and I am not authorized to change it.

4 October 2007

What exactly will be best is very difficult to say because no one can say what the future will bring. On the whole it seems that although your struggle to stay unmarried has been glorious and fruitful in terms of service, it is wise to face the reality that you cannot go on struggling like this forever, and should prepare yourself for marriage.

There is no need to be disappointed. Just take it as another step in your journey back to Krsna. Everyone has individual needs and for most a period of family life is one of them.

I've added *** Prabhu as a receiver here so that you may further discuss this with him and +++ Prabhu.

20 October 2007

My best wishes are with you, as always, if you wish to accept them.

The other day when I opened my email, I was happy to see that there was a letter from you. But naturally I became unhappy on seeing that it was a declaration of your being my "ex-disciple."

I understand that you are upset with many things in ISKCON. But we have always had an affectionate relationship—at least, I always liked you, and thought that you felt the same way about me. According to sastra there are grounds for rejecting a guru, but I do not fit that description. Mahabharata, Udyoga-parva, 179.25 (quoted, without translation, in SB 8.20.1 purport), states:

A depraved charlatan who is wallowing in carnal pleasures and material comforts, who is confused about the human goal of life and is devoid of bhakti, and who simply poses as a guru, must be rejected.

As you know, I am also disappointed in perceiving that much of ISKCON today is adrift from the ideals of Srila Prabhupada. However I do not feel that it is irrevocably corrupted, and thus consider it my duty as Srila Prabhupada's disciple to do what I can, within my admittedly limited capacity, to try to make ISKCON as good as it can be within this age of quarrel and hypocrisy. Maybe you know that when Giriraja Maharaja asked Srila Prabhupada how his disciples should face problems in ISKCON after Srila Prabhupada had left, Srila Prabhupada replied that they should not leave, but should stay and try to rectify the situation.

The immediate cause for your anger is your suspicion that ISKCON authorities got cancelled *** Prabhu's US visa. Maybe they did. Or maybe the US authorities themselves cancelled it. These days they are getting much tighter on letting people into the country. Quite likely the immigration authorities asked him which specific ISKCON center he was going to and for what purpose, and seeing him unable to reply properly, rightly cancelled his visa.

But even if it was ISKCON authorities who had the visa cancelled, they were in their rights to do so, as *** Prabhu was not serving in an approved ISKCON project. And why should *** Prabhu try to enter USA on an ISKCON-sponsored visa if he was not going for ISKCON service? That is not ethical.

Please do not be so bitter. Bitterness is unbefitting a sadhu, and blocks bhakti; the sweet fruit of love of Krsna cannot grow in a bitter heart. Bitterness arises from blaming others for misfortunes. But sastra teaches the individual to see himself, not the perpetrator, as the ultimate cause of his distress (see for instance Bg 13.21, SB 10.14.8, SB 11.23—The Song of the Avanti Brahmana). A devotee sees Krsna's benign hand in everything, and accepts that Krsna has a purpose in awarding various difficulties.

It is good that you wish to serve Srila Prabhupada, but you should know that to disciples who complained about wrongs in ISKCON, Srila Prabhupada would often challenge them to do better. Srila Prabhupada himself, when he had difficulty with his godbrothers, went out and did better than all of them together. So you do that. Surely Srila Prabhupada will be very happy if by dynamic preaching you attract many persons to Krsna consciousness and set an example that others will take note of. At least try to distribute many of Srila Prabhupada's books. You surely know that simply sitting and peacefully chanting Hare Krsna was not approved by Srila Prabhupada. He wanted his followers to preach vigorously.

I see you as very much in need of guidance and have thus attempted to give some in this letter. No good will come by rejecting me as guru, and neither Srila Prabhupada or Lord Krsna will be pleased by this unwise move. I still retain affection for you and am willing to accept you.

27 October 2007

(In response to a letter regarding a dream about Krsna)

Very nice. Catch on to all the mercy however Krsna reveals it to us, while always concentrating on the principal activities of Krsna consciousness based on hearing and chanting.

6 November 2007

Your husband has written to me that you are suffering from continuing and quite severe sickness. I am of course sorry about this, and hope that you may recover soon. I understand that even apart from this you are going through a very difficult period, but actually all over the world it seems that everyone, devotees included, are increasingly harrassed by innumerable and often apparently unsolvable problems.

Really the only recourse is to take shelter of Krsna:

> samasrita ye pada-pallava-plavam
> mahat-padam punya-yaso murareh
> bhavambudhir vatsa-padam param padam
> padam padam yad vipadam na tesam

"For one who has accepted the boat of the lotus feet of the Lord, who is the shelter of the cosmic manifestation and is famous as Mukunda, or the giver of mukti, the ocean of the material world is like the water contained in a calf's footprint. Param padam, or the place where there are no material miseries, or Vaikuntha, is his goal, not the place where there is danger in every step of life." Srimad-Bhagavatam (10.14.58)

Although I am unable to offer you help in any form that might be considered tangible, I hope this little reminder may bring you some solace and inspiration.

13 November 2007

I do not agree that it is best for you to desert or divorce ***, therefore, as Mother +++ was already aware of your problems, I asked her to contact you to help you in this difficult time.

However it seems that you have decided that there is no solution, and are not prepared to take anyone's advice in this matter. That is not good.

21 November 2007

I do not feel appropriate to take Lakshmi from Guru Maharaja. She may rather be engaged in furthering Srila Prabhupada's mission as deemed appropriate by Guru Maharaja.

Thankyou, J. I very much appreciate your spirit of selfless service. But I prefer in such cases to arrange payment from previously collected funds. If it becomes standard that devotees purchase whatever I request, some people might misunderstand that I am inappropriately burdening others, and in fact it could happen that a devotee who is not very willing to donate may feel pressured to do so.

I sometimes request devotees who I know will not feel burdened to buy inexpensive items. But this computer will come to more than $500, including taxes.

Donations are always welcome, but better they are given to my fund for book publication, from where payments for major items like this computer can be made.

5 December 2007

I suggest that instead of asking so many questions, you commit yourself to a thorough patient study of all of Srila Prabhupada's books, under the guidance of a devotee who lives according to those books, and yourself follow the basic sadhana practices given by Srila Prabhupada. That will benefit you more than trying to swallow the ocean of knowledge in haphazard gulps.

5 December 2007

Please ask *** Prabhu to follow standard sadhana programs, engage fully in service, and when he has time, to thoroughly study

Srila Prabhupada's books. Even if he has read them before, he should read them again and again.

14 December 2007

Thankyou *** Prabhu for your long, interesting realizations.

Regarding +++: I cannot force her or anyone into any kind of relation with me or anyone else. Many people take vows and later regret doing so. Better they seriously considered in advance. She is confused. This business of "I'm following Srila Prabhupada" is laughable in people who simply follow their own minds, and thus are led around by maya like an animal on a tether.

It would be too much of a circus to adjust myself to each aspiring disciple's expectations. Better they see what is there, decide if they want to live with it, and if so go along with it. It is unfair to accuse the guru of not being what one wants him to be when he never professed to fulfill such a role.

Anyway, it's nice she informed me that she no longer considers me her guru. It would be better if someone feeling uncomfortable in a relationship tells the other, "Look, these are the difficulties—what can we do to improve the situation?" rather than just unilaterally walking out. Of course, she is not the first to reject me and won't be the last. Gurus in the modern age get used to people rejecting them on the most flimsy grounds, or even on no grounds except that the disciple no longer wants to be a disciple. And sometimes gurus decide that they no longer want to be gurus.

I wish her all the best, and suggest (if she is at all willing to take any advice) that she take guidance from someone she can respect, if not me; for surely she is in need of guidance. But maybe that is the problem: she doesn't trust or respect anyone sufficiently to take the guidance she so much needs.

Congratulations for continuing to try to help her despite her self-imposed helplessness.

17 December 2007

Gita Govinda should not be translated. It is meant only for the most elevated devotees. It will be like poison to anyone else.

21 December 2007

Thankyou for your concern for ***. His position is lamentable, and we should pray that he reforms. It is up to him to decide whether he wants to serve Krsna or maya. If he wants to stop all that nonsense then he should leave that bad association, associate with devotees, become humble, and realize that he is meant to be the servant of the servant. Because he was not granted brahminical initiation does not mean that he should become so upset as to stop following the principles of Krsna consciousness. That is just an exhibition of egoism and proves that he was not fit for brahminical initiation. The following anecdote is relevant in regards to him.

In Bombay a man approached Srila Prabhupada, bowed before him, and said, "Swamiji, you will save me." Srila Prabhupada replied, "No, I cannot save you; I can teach you how to save yourself, but you must do the work."

Srila Prabhupada also said:

"We should be very serious. Why should we wait for another birth, either in very pious family or rich family or in other planet? This human body can give you the highest perfection. But we have to be very serious and try for that perfection. But we are not serious. We are not very serious."

Try to convince him to give up his foolishness, for which he is suffering now and will have to suffer more in future, unless he at last gives up attachment to sense enjoyment and becomes serious about Krsna consciousness.

24 December 2007

Food cooked by nondevotees is not fit to offer to Krsna. If you have to travel a lot, you could contact devotees in various cities (I'm sure if you try you'll find there are some everywhere) and ask them to prepare prasada that you could honor. You could reciprocate by giving gifts like prasad from Vrindavan, or Krsna conscious books.

Or do as Srila Prabhupada did: cook for yourself with a tiered cooker, which cooks rice, dal, and vegetables all at once. Carry it with a few ingredients and an electric stove.

Or, for one or two days you could get by on dried fruit, yogurt, etc.

Best would be to get a job that allows you to stay at home with your family more. Too much travel is bad for physical health and for sadhana.

2008

9 January 2008

There is no harm if at present you feel disability to distribute books. There are many other services in the sankirtan movement and any service sincerely executed is pleasing to Krsna. So please go on with all enthusiasm in your present service. Try to chant the mahamantra without offenses and in this way be assured of your gradual progress toward the kingdom of God.

27 January 2008

Please don't beat your wife; by doing so you fall into passion and ignorance and cannot be considered better than her. Tolerate, understand she won't come to your exalted level very soon, and discuss and take guidance from your brother. Separation is not a good idea.

28 January 2008

Thankyou for your concern, dear *** Prabhu. For many years I have been in difficult and dangerous situations serving Srila Prabhupada's mission and Lord Nrsimha has kindly protected me. Please pray to Him that he may also do so in our upcoming trip to Sri Lanka.

23 January 2008

I was thinking of how your great misfortune was counterbalanced by the great fortune of living in Srila Prabhupada's temple and being able to have darshan of Sri Sri Gaura Nitai, Sri Sri Radha Krsna, Lalita and Visakha, and Sri Sita Rama Laxman, Hanuman.

But it seems you are not taking advantage of that opportunity, which reminds me of Locan dasa: *nire kari vaas, na gelo piyaas* (I live in water but my thirst did not subside). Whatever the reason may be, remember the gopis who didn't care about anything else, who were ready to accept all insults and ostracization, as they ran to Krsna. I'm sure that if you get yourself up and out in front of the Lord, you will be much more happy, and healing will go faster.

Another suggestion is that you could keep some copies of my books and do a little transcendental book distribution to the many devotees who are kindly visiting you. If you like the idea, I'll arrange to get some to you.

12 February 2008

You have asked for a method by which you can again get up early and engage in spiritual activities. But there is no method. You just have to decide to do it and then do it. You can pray to Krsna for strength but ultimately it is up to you to decide whether you want excessive sleep or you want Krsna consciousness.

To gain spiritual enthusiasm, try to distribute Srila Prabhupada's books.

3 March 2008

Please try to arrange that as much as possible devotees are with Nrityanandini.

This note may be given to her.

I have called you Nrityanandini, which means one who takes pleasure in dancing. You always loved to dance for Krsna but just now you are not able to do so. But please keep on chanting Hare Krsna, at least in your mind, and pray to Srila Prabhupada intensely, and very soon you will have the opportunity to dance eternally with Krsna in a spiritual body in the spiritual world.

There is nothing to be regretted. We all have to pass on at some point. A devotee does not die but simply passes on to another situation to serve Krsna.

When Srila Prabhupada's dear disciple Jayananda Prabhu passed away, Srila Prabhupada wrote the following letter to him, which is applicable to you also.

> My Dear Jayananda,
>
> Please accept my blessings.
>
> I am feeling very intensely your separation. In 1967 you joined me in San Francisco. You were driving my car and chanting Hare Krsna. You were the first man to give me some contribution ($5000) for printing my *Bhagavad-gita.* After that, you have rendered very favorable service to Krsna in different ways. I so hope at the time of your death you were remembering Krsna and as such, you have been promoted to the eternal association of Krsna. If not, if you had any tinge of material desire, you have gone to the celestial kingdom to live with the demigods for many thousands of years and enjoy the most opulent life of material existence. From there you can promote yourself to the spiritual world. But even if one fails to promote himself to the spiritual world, at that time he comes down again on the surface of this globe and takes birth in a big family like a yogis' or a brahmanas' or an aristocratic family, where there is again chance of reviving Krsna Consciousness. But as you were hearing Krsna-kirtana, I am sure that you were directly promoted to Krsna-loka.

janma karma ca me divyam
evam yo vetti tattvatah
tyaktva deham punar janma
naiti mam eti so 'rjuna [Bg. 4.9]

Krsna has done a great favor to you, not to continue your diseased body, and has given you a suitable place for your service. Thank you very much.

Your ever well-wisher,
A. C. Bhaktivedanta Swami

8 May 2008

Having gone so far it is best to work hard and finish the thesis. But if you feel that there is little point in struggling without making any progress, then if your parents agree it might be better to leave the thesis unfinished. Either way, please keep on chanting Hare Krsna. That is the most important thing and is more valuable than millions of doctorates.

22 May 2008

I was informed that a senior preacher in USA was disturbed by some of your writings, and asked him to detail why. Please note that this devotee is not what we might call a liberal. He is a mature preacher of Krsna consciousness who I personally know and whose opinion I respect.

Considering his response, better you stop writing on loaded issues. Cultural maladies should be addressed from a higher standard of culture; by stooping to the level you claim to transcend, you have actually become part of the problem. By freely using pejoratives like "prostitute" you give the impression that you consider most women as such, and that you are fixated on unchaste women. Particularly you must desist from openly criticizing devotees much senior to you, even if you abhor their views.

Remember that your writing reflects on me. I am often blamed for my outlook, but would prefer that any blame that might accrue to me be for my own perceived faults. It really doesn't help that a disciple re-stoke the smoldering fire of animosity against me.

Don't emulate the gutter journalism typical of too many "internet theologians." Unsubstantiated and often warped presumptions, banged out with plenty of vitriol, are daily fare for a lamentably large number of Vaisnavas strong on opinions but weak on reason. However, writing that truly represents and glorifies our parampara requires serious thought and realization. A good standard of polemic writing is when your adversaries respect your erudition and delivery, even if they do not accept your message.

I suggest that for the time being you concentrate on writing about the good things you find in life in Bangladesh, without overly contrasting it with the worst of the West—as I did in "Glimpses of Traditional Indian Life." Or better still, glorify Uttama-sloka, the Supreme Lord who deserves and desires to be praised in the most glorious ways.

22 May 2008

Then I would come to India after Janmasthami. Please tell me if you agree with this plan.

Yes.

Please bless us that the Book Distribution mission here in S will expand nicely.

Work hard and Srila Prabhupada's blessings will always be there. I must also offer blessings for this noble endeavor.

If you can please clarify what is the best standard and engagement for the temple devotees? What was Srila Prabhupada's mood?

Both preaching and sadhana are required, and a proper balance between them. What constitutes a good balance will vary among individuals. Basic sadhana must be there, but preaching and book distribution must also be strongly pushed. It probably won't work to try to transform spirited book distributors into peaceful pandits. If possible varying programs may be offered for devotees of different propensities. *** Prabhu will have to preach in the colleges to recruit the kind of person suited to study all day. Yes, keep the traveling sankirtana party alive. There are profuse quotes from Srila Prabhupada extolling book distribution, so you have plenty of powerful ammunition.

1 June 2008

C Prabhu: *** Prabhu mailed to me a letter of yours from 30 May. I quote some of it below.

Throughout all of your posts talking about "dynamic unity," "accepting everyone" etc, I do not recall seeing you make the statement "Simply accepting Srila Prabhupada's teachings as it is."

The tone of your letter is accusative, as if you presume that *** Prabhu does not accept Srila Prabhupada's teachings as it is. You may feel like that but be sure that he doesn't. You could have stated that "dynamic unity" and "accepting everyone" are noble sentiments but must be within the parameters of accepting Srila Prabhupada's teachings as it is (or, as they are), and explained why you see a danger in stressing "dynamic unity" and "accepting everyone" without simultaneously stressing accepting Srila Prabhupada's teachings as it is.

No. People who simply accept Srila Prabhupada's teachings as axiomatic are "immature," "unbalanced," "fanatic," etc.

Did *** Prabhu state that? If so, I agree that communication with him will be very difficult (but then why are you trying?).

If he did not directly state that, then you are accusing him of something he didn't say.

And actually not everything Srila Prabhupada said should be accepted at face value, for instance when His Divine Grace sarcastically told a disciple to cut his own throat. Srila Prabhupada sometimes said different things in different circumstances, and to understand and intelligently apply his teachings takes much sagacity.

What was the purpose of your letter to *** Prabhu? (Please answer this question.) If it was to make him feel insulted and alienated from you, it has been achieved, but what is the use of that? How does that help anybody or help promote the purposes of ISKCON?

Admittedly I've not visited ***'s blog so I don't know what he's saying, but on principle cultivating bad relationships is generally better avoided. Srila Prabhupada gave the example that "two lawyers in the courtroom may fight vigorously about a law point, but upon returning to the law library, they talk and embrace like friends." So discuss with gusto, but philosophically. Deviations should be addressed, but not by mere vilification. I have as little taste for slanging matches as I have for deviations. Neither are helpful for bhakti.

Of course I'm not in favor of fanciful interpretations, but my experience in attempting to combat head-on various striking deviations in *** is that it didn't change the perceptions of those who subscribed to them.

As S Prabhu recently wrote:

Getting angry with the situation is simply not enough. ... unless I am willing to patiently spend time dealing with a person better not to get involved because I will tend to get frustrated and then angry.

So again, your intention is good but your style needs a lot of refining if it is going to be effective and not instead reinforce perceptions of traditionalists within ISKCON as being "immature," "unbalanced," and "fanatical."

You cannot change the world overnight, so be patient. *Satyam eva jayate nanrtam.*[21]

12 June 2008

I hope that you are happier now that you are in ***. It is good that you have distributed books and please continue to do so. I especially wanted that you would regularly go door to door distributing books. That would be good for you and good for others.

I'm happy that there is good attendance for Mahabharata classes but am concerned that it will be detrimental for you and others if you become a popular speaker but your sadhana is poor. Preaching should be accompanied by proper practice, otherwise it becomes cheap. So please seriously strive to improve your sadhana.

24 June 2008

Such cases can be difficult to adjudicate. The liberality Srila Prabhupada showed in the Bowery is not necessarily applicable in all circumstances. We want to help everyone but certain people need special treatment. It might be merciful to allow to a preaching program a person reeking of alcohol and tobacco, but it might not be wise to do so if in doing so we turn off other visitors. Ultimately someone has to decide and as with any decision it is likely that not everyone will agree with it. Nevertheless decisions have to be made.

---

21. "Truth will surely prevail, not untruth."

9 July 2008

One reason I am cautious about allowing devotees to worship deities is because in all circumstances worship has to be performed by suitably qualified devotees, which may not always be possible. Before starting worship your friend should have thought who will worship the deities when she gets sick. Worship of Radha-Krsna deities requires a high standard that I doubt either you or she can fulfil. As you know I do not like that non-brahmin initiates perform deity worship, as this is a significant step down from the standard given by Srila Prabhupada and all previous acaryas. However if you like you may continue temporarily.

17 July 2008

I hope you make it to *** and that we can spend considerable time together.

I also have the insane tendency to want to help others, seeing myself as a benefactor, despite my inability to do anything to actually help anyone—except, of course, to repeat Srila Prabhupada's message, which method of help some devotees (?) see as unoriginal and impersonal.

And now I am thinking I have to help you! But what can I do but offer sympathy? And sastric quotes.

Really it's true that we have to fly our own plane. Although it can help to know that someone cares whether or not we survive.

I'm just waiting for Krsna's gift to me in the form of severe testing. I don't know what form it will take but I know it must be coming.

Hare Krsna! Again: Hare Krsna!

Pray that I keep on chanting Hare Krsna. *Nama bina kichu nahika aro* (there I go again with my terrible vice of quoting sastra).

21 July 2008

Everything stated in sastra about the lower nature of women is true and everything Srila Prabhupada said about this is true. Women should not be independent and, for their own good and that of broader society, need to be controlled. No-one, even in ISKCON, wants to accept this as true and the result is disaster. An atmosphere has been created both in karmi society and in ISKCON wherein these points cannot be stated. Therefore there is no hope of social sanity either in karmi society or within ISKCON.

Women who are controlled and who are trained in the culture of submissiveness and proper feminine behavior can overcome the lower womanly tendencies and make the natural female contribution to society as mothers of worthy children. "Mother" does not mean just one who performs the biological function of giving birth, but one who is revered as the first guru because she gives herself completely to her children and acts selflessly for their all-around benefit.

I have written much more on this and many other topics. Please pray that I may be able to serve Srila Prabhupada's mission by collating these points into books that can help guide devotees and society at large.

PS: here's something else I just wrote.

ISKCON is like a desire tree; one may get from it the fruits of karma (sense gratification), jnana (mental speculation), or if one really desires it, suddha-bhakti. But ISKCON is meant to be a kalyana-kalpataru that delivers only suddha-bhakti without the distractions of karma and jnana. As karma and jnana become prominent, ISKCON increasingly resembles general Hinduism in which all strains of religion are present and suddha-bhakti is only one dish in a large smorgasbord.

It is extremely frustrating to have the answers that the world needs yet to be part of an institution that is largely dysfunctional in applying those principles even within its own walls. Any intelligent person who takes a look at ISKCON will realize that we have myriad problems of our own and are not in a position to offer solutions to anyone else, let alone pontificate on the welfare of the world. Thus we are only able to attract yet more dysfunctional people, some religious sentimentalists, and a few genuine truth-seekers and people of high ideals who are prepared to grit their teeth and live with ISKCON despite its problems. But the gap between the philosophy in the books and our application of it is so great that even nondevotees cannot help but notice it.

Here's something I wrote a few weeks ago:

Feminism resembles communism inasmuch as it pinpoints inveterate social inequities and proposes specious corrections. Both communists and feminists presume that all social systems were wrong until they came along as messiahs. They accept their panaceas as axiomatic and virtually sacred, maintaining zero tolerance for anyone who dares to disagree. Communism had a mission to convert the world by any means including war. Similarly, women's rights is cited as a major justification for the US-led invasions of Iraq and Afghanistan. Communism sounds noble but is fundamentally flawed, and therefore even though able to win enough mass support to take control in many countries and thus become a major world force, ultimately it had to resort to most ignoble methods to retain power, and finally collapsed. Feminism may be predicted to go the same way: it is likely to eventually crumple when its inadequacy, impracticality, and hypocrisy become obvious in the wake of inflicting untold suffering on millions.

27 August 2008

Now you have a good opportunity for material progress, but don't forget your opportunity for spiritual progress. Chant Hare Krsna seriously and go to Krsnaloka, which is infinitely superior to America.

27 October 2008

I read the whole file you sent me. You have yourself upheld your position in your reply to ***.

I disagree with +++ Prabhu that we should only preach to the innocent and not bother with the bigger cheaters.

You actually dealt with B very mildly. You should expose him as a foolish rascal for daring to call himself God when no one else recognizes him as such and he cannot even control his passing stool. Isn't that what Srila Prabhupada would do?

Even if you are "too aggressive" it is just a small counterbalance against the mush that typifies the average so-called devotee today.

See "Heroine Govinda Dasi" in the Vedabase, for the reply to "you are not emanating love."

31 October 2008

As it seems is the fate of many disciples of Srila Prabhupada directly involved in the preaching mission, I am also very busy these days. I could try to give you advice but only according to general principles as it would be unwise for me, being so far away, to think that I could fully understand the details of the circumstances you are in. I would prefer occasional phone contact, which I find better for this kind of communication than email.

31 October 2008

It is not wise to trust either a woman or one's own mind, nor to go against acceptable standards of male-female interaction, nor to unnecessarily invite criticism. Even though gross falldown is not expected, just having a woman living with you when your wife is away would be a violation of appropriate human behavior, and one that others would rightly criticise you for. Persons with improper motives may in future do the same thing, citing you as an example. So in my opinion you should tell *** that under the circumstances you cannot let her stay with you. It will be hard on her, but you should not take the risk.

12 November 2008

I have the highest respect for K Prabhu as a Vaisnava and a gentleman; yet I also have marked reservations about the approach to Krsna consciousness of himself and several other devotees. It is not always easy for me to keep these two conflicting perspectives balanced, and it is unlikely that devotees deeply committed to him would be able to appreciate that the differences between us are less important than the similarities.

P.S. Dear Guru Maharaja, by your mercy I previous month distributed more than 600 maha-big Srila Prabhupada's transcendental books.

That is really superb; the kind of news that gives me real pleasure, knowing that Srila Prabhupada is surely pleased by it.

26 November 2008

Throughout most of my formative years in this movement I had little direct strong association, so I took shelter of Srila Prabhupada's books by studying them thoroughly. I suggest you do the same. Study every day for two hours even if it means doing less of other services.

Why do you want to go back to work? Now you have given your life for Krsna's service. Don't look back. Preach more and be happy in that. Now the December book distribution marathon is at hand so try to do what you can do for that.

3 December 2008

I strongly feel that *** Prabhu needs a program of simple, regulated, menial service, especially going out on book distribution. He has never been an ordinary brahmacari living in an ashram under an authority. He started his ISKCON life with Sanskrit and needs to get immersed in the basics of Srila Prabhupada's mission. I am afraid that at this point, becoming the traveling teacher of an ISKCON guru and sannyasi would carry him further out into the clouds. He needs to be brought down to earth soon before it is too late.

+++ Prabhu asked me if I could release him to stay and teach at G but when I explained my outlook, he acceded. I told +++ Prabhu that *** could be back with him after a year and I plan to stick to that.

I know of your strong desire to please Srila Prabhupada by going deeper into sastra and presenting it for the benefit of others. But I am afraid for ***, because as you know competency in Sanskrit has often given rise to pride and offensiveness. Nitai fell down even in the personal association of Srila Prabhupada. It is a pleasure to know that *** is doing so well in Sanskrit, but first let him learn what it means to be a humble disciple before he becomes a guru.

Please forgive me for disappointing you and please still consider me as your servant.

9 December 2008

Please always stay strong in Krsna consciousness. Finish your family duties as soon as possible and come back and join me again. Avoid getting married. Give your life to Krsna. I am waiting for you.

15 December 2008

I heard of your present situation and naturally am not happy about that. I last saw you in L, where everyone including myself was impressed and inspired by your jolly serving mood. But now we are all disappointed. Of course, these things happen. You are not the first and will not be the last to have been apparently doing well in Krsna consciousness, but then change for the worse.

Probably you are not very willing to take advice or instruction from me, but I can only request with folded hands that you reconsider your course. You are of course always welcome to take a spiritual break or a fresh start here with us in India.

17 December 2008

Be blessed to expand the family of Vaisnavas. Please do not think of children as a burden or an impediment to bhakti. See them as a joy and an opportunity to serve.

23 December 2008

I received the following message from you, via *** Prabhu: that you are tired of politics among devotees and that you want to stay outside and continue chanting your rounds, that you are tired of Ramayana and the debts for it, and that you are very inspired to serve during the summer tour of H.H. +++ Swami.

I sympathize. I'm also tired of devotee politics. But it's not a good sign that you want to stay away from devotee association. Politics isn't everywhere, but opportunities to preach and serve Srila Prabhupada's mission are everywhere, so best is to place oneself in a situation where negative influences are minimal and one can serve in a positive manner.

It is very good that you are enthusiastic to serve with +++ Maharaja. Maybe you could ask him for some way to remain always preaching under his inspirational guidance. He sets a superb example of avoiding negative factors and keeping himself and others focused on the essence.

I appreciate the tremendous sacrifice you went through to produce Ramayana in P and am surprised that it is not selling better. Please see another letter with a suggestion for what we can do about clearing the stock.

2009

1 June 2009

I believe not many men would stay around under these circumstances.

True. Congratulations for accepting Krsna's mercy and being true to the *tat te 'nukampam* verse. Everyone receives Krsna's mercy in different ways. Your old partner, *** Prabhu, accepted Krsna's mercy in a completely different way, as a means to degrade himself. Still, Krsna will not forget his contributions. But for you, years of austerity in distributing thousands of books has qualified you for concentrated mercy in the form of extreme domestic distress. Krsna is kindly showing you the true face of material nature and burning out the reactions to all traces of past sins, while simultaneously destroying any remaining illusion you might have had of this material world being a nice place. You are most fortunate to get such intense purification, and your aggressive wife is, unknown to her, your best benefactor. You might even thank her for the great service she is rendering you. I am not so fortunate to get such mercy. I am surrounded by doting disciples in the illusion of thinking me a big guru. Your situation is most favorable for going back to Godhead very soon, whereas I am in serious danger of becoming a worm in stool.

9 June 2009

A couple of points I remember: Srila Prabhupada was very critical of his godbrother Bhakti Vilasa Tirtha Maharaja, yet

378

after the latter passed away, Srila Prabhupada said he went back to Godhead, by the mercy of Srila Bhaktisiddhanta Sarasvati.

Some years ago a godbrother who often complained to me about what you would call an MTD ["Me The Doer"] afflicted devotee told me of a dream he had had in which he brought his complaints about that devotee to Srila Prabhupada. But Srila Prabhupada just brushed aside all the complaints. Then that devotee noticed that (in the dream) he was sitting above Srila Prabhupada. He surmised that by this dream Srila Prabhupada taught him that it is his (Srila Prabhupada's) job to correct his disciples.

Now it's true that I've had some heavy public run-ins with certain godbrothers. But I try to keep it issue-based. It got difficult in the case of *** Swami, who diverted away from the issues by presenting it as merely a personal attack on him, an impression that still today many devotees hold. My strategy didn't produce the desired result, so in that sense it was a failure.

So my experience is that it is best to stick to the issues or the syndrome at hand, even if directly involved in an ideological battle with others. There are many devotees who maintain high respect for A Goswami and B Goswami, seeing them as men who one way or the other have maintained a lifelong commitment to Krsna consciousness, which only a small percentage of Srila Prabhupada's disciples have done. I'm trying to learn the art of speaking strongly yet not being or coming over as disrespectful to godsiblings. It's not easy and it doesn't come to me naturally, barbarian as I am.

Please pray to Srila Prabhupada that he gives me intelligence, purity, strength and energy to properly represent his mission.

I hope my own biodata in my books doesn't come over as egoistic.

18 June 2009

Your posting was funny. But the light tone might undermine the importance of the message. Also, the humor seems typically British, and much of it may be lost on non-Brits.

A website giving a directory of questionable books would be a valuable resource. If presented soberly it would be taken very seriously by discriminating devotees.

*** Prabhu's recent posts on Sun, regarding the +++ CPO case, is probably the best example I've seen of a dispassionate indictment.[22] He doesn't condemn or slander anyone, just lets the facts speak for themselves. Facts that are significant, if presented clearly, don't need highlighting to be recognized by intelligent people. Personal commentary, especially if highly opinionative, may serve to alienate rather than win over the reader.

28 June 2009

Satire is an artful medium of criticism: it only works if true, is difficult to reply to, and indirectly scorns those who deserve it (which in this case they certainly do).

28 June 2009

Thankyou dear J Prabhu for your positive reply. I was thinking to speak (at my convenience) on Ramayana—traditional pATha style, mostly reading with a few comments—and have that redacted by others into written commentaries.[23] Caitanya Candramrta, although much smaller, seems to me a much greater challenge. It would require considerably more work than I am ready for soon.

Thankyou for the offer, but I am not much in favor of anyone trying to make disciples for me. I prefer that an interested

---

22. CPO—ISKCON's Child Protection Office, formed to guard against child abuse.

Sun—abbreviated name for the website "Sampradaya Sun."

23. Pāṭha refers to the recitation of a sacred text, typically in an ashram or household, and basically entailing the systematic reading, consecutively from beginning to end, of a small portion of the text at the same time each day, and also reading a written commentary on it, and sometimes including occasional brief explanatory asides interspersed by the reciter.

devotee may approach me if they feel drawn to my preaching, and that they make an informed, intelligent decision, having learned what I stand for and desire of my disciples.

I am very happy that your visit to India has been rewarding and that you are feeling spiritual strength and enthusiasm.

28 June 2009

Your plan to focus on scientific research and publication is approved by me. I suggest that you seek official recognition for your weekly satsang in D.

Please tell *** Prabhu that I fear his unwillingness to go to S signifies a lack of desire to commit himself to discipline and surrendered service. If he wishes he can join VG Prabhu, but it is better that brahmacaris accept the direction of their guru; otherwise what is the point of having one?

30 June 2009

It would certainly enhance the Janmastami program to have present a large murti of Srila Prabhupada, but you also have to consider how to serve him after Janmastami. Where will he stay? The temple room is not very big, and with curtains around him much of the temple room would be taken up. Who will dress him daily? There are not many devotees there and everyone is already busy.

30 June 2009

Thankyou for informing me. Please ask *** Prabhu to proceed to padayatra as we had discussed by phone. Tell him that I have great hope for his flourishing in Krsna consciousness but he has to find a steady situation. There is a great need for many padayatras and if he can spearhead that, it will be very pleasing to Srila Prabhupada.

30 June 2009

There is no emergency, but as you may remember, I had discussed with you previously that I wanted you to concentrate on editing Srila Prabhupada's books in [name of language], which is a most important service. And I was concerned that in *** you were entangled in extraneous matters.

This impression was reinforced when X Prabhu told me that among other things you had organized a tour to Vrindavan without informing him—which is clearly undermining to his managerial authority. Of course there is always more than one side to a story, but it is exactly this kind of thing—getting involved in tours—that will distract you from your main service.

And for whatever reason, whether valid or not, that X Prabhu has some misgivings about your staying in *** will make it difficult for you to do so. That he suggests that you go to +++ or a similar place indicates that he doesn't wholly distrust you, but that he feels that you need to shift location.

It is thus better that you go to a smaller center and simply concentrate as far as you can on [name of language] books (and now also BTG). Of course, there are also my books to produce— we need to expand the team working on these to free you further.

Your suggestion of going to V or P is good although you might need to rent a place close by either center to get work done. You should be able to concentrate on your service without having to arrange prasada and other minor details of your staying.

I'll take this opportunity to thank you for the dedicated service you have put into bringing out [name of book] and I'll look forward to eventually seeing it in print. Which destinations is it being sent to?

It's past midnight now and I have to board my flight to Munich.

25 July 2009

From my research on Srila Bhaktisiddhanta Sarasvati I learned that someone sometimes says something or puts it in writing and it becomes generally accepted as a fact even if it is not. Like "Prabhupada said."

25 July 2009

I don't read Maharaja as being against meetings, but that he wants them to be focused and thus fruitful. Possibly he has much experience of unfocused, unfruitful meetings, or specifically feels that meetings with you have been like that. This is what I deduce, but as you rightly point out, it is difficult to understand others' feelings from emails.

13 August 2009

I received a letter from A Prabhu of ISKCON T stating that you wish to join him there. I have no objection to this and I trust you can do well there. However I'm not happy that you decided to leave India without consulting anyone, even me. Please have a little trust that I have your best interest at heart. I can understand that you find difficulty in staying in India. Nevertheless it will be better if you complete a full year before returning to Russia. Srila Prabhupada wanted Western devotees to come to India, both for their own benefit and to help the preaching. You might not understand how you are benefiting by being there, but at least you might appreciate that the opportunity to pick up some English will provide an asset that will remain with you throughout your life.

21 September 2009

Krsna has revealed to you a little taste of the eternal bliss of his association that awaits us all when we have finished our plans for anything other than surrendered service to him. Your dream was a precious rendezvous with reality, and waking up brought you back to the dream-like condition of this crazy world. To understand why Krsna revealed that vision to you and then withdrew it, please see a similar description, of Krsna appearing to Narada, in SB Canto 1.

I am glad to know that your home situation is easing up. Please go on as usual, executing your family duties in Krsna consciousness, being confident of the reward that awaits you very soon. It is best that at least for the time being you keep this dream as a cherished secret.

29 September 2009

Despite garlic having reputed medical benefits, according to sastric classification it is equivalent to meat, and thus it is forbidden for Vaisnavas. The intensity of smell and flavor of onions and garlic resembles that of meat, and it is likely that vegetarians who start to eat onions and garlic will next want to eat meat. When cooked with vegetables, dal etc., it completely overpowers their subtle flavors. Onions and garlic are highly heating foods, and are most unsuitable for persons attempting to cultivate sattvik consciousness.

After cancer and chemotherapy, you need restorative food and medicine, but there must be natural and ayurvedic alternatives to garlic. Possibly the Kerala ayurveda clinic in Trivandrum, who I have added as a receiver here, can offer relevant advice.

11 October 2009

Srila Prabhupada said that Krsna consciousness is simple (easy) for the simple (those who simply want to serve Krsna), and difficult for the crooked (those who have interests other than to serve Krsna). Psychology, and many other subjects, are interesting to persons whose interest is in the material world, material objects and the material mind. As such, psychology and similar subjects may be presented by expert devotees as a

385

technique to gradually interest people in Krsna consciousness. However, devotees who have understood the essence of Krsna consciousness participate in it happily, without many reservations and without remaining stuck on the mental platform (manomaya or jnanamaya—see Bg. 13.5 purport). By understanding Krsna one can understand everything in proper perspective (see Bg. 15.19). But Krsna can only be understood through bhakti (see Bg. 18.55). Psychology, specially the strains of modern psychology propagated by various speculators, is not a means to understand Krsna. He can be approached by sravanam, kirtanam etc. and there is one important secret; yasya deve para bhakti ... (see Bg. 6.47 purport).

Do not try to understand everything about Krsna and Krsna consciousness as a prerequisite to surrender—rather one should have the simple faith that Krsna is the Supreme Lord and He is my well wisher and on this basis one can take to Krsna consciousness with full determination. Krsna gradually reveals everything within the heart of such a sincere devotee.

You have mentioned prescribed duties. You should know that the prescribed duty of every jiva is to surrender to Krsna, and duties in this world are subservient to that. Specifically as an initiated devotee your prime duty is to chant at least 16 rounds of the Hare Krsna maha-mantra daily. Unfortunately you have found many reasons not to do so. I am surprised that while not being fixed in the vow taken at first initiation you are requesting brahmanical initiation.

If you simply follow the simple and joyful process given to us by Srila Prabhupada, all success will be guaranteed. Apparent difficulties that you face in doing so are tests of maya. Do not be deterred but remain steady on the path. For all devotees but for you especially it is most important to read Srila Prabhupada's books and not be distracted by peripheral or so-called esoteric writings.

13 October 2009

I am informed that many translations of Srila Prabhupada's books into Indian languages dilute Srila Prabhupada's strident style. Possibly the translators are alarmed by Srila Prabhupada's heaviness. Please be sure that the tone of SBV is maintained in the translation. Unless the undiluted power of our acarya's message is allowed to come through, it will not be bhakti-siddhanta but mere sentimentalism.

28 October 2009

What do those devotees do who "have not understood the essence of Krsna consciousness" yet, cannot enthusiastically practice without many reservations? What do those devotees do who have not known Krsna yet and can not "understand everything in proper perspective?"

They should become sincere. Krsna helps those who want to know him. Those who want something else in the name of Krsna consciousness get something else, such as adulation from other insincere people. Be happy with your esoteric books and I will keep faith in *Bhagavad-gita* as presented by Srila Prabhupada.

7 November 2009

I wrote to B Maharaja about you but as I have not received a response, I will not delay further in replying to you.

Your queries reveal serious misconceptions about the nature and practice of Krsna consciousness. I am not much inclined to further respond to your queries as (a) you do not seem to accept the previous answers I sent, and (b) you have more faith in subjectivity than in sastra, and I am not going to deal with you on that platform. As a guru it is my duty to speak and act according to guru, sadhu, and sastra, among which sastra is the center. If after all these years you have not understood the importance of sastra, and consider so-called esoteric literature better for you, then there is very little I can do to help you.

Krsna helps those who want to know him. Those who want something else—even in the name of Krsna consciousness—get something else.

7 November 2009

Thankyou for informing me of this. I suggest that you concentrate on the marathon and after that consider soberly and decide what you want to do in life, i.e. marry this young lady or not. Obviously she would have to quit smoking and coffee if she is to remain with you. If you want to remain unmarried then you have to quit [name of country] forever.

Please let me know when you decide.

13 November 2009

Wishing Grahila Prabhu the courage to face all that Krsna deems best for him in this difficult time.[24]

4 December 2009

Concerned that *** Prabhu lacked grounding in the essentials of understanding what it means to be a follower of Srila Prabhupada, I took him from G for a year for basic ashram training. That year is almost over but I'm afraid that he hasn't made much progress in the direction I had hoped he would.

As you know, he is very good-natured and committed to spiritual life. Yet (as I see it) he is also undisciplined and unfocused, and, more worrying, still seriously lacks an understanding of Srila Prabhupada and his mission. He proposed to me that he study mimamsa and nyaya under a Mayavadi in X (where there is no proper ISKCON center); but he was the only one in a class of thirty plus who did not pass the Bhakti-sastra exam, based on study of

---

24 Grahila Prabhu was diagnosed with cancer and not long thereafter passed on.

Srila Prabhupada's books, because he failed to write any of the essays set as homework. Devotees in Y (where he studied Bhakti-sastra) told me that in classes he presents some impressively detailed philosophical points, yet does not have a hold on some basic ones. He is not familiar with Srila Prabhupada's books and (being more inclined to [another] siddhanta) seems to have little enthusiasm for becoming familiar with them.

I told him that for his own spiritual safety he should conduct his scholastic pursuits under your guidance, but am re-considering. Notwithstanding his strong desire to become learned in traditional philosophy, probably better for him (if he can accept to do so) is to distribute Srila Prabhupada's books and perform similar services unless and until he "gets the point." I want my disciples first and foremost to be followers of Srila Prabhupada, compared to which their being scholars or accomplished in any other field is of minor import.

What do you think?

8 December 2009

Please keep on shouting, but know for sure that the best shouting is book publication.

26 December 2009

Thankyou for contacting me at this critical stage of your life. I appreciate that as a good disciple, you have revealed your thoughts to me and will not make a major change in your life without consulting me.

However, I am not much in favor of you marrying at this late stage of your life. But even if you are to marry, you should first become more realistic. It seems that you are largely on the sensual and emotional platform, and thus unfit to make a sober decision regarding the future course of your life. Nor in such consciousness are you fit to accept the heavy responsibility of caring for a wife and children, nor would it be proper to entrust any woman to you. A family man should be responsible and mature, but your state is like that of a child who insists on getting what he wants. However, caring parents only give their child what is beneficial for him, even if he screams when denied what he foolishly desires.

Please come to the Mayapur festival, or better still come to India earlier, as I have to leave India by mid-Feb and might not be able to attend the Mayapur festival, due to new Indian visa regulations. Spend a month or two in India, and if and when your mind becomes somewhat less agitated, we could discuss your situation in a cool-headed way.

I hope that you will heed my advice. If not, I am afraid that you will follow your mind and thus cause untold difficulties to yourself and others.

Please read daily minimum one hour, concentrating on *Brahmacarya in Krsna Consciousness* and *Bhagavad-gita As It Is.* You should especially read and pray for realization of Gita Chapter Three verses 37 to 41.

Please have faith that I am your well-wisher and that you will benefit by following my advice rather than submitting to the urges of your senses—even if my advice contradicts everything that you desire.

18 December 2009

To Kisora das[25]

Any comments that you feel could be relevant are welcome. I am open to any kind of critique if it could possibly help serve our acaryas better.

---

25. This letter refers to Kisora Prabhu's checking the manuscript of *The Story of Rasikananda* prior to its re-publication.

As re-publication is not urgent, please take whatever time is needed to do a thorough job, although please also do not inordinately delay.

Unknown date

I am glad that you wish to become my disciple based on reading my books and listening to my lectures. This is the proper way to approach a spiritual master: by submissive hearing. So please go on distributing Srila Prabhupada's books and performing whatever other services you are asked to do by your local temple authorities. You are very lucky to have the chance to engage in Lord Caitanya's mercy mission of sankirtana, so please continue it with all enthusiasm and in this way qualify yourself to be accepted as a disciple.

2010

4 January 2010

To Mahavisnu Gosvami[26]

Unfortunately I have not been able to have your association for quite a long time, and it might be that we may not meet again for a considerably longer period. As I am not able to convey this to you personally, through this little note please accept my appreciation of your many years of service to Srila Prabhupada's mission, your deep love for sastra especially Srimad-Bhagavatam that you have also inculcated in your disciples, and the example of the simplicity and detachment of an ideal sadhu that you set by your very life.

22 January 2010

Thankyou for your ever kindness on me. Such skyhigh praise makes it difficult for me, however, because the expectations are so high, and I am after all (if you would just take off your rosy glasses) very ordinary and frail. Please don't take me for something that I am not. Like any of our surviving godsiblings, I live solely on Srila Prabhupada's mercy and would be doomed if I were to accept any suggestion that it might be otherwise.

X is clearly a special child. She still needs your careful oversight.

---

26. Shortly after this letter was written, Mahavisnu Goswami departed this world.

Suggestion: selling sets of SB can generate income. Go temple to temple. Hold preaching programs. Glorify the books. Most congregational devotees don't have them. What do you think?

30 January 2010

You decided to go to Europe to make a change in your life, but are just as confused and directionless as ever. As there is no sign that your confusion will soon end, I suggest that you return to India, where at least you will get service and supportive association. This is only a suggestion as I expect you to follow your mind as usual. But if possible you might try to consider to seriously consider this suggestion. If you were prepared to accept my direction, I could give you a service to focus on, and that would largely solve your disorientation.

6 February 2010

I understand that living in India is in various ways difficult for you. I went through the same syndrome for the first several years I was in this part of the world: sickness, difficulty to relate to pretty much everything.

But looking back and seeing that the great majority of my godsiblings in the West have not maintained even their initiation vows, I feel that it was Krsna's kindness that he kept me here.

I also understand that the service I have given you probably seems pretty dry. I have asked *** Prabhu to give you some outgoing service to intersperse with the file checking you are doing.

I suggest that you finish the present phase and then I will turn it over to someone else. Your godbrother +++ and his wife will soon be joining me to work full time on book projects and they could take it up from there. That would leave you freer for preaching and other similar more inspiring activities.

I want you to be happy and flourish in Krsna consciousness. I also want that you make more effort to stay on in India. You have the spirit to be a surrendered servant, and you can be one by facing the tests that qualify a devotee to enter the realm of pure devotional service. Krsna consciousness can be performed in all times, places, and circumstances, and a devotee might consider one situation more favorable for his spiritual progress than his present one. But wherever one goes the tests still have to be faced.

7 March 2010

When immature people approach you for initiation, you could see them as being sent by Srila Prabhupada, who is in effect telling you: "You are expert in analyzing the defects of others, of pointing out what should not be. Now you must show others, and me too, what actually should be done."

You cannot forever avoid taking this responsibility without being charged with the hypocrisy of which you accuse others. The preacher's fate has caught up with you. Please accept it, humbly, and discharge it in a manner that will be very pleasing to Srila Prabhupada.

An important consideration is that by accepting such a position of authority, you could better fulfil your life's mission by inspiring exponential increases in book distribution.

You don't have to lobby your way through the institutional system. You can simply submit to the concerned authorities that several devotees have asked you about guruship and that you request the Vaisnavas to consider this proposal and accept or reject it as they see fit. Then see how Krsna inspires those Vaisnavas, and accept their verdict, either way.

That is my opinion. Before writing Caitanya-caritamrta, Krsnadasa Kaviraja Gosvami submitted himself to Sri Madana-mohana, and I suggest you do the same.

12 March 2010

Best for newcomers that you stick directly to Bhagavad-gita and Srimad-Bhagavatam, lest they misunderstand Bhagavad-gita and Srimad-Bhagavatam to be less important. Especially newcomers should first focus on Srila Prabhupada's books, not Gita Press or any other books.

It is good that you have developed attraction for this Vaisnava scripture, Jaimini Mahabharata, but do not elevate it above Bhagavad-gita and Srimad Bhagavatam. A good way to serve it would be to translate it into English.

May Srila Prabhupada and Krsna bless you and your family always.

12 March 2010

It is good that you wish to perform deity worship. Please do so. But better that you request opportunities to serve the local temple deities. Srila Prabhupada clearly stated that devotees living in temple communities focus on the temple deities rather than undertaking separate deity worship.

3 April 2010

It seems that Krsna has a plan for you. Certainly, the opportunity to continually hear Srila Prabhupada will give you much shakti. If we consider Srila Prabhupada's life, at one point it seemed helpless. His family was uncooperative, his spiritual master's institution was shattered and he had been cheated of everything in business. There were many big sannyasis but unexpectedly, he emerged to do more than all of them put together.

Remembering this, we can understand that anyone who remains faithful in Krsna consciousness and does not become discouraged, despite the whole world apparently being against him, can be blessed with extraordinary mercy.

6 April 2010

I have received a letter from X Prabhu concerning yourself. He states therein that you are pushing to return to A rather than he calling you. He appreciates the service you have done in *** but agrees with me that you should not return there very soon.

I am not sure why you are so anxious to return to A. Of course it might be natural that you are attached to the service of Sri Sri Radha Krsna, having served Them for several years. Still you should realize you have had a serious falldown and that under the circumstances it is better that you stay far away from the place of your falldown. In several places (for instance 5.6.5) Srimad-Bhagavatam warns not to trust the mind but you seem to take your dangerous position too lightly and not heed such warnings.

I appreciate your enthusiasm to continue devotional service, but you should also understand that devotional service executed in any place is transcendental. Considering that the female who you became involved with is a regular visitor to ISKCON ***, it is better that you give up the idea of returning there, for the mind is fickle and old attachments die hard. Please continue whatever services are allotted to you in B, and I will look forward to seeing you there next month.

I mentioned to Y Prabhu your desire to wear saffron clothes. He was wholly opposed, and I agree with him. You have asked me for my mercy but you should know that mercy does not mean allowing the disciple to do as he wishes, but in instructing him for his ultimate welfare.

6 April 2010

It seems clear from Srila Prabhupada's direction on this point that he wanted devotees living in a temple community to focus on service to the temple Deities rather than conduct private worship. That many devotees do not follow this instruction does not lessen its weight. If you are not able to get service in the main pujari department, you could request service to the Deities in the gurukula or the bhajan-kutir or in Srila Prabhupada's samadhi. Many services are possible. If you are not immediately allowed to offer arati, you could maybe clean vessels, cut vegetables, string garlands, or whatever. After some time of steadily performing such service, you would probably be given the opportunity to offer arati or help in the early morning puja.

16 April 2010

You have asked me about overcoming attachment to palatable food, and about appreciating the spiritual value of Krsna-prasada.

I have two suggestions.

Make a point to read sections of sastra which describe the necessity of controlling the tongue and which extol the glories of Krsna-prasada. Before taking prasada remind yourself, and others also, that it is purely spiritual.

Another suggestion is to cook. When, in my youth, I started cooking for Krsna and his devotees I soon found my fascination for delicious prasada transformed from being enjoyment-oriented to service-oriented. While meditating on delicious food, I was thinking how to prepare such items to please Krsna and his devotees. Of course, you cannot now cook for Sri Sri Radha-Krsna but when I go to America after Janmashtami you could take brahminical initiation and after that start to cook. In the meantime, you could serve prasada and take pleasure in others relishing Krsna in this form.

30 April 2010

L Das recently spoke to me about his son, A, age 10. His relatives had been pushing for his upanayana ceremony but L doesn't want to do it unless it is done by Vaisnava vidhi.[27] A is chanting 16 rounds and coming with his father regularly to mangala aarti. Although he is still young, I am considering giving him Harinama initiation. After some time both he and his father could be given Vaisnava brahmana initiation. Although I am nowadays quite reserved in giving brahminical initiation, especially to congregational devotees, I have always given it liberally to males from brahmana families to save them from the pressure of their families and of their own minds, also considering that many persons even today from brahmana families have never indulged in gross sinful acts, and thus may be trusted not to do so after coming to Krsna consciousness.

What do you think?

30 April 2010

I pray that you can find peace and stability, which is however difficult to find in this world, especially in family life, and especially in Kali-yuga.

Please consider that one instruction can be qualified by another. For instance, some ISKCON devotees quote Srila Prabhupada as saying that all Vaisnavas should be addressed as Prabhu and that thus women devotees should also be addressed as Prabhu. But they do not consider another statement of Srila Prabhupada, that all women should be addressed as mother.

I am not enthusiastic about observing the formality of upanayanam without delivering the substance. It is absurd and a mockery of the real process; even more if performed by people who should know better.

---

27. *Upanayana*—ritual initiation, accompanied by investiture of the sacred thread; *vidhi*—ritual.

3 May 2010

It is true that ISKCON does not as yet provide educational or occupational possibilities to the standard that Srila Prabhupada envisaged. However this can only come about if devotees are prepared to take the risk, work hard, pray, and do all else that is required to establish such systems. It will never happen as long as everyone waits for everyone else to get started.

I spoke with *** Prabhu about the possibility of your serving the temple and he told me that you wanted more money than he was willing to offer. You can't have it all ways.

As you have already married outside your caste, it seems even more meaningless (if that is possible) to be concerned with caste rules for your sons. Hopefully they will identify with the community of devotees more than with any caste.

Rules concerning asauca and other similar stipulations may be followed as far as they are favorable to or compatible with bhakti. See Bhakti-rasamrta-sindhu 1.2.200 quoted in Cc. 3.13.113.

22 June 2010

Thank you for your concern. B Prabhu is certainly capable and productive but he is also spiritually weak and neither under any authority nor particularly inclined to serve under any authority. He initiated some gundagiri in *** for which he had to be removed, but no one including myself could convince him that his actions were wrong.[28] That is only one act in a long drama. So you can understand that, for all his excellent service, he is not well-situated and is difficult to correct. C Prabhu convinced him that he is not fit for lifelong brahmacarya, which I agree with and which he has accepted. He wants to marry a devotee girl he has never met except on Facebook. What do you suggest can be done for him? Might you be interested to try to advise him?

---

28. Gundagiri—rowdyism.

21 October 2010

Actually it is a fact that the ... service pioneered and developed with much labor by yourself has exponentially increased my service, and I am ever grateful to you for that. You may quote that to whoever you like.

However it is not that you are all right and others are all wrong, as you seem to perceive.

With so many technicalities involved in ... work, there are certain to be mistakes, all of which detract from the quality of the service. I have several times told you that it is better for you to concentrate on the most essential services and do them properly, rather than taking on multiple projects, becoming overloaded, and not being able to do any of them satisfactorily. You have many good ideas but are not practical about the limits of your capability.

When you first started this service, and in the years that followed, I several times asked you about financing, but you told me that you could manage all expenses. I never said that you could not take laxmi, and more than once offered financial assistance, which you always refused. It was always your policy to keep low the price of [certain items], overriding my reservations and insisting that there would be no problem in low pricing. But now you are complaining about not being financed, as if you were the victim of unfair treatment.

But it is you who are unfair, for making such imbalanced insinuations. This typifies what you call your straightforward dealings: your expectation that others see you in the unrealistic light you see yourself. Due to this attitude, and your inability to accept guidance, I have not been able to prevent your downward spiral into your present state of self-righteous confusion and lamentation.

To tell you the truth, I have put so much energy and blood for [this] seva but in return i only get chastised by everybody.

It is untrue that you only get chastised by everybody. As I perceive it, you are not open to correction, and take as an insult even suggestions that you might be wrong. I doubt if you will accept it, but you have a serious ego problem.

> any person would prefer to serve in somewhat peaceful situation where people are not always bombarding me.

Again, a ridiculous assessment. People are not always bombarding you. The main cause of your lack of peacefulness is your own disturbed mind.

I will not reply to all your accusations, and shall also be more cautious about making comments about you that are liable to get back to you in exaggerated or otherwise distorted form.

I wish that you be happy and continue this service. As you state, a systematic approach is required to properly effect these services, and we should work toward that. Some adjustments are required, the main one being in your consciousness. I have repeatedly tried to impress on you the need for a solid spiritual basis in hearing and chanting. Until you are solid in sadhana, you will continue to have multiple mind-born problems.

An option that you previously refused is still open, of shifting to H, where much support at all levels is promised.

Thankyou for your time and patience.

9 December 2010

You are a sincere and hard-working devotee and better than millions of karmis, but you still have many things to learn. I would be happy if you make a great effort to try to work with others, even if you think they don't like you. If you feel that your nature is a problem then you should work on rectifying it (ceto darpana marjanam) rather than citing it as an excuse to continue with it. Unless you improve in communication and dealings, you will continue throughout your life to unnecessarily face problems. And your problems become my problems. So please make self-improvement a priority.

Acknowledgements

My thanks to everyone who helped produce this book, prominent among whom were:

Cover design—Rasikaśekhara Dāsa

Editing—Guru-Kṛṣṇa Dāsa

Index—Bhāgavatī Dāsī

Layout—Bhīṣma Dāsa

Printing supervision—Śrīdhara Śrīnivāsa Dāsa, Śrī Giridhārī Dāsa

Proofreading—Gaura Bhagavān Dāsa, Harilīlā Devī Dāsī, Indirā-sakhī Devī Dāsī, Kiśora Dāsa and Ananta-sarovara Dāsī, Nārāyaṇa Śrīnivāsa Dāsa, Priya Govinda Dāsa

Text Organization—Kiśora Dāsa

Index

403

see them philosophically, 331

Discipleship
  be follower of Srila Prabhupada, 388
  blessings for, 22
  deviating to cheater guru, 324
  do not be a burden on guru, 131
  qualify for via sankirtana mission, 390
  standards for, 49

Disobedience
  of guru's instruction, 328

Divorce, 358
  adharmic, 283, 292
  avert it by joking, 317
  in ISKCON, 291

Donations
  accept them for service, 222
  best given for books, 359
  purify laxmi via, 240

Dramas
  for absorption in Lord's lila, 164

Dreams
  of acaryas, 313
  of guru, 277, 379
  of reality, 384

E

Ekadasi
  book on, 176

Empiricists
  critique of, 297

Enthusiasm
  for Krsna's service, 354
  sign of advancement, 39

Envy
  to be purified not dovetailed, 56–57

F

Faith
  broken and rebuilding, 167
  cannot be legislated, 306
  faithless offensive persons, 179
  in Bhagavad-gita, 386
  in guru, sadhu and sastra, 297
  in guru's instructions, 156
  in ideal spiritual life, 347
  that Krsna is Supreme Lord, 385

Falldown, 159
  do not risk, 87
  failure is pillar of success, 170
  issues around, 176
  stay away from place of, 395

Family matters
  and bad press about ISKCON, 209
  dealing with family demands, 208, 334, 343
  finish up your duties, 376
  keep good relationships, 46
  meat-eating family members, 316
  opposed to joining ISKCON, 210
  patiently encourage, 199
  respect parents but, 152

Farm development, 91, 331

Fear
  of death, 250
  of maya, 194

Feminism, 373

FOLK, 2

Fundraising
  by donating blood, 149

G

Ganga
  different names for, 117

Garlic, 384
  affects the consciousness, 10
  tamasic, 33

Other Books by Bhakti Vikāsa Swami

A Beginner's Guide to Kṛṣṇa Consciousness

Read this book and improve your life!

All you need to know to get started in Kṛṣṇa consciousness. Easy-to-understand guidance on daily practices that bring us closer to Kṛṣṇa. Packed with practical information. Suitable both for devotees living in an ashram or at home.

Guaranteed to make you a better, more spiritual person

120 x 180 mm • 132 pages • line art • softbound

Available also in Bengali, Croatian, Gujarati, Hindi, Indonesian, Kannada, Malayalam, Marathi, Nepali, Polish, Russian, Slovene, Tamil, Telugu, and Urdu

A Message to the Youth of India

Youth of India, Awake!

Your country is destined to lead the world by spiritual strength. Understand the power of your own culture, which is attracting millions from all over the world.

Religion, philosophy, social and historical analysis. Compelling insights, not only for the youth but for all interested in the future of India and the world.

Arise, come forward, be enlightened

120 x 180 mm • 128 pages • softbound

Available also in Bengali, Gujarati, Hindi, Marathi, Tamil, and Telugu

Brahmacarya in Kṛṣṇa Consciousness

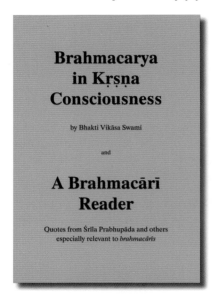

A "user's guide" to *brahmacārī* life. The first part consists of elaborate discussions and practical guidance regarding many aspects of *brahmacarya*. The second portion is a compilation of quotations on *brahmacarya* from Śrīla Prabhupāda's books, letters, and recordings.

Invaluable not only for *brahmacārīs* but for all devotees seriously interested in improving their spiritual life.

135 x 210 mm • 272 pages • softbound

Available also in Bengali, Croatian, Gujarati, Hindi, Indonesian, Italian, Mandarin, Portuguese, Russian, and Tamil

Glimpses of Traditional Indian Life

Journey to the real India. Discover the wisdom and devotion at the heart of Indian life. Meet people who were raised in a godly atmosphere and learn how it shaped their character and enriched their life. Explore the adverse effects of India's technological development, the downfall of her hereditary culture, and other causes of India's present degradation.

135 x 210 mm • 256 pages • 16 color plates • softbound

Available also in Croatian and Russian

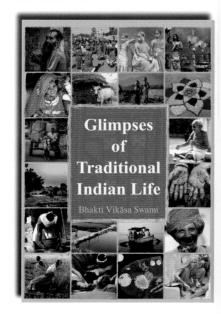

Jaya Śrīla Prabhupāda!

There is no limit to Śrīla Prabhupāda's transcendental attributes, nor do we wish to ever stop describing them. His qualities, combined with his achievements, undoubtedly establish Śrīla Prabhupāda as an extraordinarily great transcendental personality.

Śrīla Prabhupāda is still with us, watching over the continuing expansion of the Kṛṣṇa consciousness movement. If we simply follow his instructions carefully, we can expect many amazing, unimaginable things to happen.

135 x 210 mm • 240 pages • pictures and line art • softbound

Available also in Gujarati, Russian, and Tamil

The Story of Rasikānanda

Śrī Rasikānanda Deva was a mighty Vaiṣṇava *ācārya* in the era after Lord Caitanya's disappearance. Along with his guru, Śrīla Śyāmānanda Paṇḍita, he inundated North Orissa and surrounding districts in waves of Kṛṣṇa-*prema* that are still flowing today. He subdued and converted atheists, blasphemers, and dacoits, and even tamed and initiated a rogue elephant! The exciting story of Śrī Rasikānanda Deva is told herein.

135 x 210 mm • 216 pages • 4 color plates • softbound

Available also in Gujarati, and Russian

On Pilgrimage in Holy India

Travel with an ISKCON sannyasi, including to some of India's less-known but most charming holy places.

210 x 280 mm • 196 pages
• full-color with 191 pictures
• hardbound

Available also in Russian

Rāmāyaṇa

Countless eons ago, when men and animals could converse together and powerful *brāhmaṇas* would effect miracles, the uncontrollable demon Rāvaṇa was terrorizing the universe. The *Rāmāyaṇa* records the adventures of Rāma, the Lord of righteousness, as He struggles to overcome the forces of Rāvaṇa. This absorbing narration has delighted and enlightened countless generations in India, and its timeless spiritual insights are compellingly relevant in today's confused world.

135 x 210 mm • 600 pages • 16 color plates • line art • hardbound

Available also in Croatian, Gujarati, Hindi, Latvian, Marathi, Polish, Russian, Telugu, and Thai

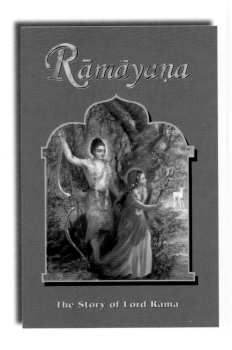

Śrī Caitanya Mahāprabhu

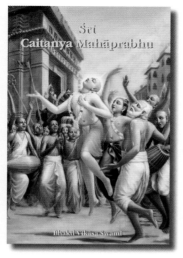

Hundreds of thousands of people throughout the world now follow the spotless path of Kṛṣṇa consciousness as given by Lord Caitanya. Chanting the holy names of Kṛṣṇa and dancing in ecstasy, they desire only love of Kṛṣṇa and consider material enjoyment to be insignificant. This book gives an overview of the life and teachings of Śrī Caitanya Mahāprabhu, the most munificent avatar ever to grace this planet.

120 x 180 mm • 176 pages • 16 color plates • softbound

Available also in Gujarati, Hindi, Russian, Tamil, and Telugu

Śrī Vaṁśīdāsa Bābājī

Śrīla Vaṁśīdāsa Bābājī was a great Vaiṣṇava who although physically present in this world, had little communication with it. His hair and beard were uncut, matted, and dishevelled. He almost never bathed, and his eyes looked wild. He wore only a loin cloth, and nothing more.

This book introduces us to a personality of such extraordinary, inscrutable character that we simply offer him obeisance and beg for his mercy.

135 x 210 mm • 152 pages • 8 color plates • softbound

Available also in Croatian, Hindi, and Russian

My Memories of Śrīla Prabhupāda

An ISKCON sannyasi recalls his few but precious memories of the most significant personality to have graced the earth in recent times.

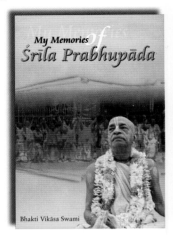

Also includes:

- On Serving Śrīla Prabhupāda in Separation
- Vyasa-pūjā Offerings

135 x 210 mm • 230 pages • full-color with 39 pictures • hardbound

Available also in Croatian, Czech, Gujarati, and Russian

Śrī Bhaktisiddhānta Vaibhava

Śrīla Bhaktisiddhānta Sarasvatī Ṭhākura altered the course of religious history by reviving and forcefully propagating pure Kṛṣṇa consciousness. His boldness in combating cheating religion earned him the appellation "lion guru"—yet his heart was soft with divine love for Kṛṣṇa.

Based in Bengal and traveling throughout India in the early twentieth century, Śrīla Bhaktisiddhānta Sarasvatī Ṭhākura laid the foundation for, and was the inspiration and guiding force behind, the later worldwide spreading of the Hare Kṛṣṇa movement.

ೞಜಿೞಜಿೞಜಿ

The result of over twenty years of research, *Śrī Bhaktisiddhānta Vaibhava* presents a wealth of newly translated material. Replete with anecdotes told by disciples who lived with him, this devotional, philosophical, cultural, and historical study gives intimate insights into the activities, teachings, and character of an empowered emissary of the Supreme Lord.

160 x 240 mm • 1576 pages • 164 black-and-white photos • 9 color photos • hardbound • decorative protective box

Śrī Bhaktisiddhānta Vaibhava is presented in three volumes

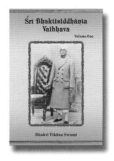 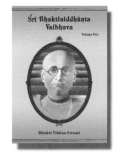 

Volume 1 features a biographical overview, plus detailed analysis of the message, mission, and personality of Śrīla Bhaktisiddhānta Sarasvati.

Volume 2 details the preaching challenge that Śrīla Bhaktisiddhānta Sarasvati faced, and also includes biographical sketches of several of his disciples and associates.

Volume 3 features an overview of Śrīla Bhaktisiddhānta Sarasvati's contributions, with selections from his lectures, writings, and colloquies, also his astrological chart, and appendixes that include important details concerning Śrīla Bhaktisiddhānta Sarasvati and the Gauḍīya Maṭha.

On Speaking Strongly in Śrīla Prabhupāda's Service

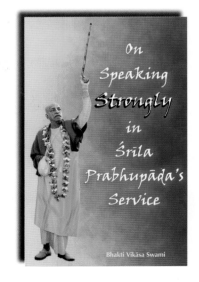

Why followers of Śrīla Prabhupāda should speak strongly, as he did. A comprehensive analysis of how to present Kṛṣṇa consciousness straightforwardly, intelligently, and effectively. Features many anecdotes and more than five hundred powerful quotes.

135 x 210 mm • 272 pages
• hardbound • multimedia CD

For more information, please visit:
www.speakingstrongly.com

From the BVKS Media Ministry

Hearing the Message "As It Is"

Lectures by Bhakti Vikāsa Swami in English, Bengali, and Hindi on
Bhagavad-gītā, *Śrīmad-Bhāgavatam*, and various topics

Free download of over 3,000 MP3 lectures and 100 video lectures:

www.bvks.com

To order books: books@bvks.com

For CDs and DVDs of lectures: media@bvks.com